CYCLING LAND'S END TO JOHN O' GROATS

LEJOG END-TO-END ON QUIET ROADS AND TRAFFIC-FREE PATHS

by Richard Barrett

JUNIPER HOUSE, MURLEY MOSS,
OXENHOLME ROAD, KENDAL, CUMBRIA LA9 7RL
www.cicerone.co.uk

© Richard Barrett 2021
Third edition 2021
ISBN: 978 1 78631 025 5
Reprinted 2022 (with updates)
Second edition 2019

Printed in Singapore by KHL using responsibly sourced paper
A catalogue record for this book is available from the British Library.
All photographs are by the author unless otherwise stated.

Route mapping by Lovell Johns www.lovelljohns.com
© Crown copyright 2021 OS PU100012932.
NASA relief data courtesy of ESRI

Dedication

This book is dedicated to my club-mate Mari, who mid-way through writing this guidebook also became my partner.

Acknowledgements

My thanks to Jonathan and Joe Williams of Cicerone for commissioning me to produce this book and introducing me to wonderful bits of country I had never previously visited. I should also like to thank Andrea, Verity and the production team, who once again made the process such a pleasure and my friend Ian Gilbert who joined me through the Scottish Lowlands.

Front cover: The obligatory photograph at the fingerpost at John o' Groats

CONTENTS

Route summary table 5
Suggested schedules. 6–9

INTRODUCTION 11
Why the End-to-End route? 12
Tailoring this route to your needs 12
Which direction to ride? 17
Selecting a schedule. 17
When to ride 18
Riding alone or as part of a group? 19
Getting there 19
Getting back. 21
How much to budget 22
First and last nights 22
Accommodation. 23
Baggage transfer. 24
What to take. 25
Preparing yourself. 25
Preparing your bike 26
Eating. 27
Phones and Wi-Fi. 27
Waymarking. 27
Maps 28
Practical tips. 28
Using this guide 29
GPX tracks 30

LAND'S END TO JOHN O' GROATS 31
Stage 1   Land's End to Fowey 32
Stage 2   Fowey to Crediton. 42
Stage 3   Crediton to Clevedon 49
Stage 4   Clevedon to Worcester 58
Stage 5   Worcester to Nantwich 69
Stage 6   Nantwich to Garstang 81
Stage 7   Garstang to Penrith 96
Stage 8   Penrith to Moffat 107
Stage 9   Moffat to South Queensferry 120
Stage 10   South Queensferry to Pitlochry 130

Stage 9a	Moffat to Balloch	139
Stage 10a	Balloch to Pitlochry	153
Stage 11	Pitlochry to Aviemore	164
Stage 12	Aviemore to Alness	172
Stage 13	Alness to Tongue	181
Stage 14	Tongue to John o' Groats	189

Appendix A	Accommodation	197
Appendix B	Cycle shops	210
Appendix C	Facilities summary	216
Appendix D	Useful resources and contacts	222
Appendix E	Official tourist information contacts	224
Appendix F	Additional contacts for rail travel	225
Appendix G	What to take	226
Appendix H	Further reading	227

Updates to this Guide

While every effort is made by our authors to ensure the accuracy of guidebooks as they go to print, changes can occur during the lifetime of an edition. This guidebook was researched and written before the COVID-19 pandemic. While we are not aware of any significant changes to routes or facilities at the time of printing, it is likely that the current situation will give rise to more changes than would usually be expected. Any updates that we know of for this guide will be on the Cicerone website (www.cicerone.co.uk/1025/updates), so please check before planning your trip. We also advise that you check information about such things as transport, accommodation and shops locally. Even rights of way can be altered over time. We are always grateful for information about any discrepancies between a guidebook and the facts on the ground, sent by email to updates@cicerone.co.uk or by post to Cicerone, Juniper House, Murley Moss, Oxenholme Road, Kendal, LA9 7RL.

Register your book: To sign up to receive free updates, special offers and GPX files where available, register your book at www.cicerone.co.uk.

ROUTE SUMMARY TABLE

Stage	Start	End	Distance (miles/km)	Ascent (m)	Riding time hrs at 12mph (19kph) + 500m/hr*	Traffic-free (%)	Page
1	Land's End	Fowey	65/105	1400	8–9	10	32
2	Fowey	Crediton	65/105	1700	8–9	13	42
3	Crediton	Clevedon	86/138	800	8–9	24	49
4	Clevedon	Worcester	91/146	700	8–9	17	58
5	Worcester	Nantwich	83/134	900	8–9	14	69
6	Nantwich	Garstang	85/136	600	8–9	46	81
7	Garstang	Penrith	70/112	1400	8–9	1	96
8	Penrith	Moffat	70/112	700	7–8	5	107
9	Moffat	South Queensferry	64/102	900	7–8	20	120
10	South Queensferry	Pitlochry	66/106	1300	8–9	25	130
9a (alt)	Moffat	Balloch	83/133	1000	8–9	56	139
10a (alt)	Balloch	Pitlochry	92/147	1600	11–12	34	153
11	Pitlochry	Aviemore	60/96	900	6–7	28	164
12	Aviemore	Alness	64/102	700	6–7	29	172
13	Alness	Tongue	66/106	1100	7–8	1	181
14	Tongue	John o' Groats	64/102	1300	7–8	0	189
Total			1000/1600	14,400		17	
Total (alt)			1046/1675	14,800		21	

*Estimated riding times are based on the time to cover the distance plus the time spent climbing.

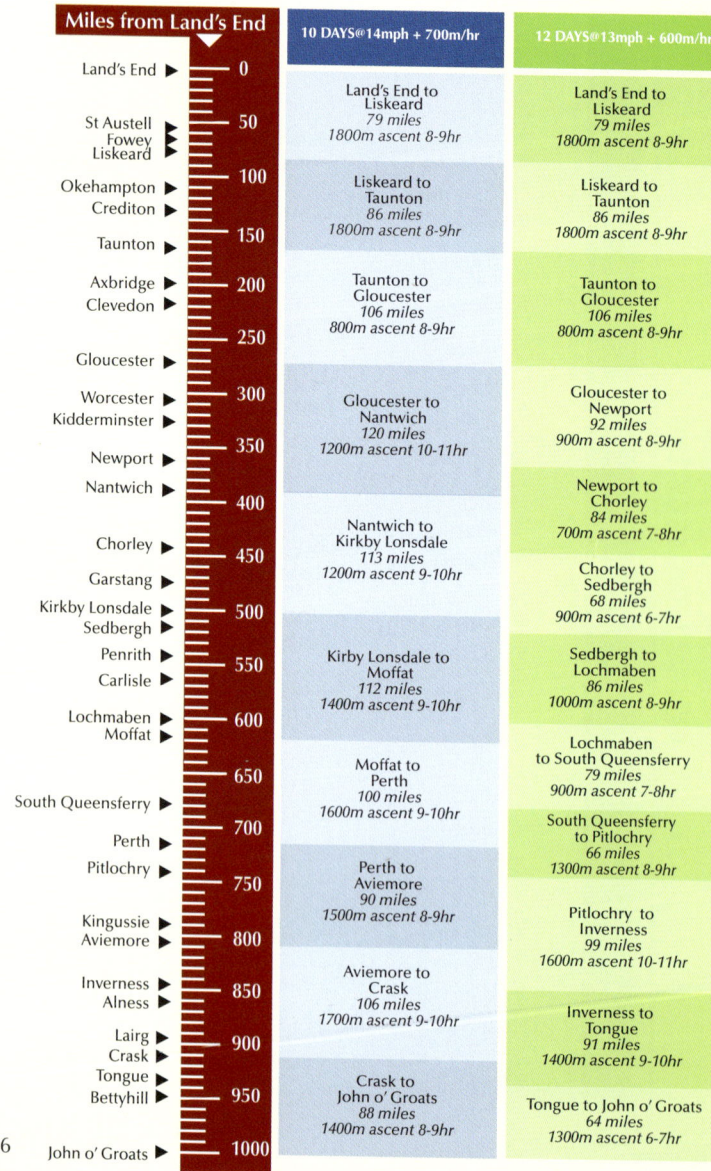

14 DAYS@12mph + 500m/hr	16 DAYS@11mph + 400m/hr	18 DAYS@10mph + 300m/hr
Land's End to Fowey 65 miles 1400m ascent 8-9hr	Land's End to Fowey 65 miles 1400m ascent 8-9hr	Land's End to St Austell 57 miles 1200m ascent 9-10hr
Fowey to Crediton 65 miles 1700m ascent 8-9hr	Fowey to Crediton 65 miles 1600m ascent 8-9hr	St Austell to Okehampton 54 miles 1500m ascent 10-11hr
Crediton to Clevedon 86 miles 800m ascent 8-9hr	Crediton to Axbridge 72 miles 800m ascent 8-9hr	Okehampton to Taunton 54 miles 1000m ascent 8-9hr
Clevedon to Worcester 91 miles 700m ascent 8-9hr	Axbridge to Gloucester 69 miles 600m ascent 7-8hr	Taunton to Clevedon 51 miles 300m ascent 6-7hr
Worcester to Nantwich 84 miles 900m ascent 8-9hr	Gloucester to Kidderminster 56 miles 500m ascent 6-7hr	Clevedon to Gloucester 55 miles 500m ascent 7-8hr
Nantwich to Garstang 85 miles 600m ascent 8-9hr	Kidderminster to Nantwich 62 miles 600m ascent 7-8hr	Gloucester to Kidderminster 56 miles 700m ascent 7-8hr
Garstang to Penrith 70 miles 1400m ascent 8-9hr	Nantwich to Chorley 56 miles 500m ascent 7-8hr	Kidderminster to Nantwich 62 miles 600m ascent 8-9hr
Penrith to Moffat 70 miles 700m ascent 7-8hr	Chorley to Kirkby Lonsdale 58 miles 600m ascent 7-8hr	Nantwich to Chorley 56 miles 500m ascent 7-8hr
Moffat to South Queensferry 64 miles 900m ascent 7-8hr	Kirkby Lonsdale to Carlisle 63 miles 900m ascent 9-10hr	Chorley to Kirkby Lonsdale 58 miles 600m ascent 7-8hr
South Queensferry to Pitlochry 66 miles 1300m ascent 8-9hr	Carlisle to Moffat 50 miles 500m ascent 5-6hr	Kirkby Lonsdale to Carlisle 63 miles 900m ascent 9-10hr
Pitlochry to Aviemore 60 miles 900m ascent 6-7hr	Moffat to South Queensferry 64 miles 900m ascent 8-9hr	Carlisle to Moffat 50 miles 500m ascent 6-7hr
Aviemore to Alness 64 miles 700m ascent 6-7hr	South Queensferry to Pitlochry 66 miles 1300m ascent 9-10hr	Moffat to South Queensferry 64 miles 900m ascent 9-10hr
Alness to Tongue 66 miles 1100m ascent 7-8hr	Pitlochry to Aviemore 60 miles 900m ascent 7-8hr	South Queensferry to Pitlochry 66 miles 1300m ascent 10-11hr
Tongue to John o' Groats 64 miles 1300m ascent 6-7hr	Aviemore to Alness 64 miles 700m ascent 7-8hr	Pitlochry to Kingussie 47 miles 700m ascent 7-8hr
	Alness to Tongue 66 miles 1100m ascent 8-9hr	Kingussie to Inverness 52 miles 700m ascent 7-8hr
	Tongue to John o' Groats 64 miles 1300m ascent 8-9hr	Inverness to Lairg 55 miles 900m ascent 8-9hr
		Lairg to Bettyhill 51 miles 1000m ascent 7-8hr
		Bettyhill to John o' Groats 50 miles 800m ascent 7-8hr

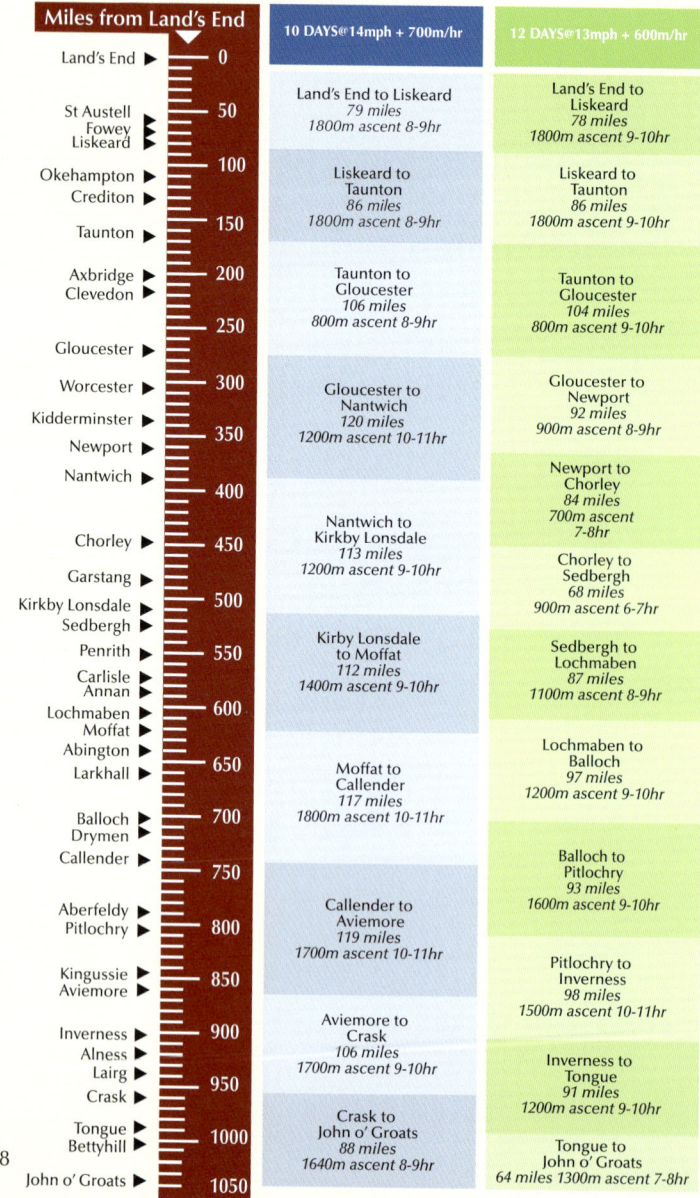

14 DAYS @ 12mph + 500m/hr

Land's End to Fowey
65 miles
1400m ascent 8-9hr

Fowey to Crediton
65 miles
1700m ascent 8-9hr

Crediton to Clevedon
86 miles
800m ascent 8-9hr

Clevedon to Worcester
91 miles
700m ascent 8-9hr

Worcester to Nantwich
84 miles
900m ascent 8-9hr

Nantwich to Garstang
85 miles
600m ascent 8-9hr

Garstang to Penrith
70 miles
1400m ascent 8-9hr

Penrith to Moffat
70 miles
700m ascent 7-8hr

Moffat to Balloch
83 miles
1000m ascent 8-9hr

Balloch to Pitlochry
93 miles
1600m ascent 8-9hr

Pitlochry to Aviemore
60 miles
900m ascent 6-7hr

Aviemore to Alness
64 miles 700m ascent 6-7hr

Alness to Tongue
66 miles
1100m ascent 7-8hr

Tongue to John o' Groats
64 miles
1300m ascent 8-9hr

16 DAYS @ 11mph + 400m/hr

Land's End to Fowey
64 miles
1400m ascent 9-10hr

Fowey to Crediton
65 miles
1700m ascent 9-10hr

Crediton to Axbridge
72 miles
800m ascent 8-9hr

Axbridge to Gloucester
69 miles
600m ascent 7-8hr

Gloucester to Kidderminster
56 miles
500m ascent 7-8hr

Kidderminster to Nantwich
62 miles
600m ascent 7-8hr

Nantwich to Chorley
56 miles
500m ascent 6-7hr

Chorley to Kirkby Lonsdale
58 miles
600m ascent 6-7hr

Kirkby Lonsdale to Carlisle
63 miles
900m ascent 7-8hr

Carlisle to Abington
68 miles
900m ascent 8-9hr

Abington to Balloch
65 miles
800m ascent 7-8hr

Balloch to Aberfeldy
78 miles
1400m ascent 10-11hr

Aberfeldy to Aviemore
75 miles
1100m ascent 9-10hr

Aviemore to Alness
64 miles
700m ascent 7-8hr

Alness to Tongue
66 miles
1100m ascent 8-9hr

Tongue to John o' Groats
64 miles
1300m ascent 9-10hr

18 DAYS @ 10mph + 300m/hr

Land's End to St Austell
57 miles
1200m ascent 9-10hr

St Austell to Okehampton
54 miles
1500m ascent 10-11hr

Okehampton to Taunton
54 miles
1000m ascent 8-9hr

Taunton to Clevedon
51 miles
300m ascent 6-7hr

Clevedon to Gloucester
55 miles
500m ascent 7-8hr

Gloucester to Kidderminster
56 miles
500m ascent 7-8hr

Kidderminster to Nantwich
62 miles
600m ascent 8-9hr

Nantwich to Chorley
56 miles
500m ascent 7-8hr

Chorley to Sedbergh
70 miles
800m ascent 9-10hr

Sedbergh to Annan
71 miles
1100m ascent 10-11hr

Annan to Larkhall
74 miles
1000m ascent 9-10hr

Larkhall to Drymen
50 miles 600m ascent 7-8hr

Drymen to Aberfeldy
67 miles
1000m ascent 10-11hr

Aberfeldy to Kingussie
62 miles
900m ascent 9-10hr

Kingussie to Inverness
51 miles 800m ascent 7-8hr

Inverness to Lairg
55 miles 900m ascent 8-9hr

Lairg to Bettyhill
51 miles
900m ascent 8-9hr

Bettyhill to John o' Groats
50 miles 700m ascent 7-8hr

The winding mechanism of the UK's largest and oldest working salt mine alongside the Weaver Navigation in Winsford (Stage 6)

INTRODUCTION

Heading towards Lochmaben on the quiet roads of Dumfrieshire (Stage 8)

Cycling the length of Great Britain between the two extremities of Land's End in the southwest and John o' Groats in the northeast is a challenge that many cyclists aspire to at least once in their lifetime. There is no official route to follow and what happens in between is entirely up to you. So there is a lot of planning involved.

The journey is commonly referred to as 'LEJOG' when ridden south to north, 'JOGLE' when ridden in the opposite direction and sometimes just as 'the End-to-End route'. But no matter what you call it, it is going to be at least 874 miles, which is currently considered to be the minimum distance if you throw caution to the wind and ride beside fast-moving traffic following trunk roads and busy city streets. The safer and more enjoyable option detailed in this guidebook links stretches of traffic-free, shared-use paths with quieter roads without adding much to the distance to give an 'optimal' route that can still be comfortably ridden by a reasonably fit cyclist in a fortnight. The 'optimal' route is 1000 miles (1600 km) with 14,400m of ascent, the majority encountered at either end of the route. A slightly longer option has alternative stages through Glasgow and the Trossachs is 1046 miles (1675km) with 14,800m of ascent.

CYCLING LAND'S END TO JOHN O' GROATS

WHY THE END-TO-END ROUTE?

Land's End is not the most westerly point on the island of Great Britain; neither is it the most southerly. And when you get to the other end you will see that John o' Groats is actually about 2 miles (3km) south of the nearby headland of Dunnet Head. So what's all the excitement about then?

The simple answer is that Land's End and John o' Groats are the two populated places on the island of Great Britain separated by the greatest distance. And it's this that has captured people's imagination and turned the journey into a challenge. Once you've completed it you will never look at a weather map in exactly the same way; mentions of rain across the Highlands will bring the memories of your ride and the friendship of the people you rode with flooding back. Your ride will also form a common bond with every other End-to-Ender you meet for the rest of your life, giving endless topics of conversation about the best route, the hardest day or the best pint you enjoyed along the way. And because you've ridden it, you can talk knowledgably.

TAILORING THIS ROUTE TO YOUR NEEDS

Every End-to-Ender starts out by developing a plan that works for them in terms of the amount of time they can spare; their budget and the places they want to visit along the way. This guidebook takes you through those considerations and gives you the tools and information to develop your own itinerary and schedule.

The route described in this guidebook sticks to traffic-free paths and minor roads. This makes navigation more complex so turn-by-turn instructions and detailed maps are included in the route description. Using the GPX tracks for the LEJOG route that is described here and the corresponding JOGLE route, which are available to download for free at www.cicerone.co.uk/1025/GPX, will undoubtedly make navigation easier.

However, many will want to tailor the route to their own needs. For instance, you may wish to make a detour to visit a landmark, friends or family or incorporate an iconic climb. You can easily do this by uploading the GPX files into one of the route planning apps listed in Appendix D, most of which can be used without

At the lighthouse on Dunnet Head, the most northern point on mainland Britain (Stage 14)

a subscription, and incorporate your detour safe in the knowledge that most apps automatically pick a route that sticks to cycle paths and quieter roads. Now it's your End-to-End route; your challenge.

A JOURNEY THROUGH A MYRIAD OF LANDSCAPES

Great Britain is renowned for its geological diversity with rocks of almost all geological ages appearing as outcrops. This route crosses the bands of different types of rock which typically run in a north-easterly direction. As a result you cycle over a rich variety of terrain. Sometimes it's flat making progress rapid, but in other places it's hillier and more challenging and it's all due to the underlying geology.

In southwest England, Devonian and Carboniferous slates, shales, sandstones and limestone are common, giving rolling hills, diverse coastal scenery and bleak moors wherever harder granites come to the surface. Once past Taunton, the Somerset Levels are a lowland landscape typically just 20–30 feet above sea level. They were formed during the last 10,000 years after the last ice age and until they were drained in the 16th and 17th centuries would have flooded regularly. Here sedimentary clays overlay older Triassic rock with numerous outcrops, typically formed from sandstone and shales that were once islands standing out above the wetlands. Look out for Burrow Mump, which is 4 miles (6km) to the east of the route south of Bridgwater and the more prominent Glastonbury Tor, which is 10 miles (16km) to the east of the route.

The route skirts around the western end of the Mendips Hills, a ridge of largely Carboniferous limestone that hides Cheddar Gorge then heads north across the flatlands along the Bristol Channel. These were formed from alluvial deposits and are riven by small rivers that were once tidal for some way inland but are now controlled by sluices or 'clysts' as they are called locally.

The wide fertile Severn Vale runs northwards through Gloucestershire and Worcestershire with the higher ground of Cotwolds Hills to the east and the Forest of Dean and the Mendip Hills to the west. Being formed from sedimentary sandstones topped with alluvial clays means it is mostly flat, giving miles of easy pedalling. However, deposits of tills and gravels left by retreating glaciers do give the occasional low hill such as Woolridge to north of Gloucester. At Kidderminster, the route leaves the River Severn and follows its tributary the River Stour which eventually turns east into the West Midlands. Here the sedimentary shales, sandstones and mudstones contain coal measures that were once mined in the Shropshire Coalfields to the west and the South Staffordshire Coalfields to the east. The route slips through a green corridor between these urban areas and then crosses a wide basin of red sandstones that runs through the eastern part of Shropshire and north across Cheshire. There are occasional geological faults which show as escarpments and low hills, such as the Mid Cheshire Range to the west. Repeated flooding 250–300 million years ago left massive salt beds mainly in the area around Northwich. The Romans extracted salt here during their occupation, but commercial extraction began in the 17th century and continues today at a mine next to the route in Winsford. The route also passes a number of pools or meres formed when worked-out mines subsided.

Sedimentary rocks such as sandstones, siltstones and mudstones also predominate through Lancashire coastal plain. Here they are shot through with coal measures in the southern industrial belt, millstone grit in the upland areas of the Forest of Bowland and the higher moors the east of Chorley and a belt of limestone between Lancaster and Sedbergh where the route follows quiet roads up the Lune Valley.

Immediately after Sedbergh the route runs around the western perimeter of the Howgill Fells which are mainly formed out of Silurian slates and gritstones, still following the River Lune and briefly snaking below the busy M6 before heading west to Shap where quarrying for limestone and blue and pink granites is the mainstay of the local economy. Once on the descent into Penrith, it is back to sedimentary rocks such as sandstones, siltstones and mudstones through the easy-rolling Eden Valley, across the Scottish border and westwards along the Solway Firth to Annan.

From a geographical and geological perspectives Scotland divides into four main subcategories. The sparsely populated Southern Uplands are mainly formed from Silurian shales and sandstones, giving gently rolling hills and broad valleys. Running between the Forth of Clyde and Firth of Forth is a rift valley generally called the Central Lowlands mainly formed of sedimentary rocks that held the coal and iron ore deposits that fuelled Scotland's heavy industries during the 19th and early 20th centuries. Next are the majestic Cairngorms which were formed 40 million years ago when volcanic granite that had been pushed to the surface was carved and gouged by glaciers to give high rugged summits and broad U-shaped valleys littered with boulders that were deposited during glacial retreat. And finally, north of the Great Glen, sedimentary rocks such as sandstone and mudstone were laid down on and then heated and compressed to form harder metamorphic rocks. Here the underlying gneisses are impervious to water giving rise to extensive bogs and peatland. But where gneiss has been forced to the

TAILORING THIS ROUTE TO YOUR NEEDS

surface and eroded by glacial action stand grand and typically isolated summits that are characteristic of the Flow Country.

And it's not just the geology and topography that change on the journey. So too do the flora, the indigenous building materials and styles and dialects. You can start the day by being waved off by a B&B proprietor with a broad West Country accent and end it being welcomed by another with a West Midlands dialect.

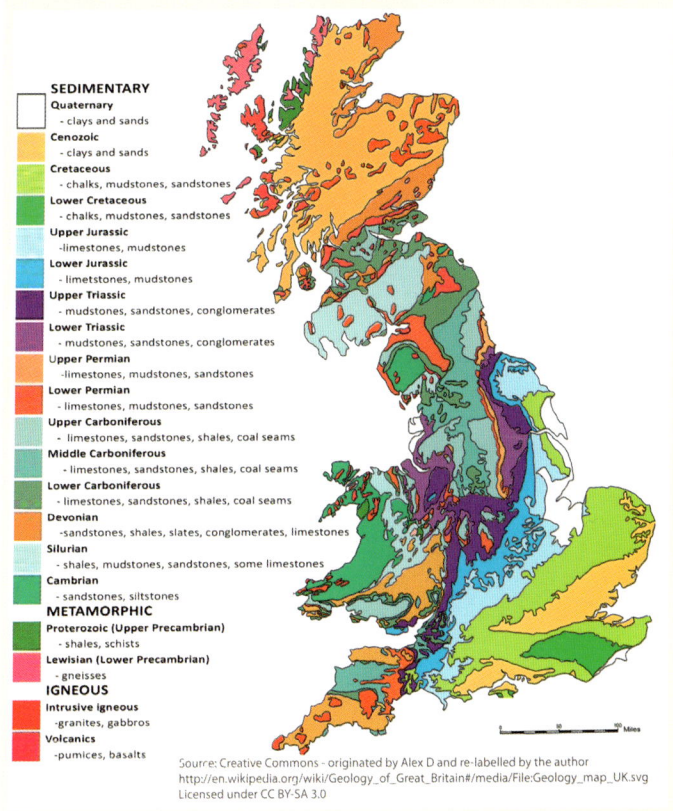

Geological map of Great Britain showing the many different types of rock encountered along the route

15

TEN FOODS TO TRY ALONG THE ROUTE

What better way to tick off the miles than trying out local foods?
- Start with the Cornish pasty which some say gained its distinctive D shape so Cornish tin miners could eat the filling and discard the crust to prevent contact with grimy hands. Then try Devonshire Splits, as scones are sometimes called locally, with jam and clotted cream.
- Quaff a little scrumpy ('rough' cider) in Somerset
- Double Gloucester cheese is ubiquitous throughout the UK, so if you enjoy meat look out for dishes made from Gloucester Old Spot pork which has been awarded Protected Designation of Origin status
- Try some piquant Worcester or Worcestershire Sauce which is a secret blend of anchovies, pureed fruit and spices used to flavour meat dishes, Welsh rarebit and the famous 'Bloody Mary' cocktail
- The welcome sign to the Shropshire town of Market Drayton on Stage 5 proudly states that it is the 'home of gingerbread', which has been produced here for over 200 years
- While passing through South Lancashire on Stage 6, try both a Chorley cake and its more popular relative the Eccles cake. Both are flat and contain fruit, but the Chorley variety is less sweet.
- The coiled Cumberland Sausage is a perennial favourite thought to have been first made in the 18th century when pepper, nutmeg and other spices were shipped into Whitehaven from the Americas
- Scotland has a wealth of foods to try such as porridge, shortbread, oatcakes, haggis, Scotch whisky, Scotch broth and Scotch pies. The Moffat Tasty, made by R. Little Bakers Ltd, is a fruit loaf with added pieces of local Moffat Toffee. It is said to be best served toasted with butter and a generous dollop of honey.
- Follow NCN 756 northwards for 1½ miles on alternative stage 9 in the centre of Glasgow and you will find the Shish Mahal restaurant (www.shishmahal.co.uk) famed for inventing chicken tikka masala

R. Little, the traditional bakers and confectioners in Moffat on Stage 8, who invented the 'Moffat Tasty'

WHICH DIRECTION TO RIDE?

Because of the prevailing south-westerly winds, it is usually easier to ride LEJOG from south to north as described in this guidebook. Riding in that direction also means you are not riding into the sun and get through Cornwall and Devon, where the hills are undoubtedly steeper, while you are still fresh. During the summer months the hours of daylight steadily increase as you ride north with John o' Groats getting over 2 hours more than Land's End on the longest day. As such you can perhaps ride at a slower pace and enjoy the Scottish landscape which increases in grandeur through the Highlands then turns to splendid isolation through the 'Flow Country'.

However, should you choose to ride in the opposite direction from John o' Groats to Land's End, (JOGLE), you will need to adapt the directions in the route descriptions or download the GPX files for JOGLE which are available at www.cicerone.co.uk/1025.

SELECTING A SCHEDULE

Inevitably the stages of this guidebook will not coincide with your personal itinerary as that will depend on the time you have available, your daily mileage and whether you visit attractions along the way. If you want a more relaxed schedule allow more time for the harder sections at either end of the route rather than the easier-rolling flatland in Shropshire and Cheshire. However, avoid having rest days as you risk stiffening up and may find it harder to get restarted the following day. So if you don't think you can sustain a consistent mileage, incorporate a couple of days when you cover fewer miles at an easier pace.

The availability of accommodation will also determine where your days begin and end, which could be at places before the end of a stage, into the following stage or perhaps somewhere off the route altogether. When planning your ride:
- First decide how many days you can spare or need
- Then use the alternative schedules to identify roughly where each day will ideally end
- Identify the most convenient accommodation that suits your budget. Inevitably this may mean amending your initial schedule so be prepared to be flexible perhaps enjoying a night in a B&B if there are no hostels nearby
- Book your accommodation and finalise your schedule. You will have more choice about where to stay if you book your accommodation well in advance
- If you are using a GPS device for navigation, download the files, which are free from the Cicerone website, and upload them into one of the many cycling route planning apps (see Appendix D for list) where you can quickly amend the route

Cycling Land's End to John o' Groats

WHEN TO RIDE

The best time to go is between April and September when the days are longer and the weather is at its best. However, if you need to 'get some miles into your legs' first it is perhaps best to ride towards the end of summer. No matter when you choose to go, you should expect the weather to change as you get further north. In July, Cornwall has an average temperate of 20°C and gets 55mm of rainfall whereas Scotland is typically 5°C cooler and gets twice as much rain. At the same time, proportionately more of the northern stages of the route are at higher altitudes where you can anticipate windier conditions. But you may get inclement days anywhere along the route so check the weather forecast before you set out and be prepared to amend your plans.

Don't be deterred by the infamous Scots midges (*culicoides impunctatus*) which are only about for an hour or so in the morning and early evening during summer and are not much of a problem for moving cyclists as they prefer still air. But if you are camping, apply one of the repellents and promptly treat any bumps with antihistamine cream if you get bitten.

Another potential hazard, particularly if you decide to ride north to south (i.e. JOGLE), is low sunlight during autumn and winter months which can dazzle other road users making you almost invisible. Draw attention to yourself with a powerful pulsing

Be prepared for misfortunes; do what you can to prevent them and ensure you can fix them efficiently and be quickly back on your way

rear light, which is more effective than a constant beam.

RIDING ALONE OR AS PART OF A GROUP?

Although you will undoubtedly meet fellow End-to-Enders along the way, you are likely to have a more enjoyable experience if you ride with a friend or two. Besides the companionship, they can take their turn at the front when you are riding into a headwind, help out with mechanicals and share any fixed expenses. However, make sure you are well-matched, both in terms of riding speed and temperament, otherwise your LEJOG could be unforgettable for all the wrong reasons.

Too large a group and you will have difficulties finding accommodation and restaurants with sufficient capacity and will need to be more disciplined when riding to minimise inconvenience for other road users. You will also need to implement procedures, such as having a designated 'tail-end-Charlie', so no-one gets inadvertently left behind.

GETTING THERE

Undoubtedly the easiest way to get to Penzance is to have someone drive you there and drop you off. If you are lucky, they may act as your support vehicle, moving luggage between stops, providing catering support and eventually taking you back home. But if you are not so fortunate, there are other ways.

One-way car hire

Rental companies with depots in or near Penzance, such as Enterprise (www.enterprise.co.uk) and Europcar (www.eurocar.co.uk) let you collect a vehicle from anywhere in the UK and leave it at their Penzance depot. So you could get to the start for the cost of a 24-hour rental and a couple of tanks of fuel, which may be cheaper than rail travel especially for a couple. You will need to check that your bike fits into the vehicle as well as the rental company's Penzance depot opening hours, factoring this into your schedule.

Some rental companies allow you to drop off vehicles when the depot is closed. If you choose to do this, it is a good idea to take a few photos of the vehicle parked at the depot to avoid any subsequent damage being attributed to you. You should also consider wrapping your bike in plastic sheeting or an old pair of curtains to minimise the risk of inadvertent damage to the interior and incurring a penalty charge.

By rail

Plan well ahead if you intend to travel to Penzance or from the far north of Scotland by rail as there will be other End-to-Enders looking to do the same and space for bikes is limited. So book your ticket and make you bike reservation early. While it is fairly

Cycling Land's End to John o' Groats

simple to book your own ticket if you are travelling cross country, you may need to make a bike reservation with every train operator involved in the journey. It can be difficult and time-consuming but is imperative as without a bike reservation you do risk getting bumped.

PlusBike (http://plusbike.national rail.co.uk) is a free tool available both within the National Rail website (www.nationalrail.co.uk) and as a downloadable app that helps you identify whether or not you need to make a reservation for any leg of your journey and which operator you need to contact. However, neither the PlusBike app nor the National Rail website provides a facility to make a bike reservation.

Online booking for bikes only works well for simple journeys where only one train operator is involved and there are no changes involved. Anything more complex and it is best to talk to a member of a support team who can confirm that your bike is reserved on each leg of your journey. Other websites and resources for making bike reservations are listed in Appendix F but if all else fails do it in person at the travel counter at your local station well before your planned departure date.

And once you have arrived at Penzance station you still need to get to Land's End which is 9 miles away. If you can't face riding it contact Anytime Taxis, (www.anytime-taxis.com) on 01736 888 888 and they will take you and your bike at any time of the day or night.

Hanging bike space on a main line express

By bus

A cheap albeit slow option is to take a National Express (www.nationalexpress.com) coach to Penzance, inevitably needing to change coach one or more times along the way. They will carry bikes as long as they are packaged and folded as small as possible, although there might be a small additional charge. However, they will only be taken if there is sufficient space in the hold, making it a bit of a gamble.

By air

You can fly to airports at Newquay (www.cornwallairportnewquay.com),

Bristol (www.bristolairport.co.uk) or Exeter (www.exeter-airport.co.uk). Properly packed, your bike could fly with you as an 'exceptional luggage item' that will incur extra costs. But once you get to your destination airport you still have to get to Land's End which will entail a one-way car hire or travelling by train from the nearest station down to Penzance and you will almost certainly need to make a reservation for your bike. Consequently, couriering it may be both easier and cheaper.

Couriering your bike
Both The Cycle Centre in Penzance and Land's End Cycle Hire in Marazion will receive your bike by courier and deliver it to Land's End. They also offer a courier service for riders completing JOGLE, securely packing your bike and any luggage in a cardboard container before handing it over to a national courier for transport home. See Appendix B for their details.

GETTING BACK

All you really want to do is lie down and sleep. But not just yet as first you have to get you and your bike home.

By car
You can ride 17 miles down the A92 and rent a vehicle from Hertz Rental (www.hertz.co.uk) in Wick and return it to any of their many depots in the UK. There are more car rental companies once you reach Inverness.

By rail
The nearest stations are 17 miles away in Wick or 20 miles back along the route in Thurso from where Scotrail (www.scotrail.co.uk) provide three or four services on weekdays and Saturdays but only one on Sundays. Competition for the limited bike space on southbound trains can be fierce, especially at weekends so book early. You can make a bike reservation with Scotrail online at the same time as you purchase your ticket. Just keep it simple by choosing a destination station within Scotland and you should not have any problems. If you need to travel over the border, make a separate reservation with the specific train operator.

By bus
John O' Groats Transport (www.johnogroatsbiketransport.co.uk) will take you and your bike down to Inverness. Either book online or ring 01463 419 160 for details. Scottish CityLink (www.citylink.co.uk), which runs bus services from John o' Groats Junction to destinations all across Scotland, carries bicycles that are boxed or bagged if there is sufficient space, once again making it a bit of a gamble.

By air
Wick airport (www.hial.co.uk) provides daily services from Wick to

Edinburgh and Aberdeen, where you can connect with UK domestic and international flights. Alternatively, you could travel by bus to Inverness Airport (www.invernessairport.co.uk) or a ferry to Orkney and fly from Kirkwall Airport.

By courier

John O' Groats Transport (www.johnogroatsbiketransport.co.uk) also offers a courier service, securely packing your bike and any luggage in a cardboard container before handing it over to a national courier for transportation. The Bike Shop in Thurso and The Spot Cycle Shop in Wick offer a similar service. See Appendix B for details. That still leaves you, but at least your bike is sorted.

HOW MUCH TO BUDGET

The cost of riding LEJOG depends on a number of factors:
- Your choice of accommodation with hotels being the most expensive and camping being the cheapest, especially if you wild camp in Scotland
- The number of nights of accommodation you need with faster schedules clearly being cheapest
- How you choose to get to the start and back from the finish
- And to some extent whether you are riding alone or in a group in that the unit cost of two people sharing a twin room is always less than single occupancy and you can also enjoy savings by sharing on-way vehicle rental charges and petrol costs

A fast and somewhat Spartan ride, camping at night and booking advance rail tickets to get to the start and back from the from the finish, is probably the cheapest option at just a few hundred pounds. While a more leisurely ride, stopping at good hotels and using first class rail or internal flights is going to cost at least a couple of thousand pounds and may be little different from the cost of a fully supported tour which is ideally suited to those with deeper pockets who wish to focus purely on cycling and let someone else take care of everything else. See Appendix D for providers of package holidays.

Whichever option you choose, it pays to populate a spreadsheet with estimated costs and then firm them up as you book your accommodation and travel, especially so if you are on a tight budget or need to justify the expenditure to a partner who is not quite so enthusiastic about your once-in-a-lifetime ride.

FIRST AND LAST NIGHTS

Land's End

Although getting you and your bike to the start may be a challenge, finding accommodation is less so especially if you are prepared to start your ride on a weekday rather than the weekend. You may struggle to find exactly the

The busy town of Penzance where many End-to-Enders overnight before their ride

type of accommodation you would prefer close to Land's End but there is plenty of choice of other types of accommodation in nearby St Just or Penzance.

The priority must be to check over your bike, find some food, lay out your kit and then turn in for the night. That way you will awake refreshed and set for an early start on what may well prove to be the hardest day of all. Take the obligatory photograph. Then see how far you can get before the rest of the world wakes up.

John o' Groats

After all the effort, most End-to-Enders spend very little time in John o' Groats, simply recording their arrival before turning around and heading off home. That is a pity because John o' Groats has benefited from the development of the North Coast 500 (www.northcoast500.com) coastal touring route which has reinvigorated many remote settlements in Northern Scotland with new businesses springing up to cater for the influx of tourists.

ACCOMMODATION

As most End-to-End routes pass through the same narrow corridor there is considerable pressure on accommodation, particularly in the north of Scotland. For this reason it pays to book your accommodation as early as possible.

Some cycle tourists prefer to camp and it is free to 'wild camp' in Scotland. The Scottish Land Reform Act 2003 confirmed that access rights extend to wild camping, meaning that as long as you do not have motorised transport, small numbers of people with lightweight tents can stay for

CYCLING LAND'S END TO JOHN O' GROATS

a maximum of three nights in any one spot. However, days of repeatedly ascending 1,000m or more are unlikely to be pleasurable with heavy luggage.

This guide makes maximum use of hostels along or near the route, but if you prefer additional comforts you will find a variety of accommodation to suit most pockets listed in Appendix A and plenty more online. You may not be able to get exactly what you want at the start or finish of each of stage so may have to curtail your day before the end of a stage, ride further into the next stage or temporarily leave the route.

Hostels are always busy during the summer months and those in the more popular locations can be full at weekends and sometimes even in the depths of winter, so it pays to book early. Both the Youth Hostel Association (www.yha.org.uk) and the Scottish Youth Hostel (www.syha.org.uk) have a number of hostels along the route and there is an increasing number of independent hostels – see www.independenthostelguide.co.uk for details.

It is worth seeking out Visit England (www.visitengland.com) and Visit Scotland's (www.visitscotland.com) star-graded B&Bs, guest houses and hotels enrolled in their 'Cyclists Welcome' scheme which provide drying facilities, bike storage and other services. Whatever you choose, if you want to arrive early to drop off your bike and go sightseeing or anticipate arriving later due to unforeseen delay, it is only courteous to ring ahead and let them know.

BAGGAGE TRANSFER

Other than arranging it yourself with local taxi operators, the only easy way

Parked up outside the Wayfarers Hostel in Penrith on Stage 7, which is perhaps the most cycle-friendly hostel in the UK

to get your luggage transferred each day is to book a self-guided package holiday. See Appendix D for details.

WHAT TO TAKE

The plethora of accommodation and the high number of cycle shops along the route means you can keep your bike as light as possible. So here are some tips to lighten your load:

- Think layers and add-ons rather than alternatives
- Use drying facilities to rinse clothing every evening
- Choose leisurewear, such as long-sleeved T- shirts, that can also be an extra layer for chilly days
- Share tools and accessories
- Buy travel-sized toiletries and give shaving a miss for the journey
- Make do with a smartphone and leave other electronics at home
- Carry a mini-bottle of lubricant and clean and oil your chain two or three times during your trip. A wet-wipe or a serviette from a café works well enough for getting rid of most of the grime.
- Use accommodation with secure storage and leave the heavy bike lock at home
- Always wear a helmet as riding without one is irresponsible and consider a high-visibility gilet in dense traffic

Adopting such guidelines produces the kit list shown in Appendix G, which totals 5–7kg for summer tours and 7–9kg during winter. Having reduced the kit list as much as possible, it should easily fit into a pair of panniers or a set of frame packs.

PREPARING YOURSELF

Completing Land's End to John o' Groats requires both stamina and motivation. Plenty of cyclists can comfortably cover 60 to 100 miles in a day. However not all have the willpower to do it day-after-day for a fortnight or more. Similarly, we all know highly competitive individuals who repeatedly take on physical challenges without first developing the right type of fitness that will ensure their success. It pays to 'get miles in your legs' as they say.

If you do not already complete 50 mile plus rides regularly and with ease, start training at least 4–6 months before your ride. Create a plan and gradually build up your distances until you can ride your target average daily distance comfortably on three or four consecutive days. Try to vary the intensity rather than just knocking off the miles perhaps with interval training or spinning classes to get your heart racing. Include regular rides with hills and supplement your riding with strength training for your legs at your local gym.

As your strength increases, try a few longer rides with loaded panniers or even a short tour around your local area. That way you will familiarise yourself with how your bike handles fully laden and be able to check your kit. You will also become familiar with what it feels like to cycle long distances on consecutive days.

Vary the training by including complementary exercises such as swimming or gym classes and try to get into a routine of stretching the major muscle groups in both your legs and upper body before and after every session. This is something you should continue when you are on your trip as it will help to prevent cramp. And when you have finished riding for the day, don't idle around in sweaty kit. Get showered, refuelled, rehydrated and rested quickly so you maximise recovery time. Many cycling professionals apparently hop in the shower with their full kit on to wash out the accumulated bacteria and sweat from their helmet linings, jersey and shorts all at the same time. Then they just remove their gear and dry it ready for the next day. After that, a light massage will help you feel much better but without a soigneur you'll probably be doing that for yourself.

For more information about training for multi-day cycling consult one of the cycling training guides listed in Appendix F.

PREPARING YOUR BIKE

You can ride the route on a road bike, touring bike, gravel bike or a hybrid/city bike, but perhaps not a mountain bike. This is because they are heavy, have considerable rolling resistance between the tyre and the road and are generally far less efficient than road bikes so you will expend far more energy over a long tour. You could even ride the route on an e-bike as long as you recharge the battery every night, use power sparingly and keep your daily distance comfortably within its maximum range. Alternative you could carry a spare battery if you don't mind the extra weight. But no matter what type of bike you choose, there are some things that you can do to make your ride more comfortable:

- Ensure your bike is the right size and is correctly set up for you. If in doubt, book a bike fitting session with an expert. It'll cost a few pounds but will be money well spent.
- Leave your best carbon frame and carbon wheels at home
- Use winter or touring tyres that are 28mm or wider as they will be more durable and more comfortable
- Fit a cassette with a 30, 32 or 34-tooth sprocket to make climbing easier
- Add bar ends to straight handlebars so you have more choice for resting tired hands

Buy a bell which is essential for negotiating pedestrians on shared-use paths. Have your bike serviced a couple of weeks before your trip, allowing sufficient time for any worn parts to be replaced and run-in before your departure.

EATING

Cycling is strenuous so keep your energy reserves topped up by eating frequently otherwise you will soon 'hit the wall' and feel tired and demotivated. However, it is best to avoid a full breakfast as it will weigh heavy for most of the morning. Get into the routine of eating and drinking little and often, say every hour rather than waiting until you feel hungry or thirsty, as by then it is frequently too late.

Many cyclists rely on things such as sandwiches, fruit cake, cereal bars, gels and sports nutrition products. Try out what works for you on a few long rides before you set out on LEJOG and assess whether you will still find them palatable after a fortnight. That is not to say you should ignore inns and cafés along the way, rather err on the side of caution and stick to energy-giving snacks and pastries rather than a full midday meal. Needless to say, always carry emergency food, such as energy bars and gels, and ample water to get through the day.

PHONES AND WI-FI

Although mobile coverage is generally good throughout the southern stages, phone users in the less populated parts Scotland may have limited access to 4G networks, so you may not be able to post your photos straight to social media. However, many cafés and pubs provide free Wi-Fi access so you shouldn't be offline for too long.

Enjoying lunch outside the cycle café in Inverness (Stage 12)

WAYMARKING

Sections of the National Cycle Network (NCN) and local cycle routes are well signed with finger posts at major junctions and small repeater signs along the way. On other parts of the route, particularly when riding through urban areas or along minor roads, you will need to be meticulous in following the turn-by-turn instructions. Having the route downloaded onto a GPS so that you get a reassuring beep at every junction is also reassuring but not a necessity.

CYCLING LAND'S END TO JOHN O' GROATS

A milestone in Cheswardine that lists the distances to Land's End and John o' Groats (Stage 5)

MAPS

This book is designed to be small enough to carry with you and includes linear maps that are entirely adequate for following the route. However, they do not show much on either side of the route, such as where your overnight accommodation is located, so it is advisable to carry separate maps, such as those in the Ordnance Survey 1:50,000 Landranger Series for such purposes, particularly in remote areas (north of Inverness for example) where poor mobile signals may compromise the use of map apps on your phone.

PRACTICAL TIPS

- Pace yourself especially during the first few days when your enthusiasm for speed may run away with you. The record for riding LEJOG has only been broken 11 times since the Road Records Association (www.rra.org.uk) was founded in 1888 and currently stands at 43hrs 25min for men and 52hrs 45min for women. Admit that it's out of reach and settle into a pace that allows you to enjoy the journey.
- Break the day into manageable chunks of say 20–25 miles with reward at the end of each leg – for instance, second breakfast or coffee break; lunch; and then afternoon cake stop.
- Use the entire day rather than arriving at the day's destination early and getting bored waiting for the hostel to open.
- To keep your spirits up arrange to meet up with friends and relatives along the way. Their enthusiasm for your ride will keep you motivated long after you've said goodbye.
- Reduce the risk of knee strain by pedalling with a higher cadence and in an easier gear than perhaps you normally would.
- Check tomorrow's weather forecast so you will know whether to keep your waterproof at the top of your pack and wear your overshoes from the start. Also consider

One of the two village greens in the unspoilt 18th century village of Askham (Stage 7)

an early, or later, start to avoid the worst of the day's weather.
- Get into the habit of riding on the drops if you have them as it is a more aerodynamic position and therefore much more efficient. Prevent sore wrists by investing in good quality bar tape and padded gloves, moving your hands around the handlebars and not gripping too tightly, especially when riding on rough surfaces.
- Look after your bottom because you can be sure no-one else will! If you need to buy a comfortable saddle, go to a bike shop that provides a saddle-fitting service and allow plenty of time to break it in. Ride commando-style with proper padded shorts (or padded undershorts if the Lycra® look is not for you) and keep your contact points rigorously clean by starting every day with freshly laundered shorts and promptly treating the first signs of soreness with antiseptic cream. Some long-distance cyclists always use chamois cream and some don't, while others, like me, carry a few sachets just in case.

USING THIS GUIDE

Although the guide is organised into 14 stages, most likely you will choose to use one of the suggested alternative schedules or work out your own itinerary. Each stage starts and finishes at a location where there is a selection of different types of accommodation and good local facilities. At the beginning of each stage, an information box summarises the practical details associated with the stage, including start and finish points (with grid references), distance, total ascent, and numbers of the relevant Ordnance Survey map sheets

Norton in Hales has enjoys repeated success in the annual Britain in Bloom competition (Stage 5)

should you wish to explore. There is an estimate of the time required to complete the stage, although this will of course vary considerably according to fitness and the prevailing weather. Details of attractions and services along the stage are also provided.

The route shown on the accompanying 1:200,000 maps is described in detail with features that appear on the maps highlighted in **bold** in the text. Distances shown in brackets in the route description are the cumulative distance from the start of the stage and the distance still to ride to the end of the stage.

GPX TRACKS

GPX tracks for both the LEJOG route in this guidebook and the corresponding JOGLE route are available to download free at www.cicerone.co.uk/1025/GPX. A GPS device is an excellent aid to navigation, but you should also carry a map and know how to use it. GPX files are provided in good faith, but neither the author nor the publisher accepts responsibility for their accuracy as sometimes GPX files misalign when transferred between different apps and devices and the route may need realigning to roads.

Also, because GPS devices calculate elevation using a combination of triangulation from satellites and air pressure, they do not record ascent that accurately. At the same time, there is considerable variance in the way different ride planning apps calculate the amount of ascent for a route. Consequently, there is often a variance between both the amount of ascent logged by riders on the same route and between the amount logged out riding and that suggested for the same route by a ride planning app.

LAND'S END TO JOHN O' GROATS

Powering along towards the Bettyhill viewpoint which gives excellent views across to Ben Loyal and Ben Hope (Stage 14)

STAGE 1
Land's End to Fowey

Start	Fingerpost at the far end of Land's End complex (SW 342 251)
Finish	Slipway to Bodinnick Ferry in Fowey (SX 127 522)
Distance	65 miles (105km)
Ascent	1400m
Time	8–9hrs
OS Maps	OS Landranger 203 and 204
Refreshments	St Buryan, Newlyn, Penzance, Marazion, Goldsithney, Stithians, Perranwell, Carnon Downs, Philleigh, Heligan, St Austell, the Eden Project, St Blazey and Par
Accommodation	Plenty of accommodation of all types in the popular coastal resorts, but not so much inland

First the obligatory photograph at the famous signpost then it's time to start. You may be raring to get some miles ticked off, but many End-to-Enders consider the first 150 miles through Cornwall and Devon to be the hardest of all. This is where riders without the physical and mental stamina needed for consecutive long days in the saddle throw in the towel. Use this first stage to ease yourself into a rhythm where you cover the miles efficiently. To minimise the amount of climbing, the stage sticks to the middle ground between the hillier roads along the coast and higher ground inland, but it is still challenging. If you have time to spare there are lots of interesting places to visit along the stage such as the Lost Gardens of Heligan and the Eden Project.

Immediately after leaving Land's End turn left along NCN 3 and follow it across Threeve Common, behind Sennen Cove and across the busy A30 making use of a shared-use path alongside the eastbound carriageway. After 3 miles, turn left along the B3283 and ride to **St Buryan** (6/59 miles), where NCN 3 turns south into hillier terrain along the coast, turn right towards Lamorna. After 2

STAGE 1 – LAND'S END TO FOWEY

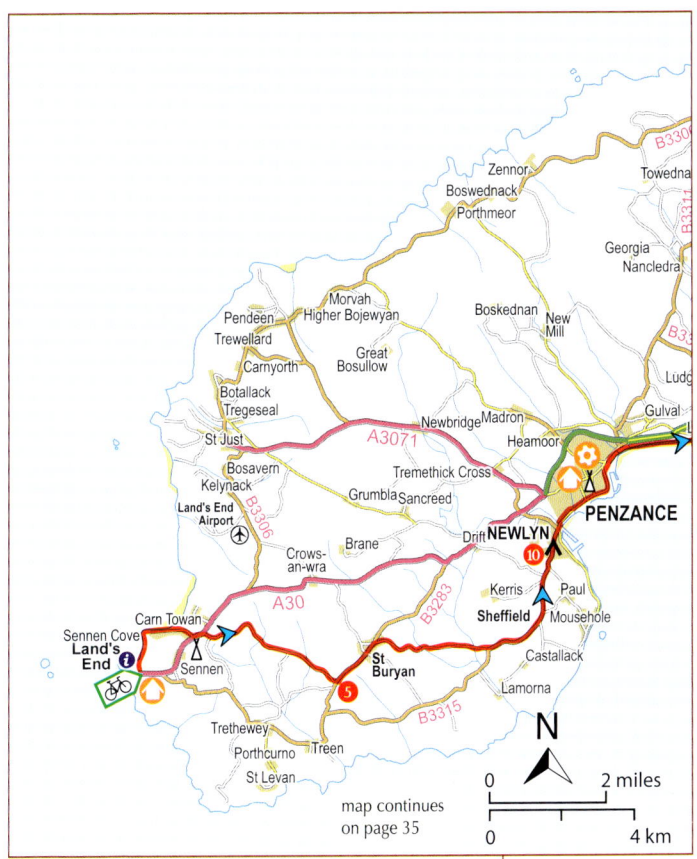

map continues on page 35

miles turn left at the T junction and follow the B3315 first through **Sheffield** and then steeply downhill to **Newlyn**. Go straight ahead at the cross roads in the centre of the village to re-join NCN 3 and follow it along the front in **Penzance** (12/53 miles) and enjoy 5 miles of easy cycling all the way around the bay to **Marazion** (15/50 miles) where St Michael's Mount is just off-shore. Here NCN 3 heads north through the once thriving mining towns

33

CYCLING LAND'S END TO JOHN O' GROATS

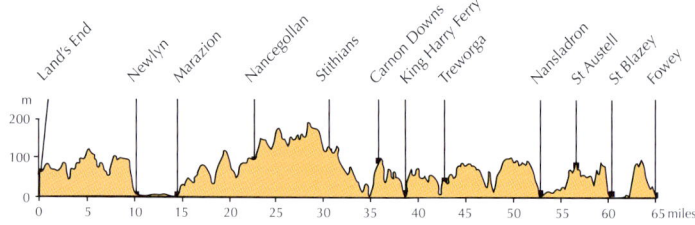

Newlyn Art Gallery celebrates the work of contemporary artists working locally who follow in tradition of the famous Newlyn School of artists who settled in the town over 120 years ago.

of Camborne and Redruth, but we meet it again later in the stage. ◂

If **St Michael's Mount** looks similar to Mont St Michel in Normandy, it's because the Priory Church on the summit was also built by French Benedictines monks who were gifted the small Cornish island by Robert de Mortain, (c.1031–c.1095), the half-brother of William the Conquerer, who controlled most of Cornwall following the Norman invasion of 1066.

The monks built the monastic buildings during the 12th century but were evicted when Henry V (1386–1422) banished alien religious orders during the Hundred Years' War (1337–1453). The tidal island changed hands many times in subsequent years until it was purchased by John St Aubyn (1613–1684). His descendants, the Lords St Levan, still live at St Michael's Mount, which is now owned and managed by the National Trust.

During the early 19th century the island had over 300 inhabitants, three schools, three pubs and a Wesleyan chapel. Today it is far quieter with only 30 permanent residents living and working on the island. You can visit St Michael's Mount castle, shops and cafés See www.stmichaelsmount.co.uk for details.

Stage 1 – Land's End to Fowey

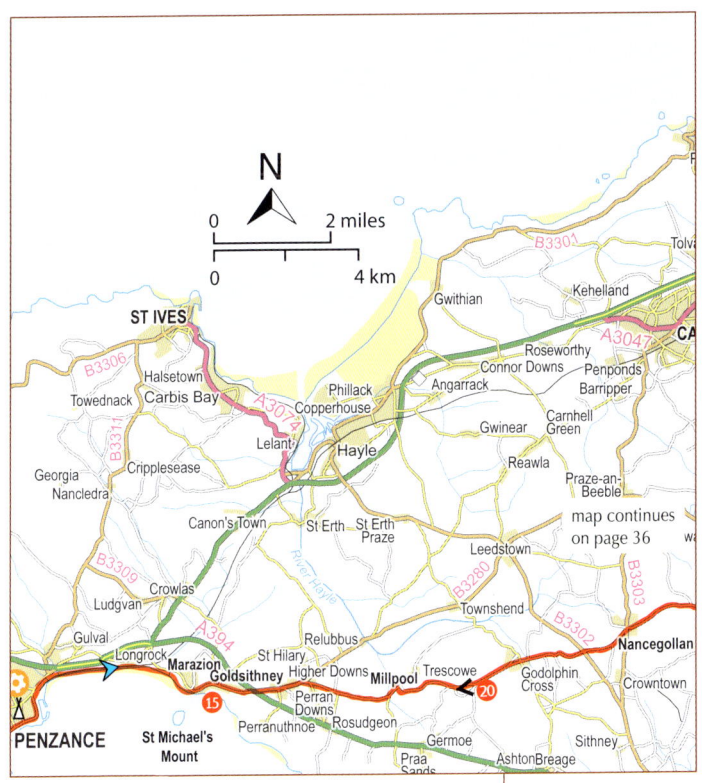

After passing through Marazion, cross the A394 and follow the B3280 through **Goldsithney** (17/48 miles) with the engine house and chimneys of the old tin mine at Tregurtha Downs to your left. At the end of the village, turn right towards **Millpool**. Ride through Millpool before turning right towards Ashton, the sign being on your right. Turn left after a mile and ride into Godolphin Cross (21/44 miles). Go straight on at the crossroads in the centre of the village and climb gently up to meet the B3302, in spring enjoying fields ablaze with daffodil which have been grown locally for over 100 years.

CYCLING LAND'S END TO JOHN O' GROATS

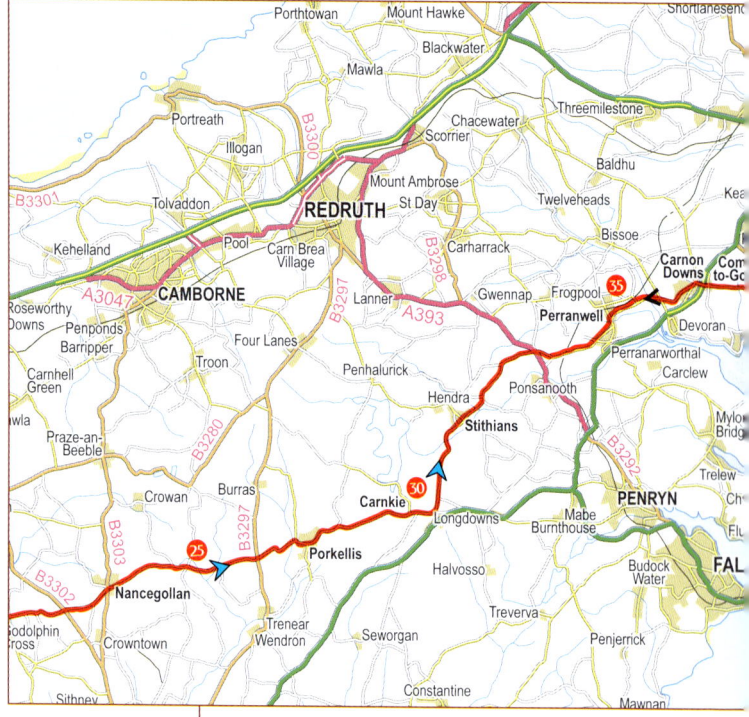

Cross the junction and continue to **Nancegollan** (23/42 miles). At the crossroads in the centre of the village, carry straight on towards Porkellis then after 2½ miles cross the B3297 and continue to **Porkellis** (27/38 miles). Turn left alongside The Star Inn and ride through **Carnkie** (29/36 miles) and **Stithians** (31/34 miles) to meet the A393. Cross over the main road following signs towards **Perranwell** (34/31 miles). Continue through the village and up Old Carnon Hill to **Carnon Downs** (36/29 miles).

Near the top of the ascent, turn right towards the magnificently named **Come-to-Good** (37/28 miles) then join the B3289 and ride through Trelissick to the **King**

STAGE 1 – LAND'S END TO FOWEY

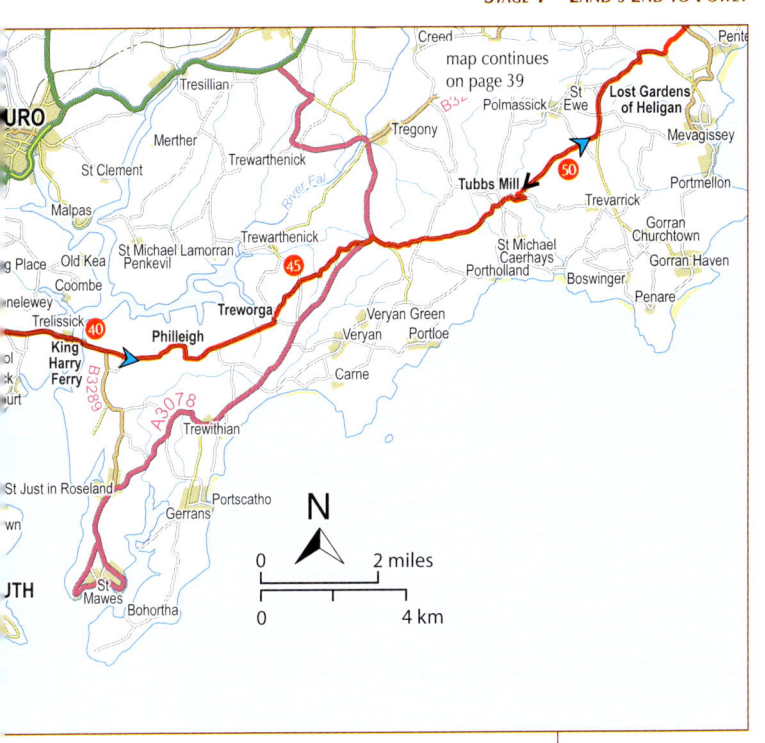

Harry Ferry (39/26 miles) by which time our route will yet again be temporarily following NCN 3. ▶

The **King Harry Ferry** (www.falriver.co.uk) across the River Fal runs continually from 7.00am (or 9.00am on Sundays) until dusk. There has been a crossing here for centuries, but the first mechanised ferry went into service in 1888 using a steam engine on the riverbank to pull the ferry along underwater chains. Since 1956 the ferries have been powered by on-board diesel-electric engines, but submerged chains remain an essential part of the mechanism.

Trelissick Gardens, which are now owned by the National Trust, were planted by the local Daniell family, whose fortune came from copper mining. The gardens were then further developed by the Copeland family of potters.

37

A contemplative sculpture of an elderly man looks out at the King Harry Ferry across the River Fal where cyclists are simply asked to make a charitable donation

Once disembarked, climb away from the river, turn left towards **Philleigh** (41/24 miles) and ride through the village. Two miles further on, turn left and ride through **Treworga** (43/22 miles). Go straight across the next crossroads, taking the unsigned road alongside the converted chapel. At its end, turn left along the A3078 towards Truro, then after 400 metres turn right towards Portholland. After another 400 metres turn left towards Mevagissey and then a mile further on bear right at a forked junction still heading towards Mevagissey, again briefly following NCN 3. At the next junction where the NCN 3 goes right, turn left towards Truro and then immediately right and descend steeply to **Tubbs Mill** (48/17 miles). Cross the river, then 350 metres further on turn sharply left towards Mevagissey and climb steadily for 2 miles. Cross the first staggered crossroads and then turn left at the next junction towards St Austell. After 1¾ miles turn right into the grounds of **The Lost Gardens of Heligan**, swing quickly left through Heligan Woods Caravan Park to pick up NCN 3 and follow it for

STAGE 1 – LAND'S END TO FOWEY

7 miles through the Pentewan Valley to **St Austell** (56/9 miles). ▶

The **Lost Gardens of Heligan** (www.heligan.com) were not really lost so much as neglected by the descendants of the Tremayne family who planted them over a period of 150 years from the mid 18th century before finding it all too much. Prior to World War I, the Heligan estate employed 22 gardeners. However, 16 were killed in action or died from their injuries immediately after the war, leaving a staff of eight who struggled to cope. Later in

In wet weather it may be better to use the B3273 which runs alongside the shared-use path all the way to St Austell.

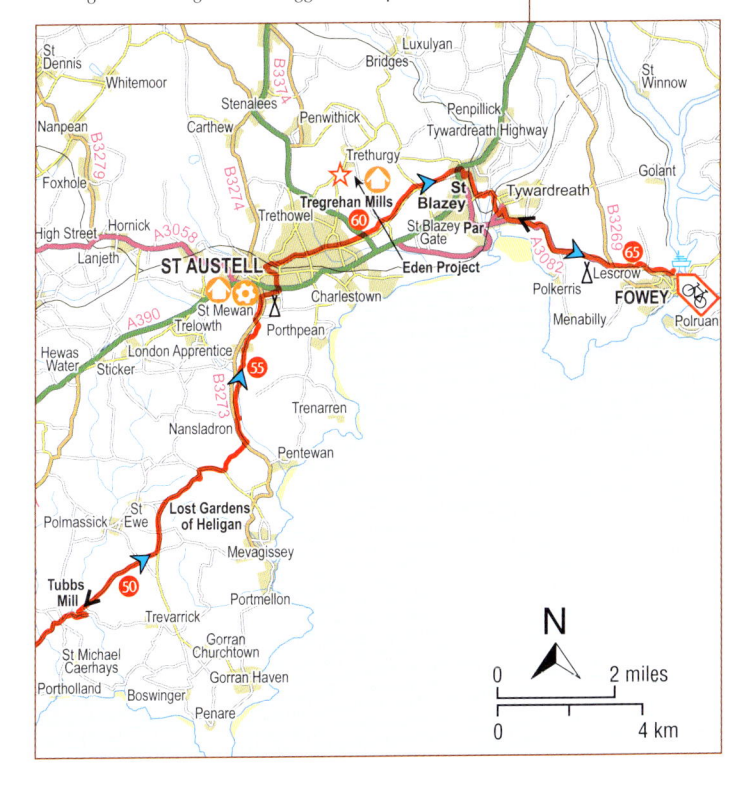

Parked up by a small thatched cob building at the Eden Project

the 1920s, the then owner Jack Tremayne decided that his first love was Italy, which had earlier inspired part of the planting, so he left Heligan and the gardens became overgrown.

After Jack Tremayne died, the Heligan estate was made into a family trust and one of the beneficiaries introduced the record producer and subsequent serial entrepreneur Tim Smit to the gardens. Together with a group of fellow enthusiasts, Smit restored the gardens to their former glory creating an important tourist attraction that has revitalised the local economy.

Follow NCN 3 right along Swales Road on the edge of the town, across the A390, through the town centre and out along Carlyon Road. Continue past the retail outlets and through the outer suburbs to **Tregrehan Mills** (59/6 miles) where the NCN 3 swings north to the Eden Project which is less than a mile off-route. It's a wonderful place to visit, take a break and stay overnight.

STAGE 1 – LAND'S END TO FOWEY

Motivated by the success of Heligan, Tim Smit conceived the idea of creating a series of biomes that could house thousands of plant species in almost natural conditions. He called it **The Eden Project** (www.edenproject.com) and set about sourcing funds to turn his vision into reality on the site of a former china clay pit that first found fame as the planet surface of Magrathea in the 1981 BBC TV series of *The Hitchhiker's Guide to the Galaxy*.

The Project was fully planted and opened to the public in the spring of 2001 and was an immediate success attracting a million visitors each year whose spending gives a tremendous boost to the local economy.

But if you want to press on, go straight on at the crossroads by the children's playgrounds at Tregrehan Mills. Climb up to the next crossroads and follow NCN 2 down through **St Blazey** (60/5 miles) to the outskirts of **Par** (62/3 miles). Bear left along the A3082 towards **Fowey**. Then after 2 miles, turn left at the roundabout following signs for Bodinnick and ride down to the car ferry in Fowey where the stage ends. ▶

> The Bodinnick ferry runs from 7.00am to 8.45pm from Apr to Sept and 7.00am to 7.00pm in winter, and starts an hour later on Sundays.

RIDING NORTH TO SOUTH – JOGLE

If you are facing a long rail journey home and don't anticipate completing your ride until late afternoon, consider breaking your trip in two with a stopover close to an intermediate station.

CYCLING LAND'S END TO JOHN O' GROATS

STAGE 2
Fowey to Crediton

Start	Slipway to Bodinnick Ferry in Fowey (SX 127 522)
Finish	Junction of High Street and Market Street, Crediton (SS 832 003)
Distance	65 miles (105km)
Ascent	1700m
Time	8–9hrs
OS Maps	OS Landranger 201 and 191
Refreshments	Lanreath, Duloe, Liskeard, Pensilva, Stoke Climsland, Horsebridge, Lydford, Okehampton, Sticklepath, Whiddon Down, Yeoford and Crediton
Accommodation	Hostels only in Okehampton, but plenty of other types of accommodation in the main towns along the stage

The day starts with quiet country lanes and a seemingly never-ending succession of short, sharp hills. Then there is a steady 6 miles from the River Tamar, where you cross from Cornwall into Devon, to the edge of Dartmoor. After that things change for the better with some easy cycling along repurposed railway track-bed now rebranded as 'The Granite Way' before returning to narrow lanes, but this time predominantly downhill into the Exe Valley to the end of the stage in Crediton.

Little need to rush out at first light as the Fowey to Bodinnick Ferry (www.ctomsandson.co.uk) only starts at 7.00am on Mondays and 9.00am on Saturdays and Sunday in summer months. Enjoy the ferry ride across to **Bodinnick**, and then follow the road upstream alongside the River Fowey and inland for 5 miles to meet the B3359 near **Lanreath**. ◄ Turn left along the B3359 towards Liskeard, then after passing under the power lines, turn right and then right again 250 metres further on. Follow this narrow lane for 3 miles dropping steeply down through **Churchbridge** and then climbing up to **Duloe**

Daphne du Maurier (1907–1989), who wrote the hugely successful novels Rebecca *and* Jamaica Inn *once lived at Ferry House overlooking the River Fowey at Bodinnick.*

(10/55 miles). Turn left and follow the B3254 through **St Keyne** (12/53 miles) to **Liskeard** (14/51 miles). Ride through the town centre, which has a number of fine buildings befitting a once wealthy stannary (tin) town, and then turn left towards St Cleer. Follow the B3254

Crossing the old bridge in the tiny hamlet of Churchbridge

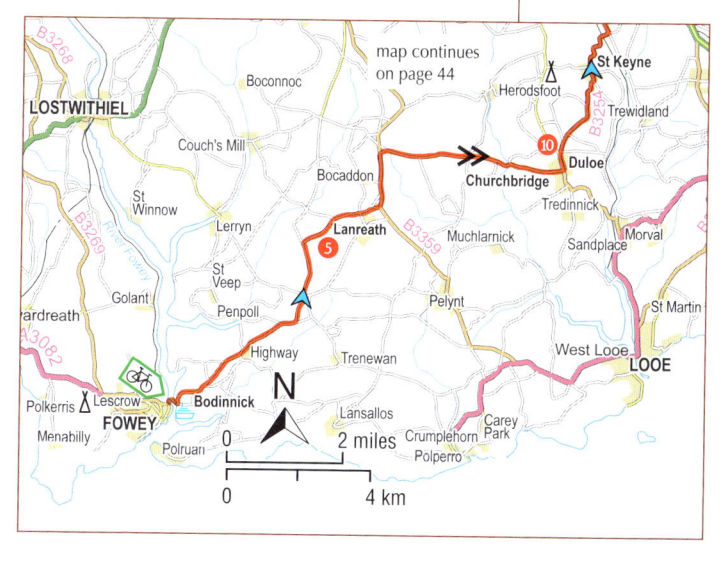

Cycling Land's End to John o' Groats

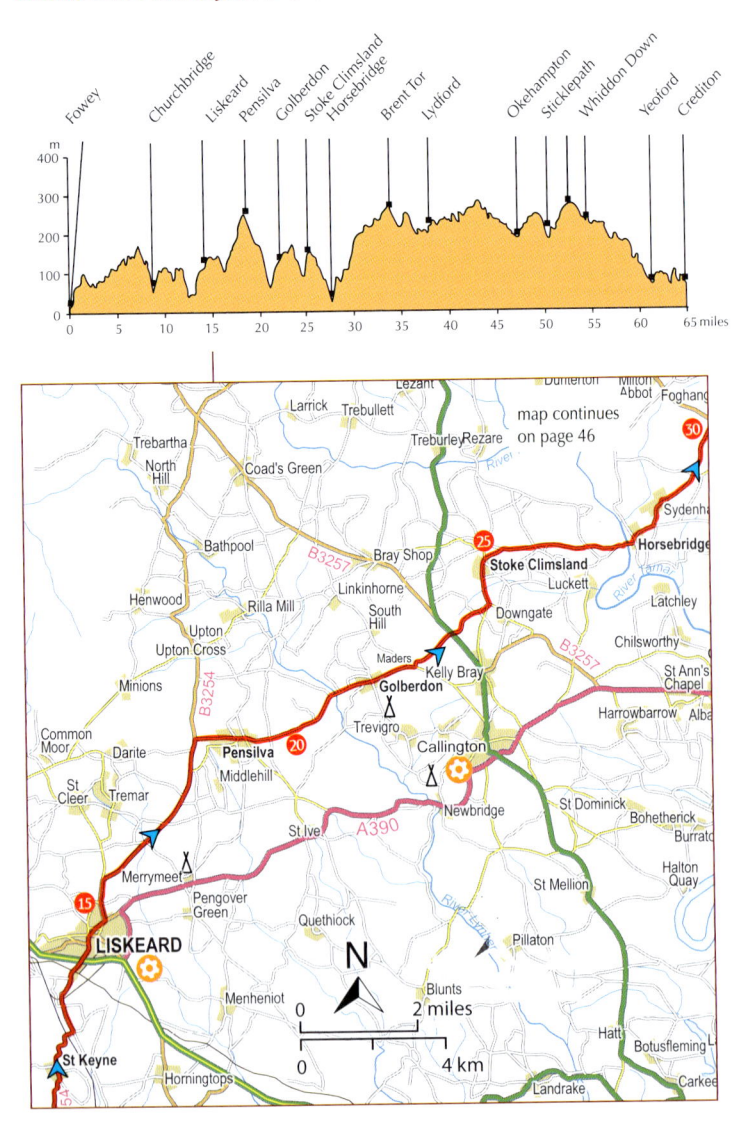

44

Stage 2 – Fowey to Crediton

for 3½ miles then turn right towards Callington and ride through **Pensilva** (19/46 miles). ▶

At the end of the village, bear left towards Golberdon. Cross the River Lynher and ride through **Golberdon** (22/43 miles). Half a mile beyond the village, turn right towards Maders and then quickly left along an unsigned lane. After a mile, cross the A388 following a sign for Downgate. After another mile, turn left towards **Stoke Climsland** (25/40 miles). Turn right into Pounds Lane by the war memorial and then at its end turn right towards Horsebridge.

Half a mile after passing through **Horsebridge** (27/38 miles), where the River Tamar forms the border between Cornwall and Devon, turn left towards Sydenham Damerel and ride through the village and across the B3362 towards Foghanger. A mile further on, turn right towards Tavistock and then immediately left into unsigned lane which runs straight for the next two miles. Cross the next two crossroads following signs for Brentor and then turn left towards Lydford at the road end where the 12th century church of St Michael de Rupe, which is still in use, sits on top of **Brent Tor**.

Continue past **North Brentor**, where the route joins NCN 272, and follow it through **Lydford** (38/27 miles) and left along the track bed of a disused railway that has been branded 'The Granite Way' all the way to the outskirts of **Okehampton** (46/19 miles). ▶

If you need a break near Pensilva, there is a choice of cake stops just a few hundred yards along the B3254 beyond the turning for Callington.

Lydford Gorge is the deepest river gorge in the South West with the spectacular 28m-high Whitelady Waterfall, the roaring Devil's Cauldron and a very welcome tea room.

The Meldon Viaduct, near the end of The Granite Way near Okehampton, was completed in 1874

Cycling Land's End to John o' Groats

The superbly tarmacked **Granite Way** largely follows the course of a stretch of the former Southern Region railway line which opened in 1874 once the Meldon Viaduct was completed. Spanning 341 feet (165 metres) the steel viaduct looks down on industrial archaeology from copper and arsenic mines and limestone quarries that were active in the area surrounding Meldon Pool during the 18th and 19th centuries. Quarrying continues today with aggregates taken out by rail link to Okehampton Station.

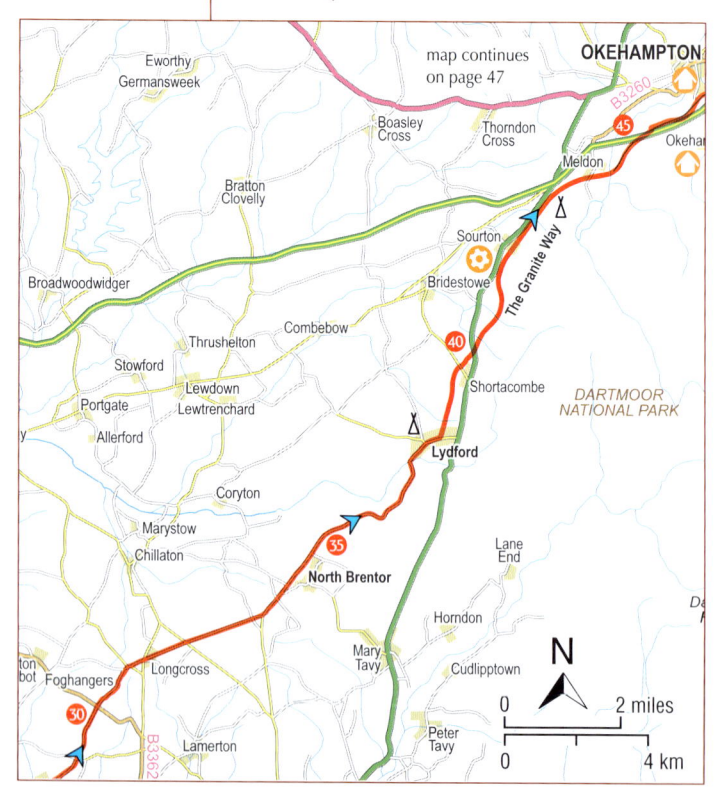

STAGE 2 – FOWEY TO CREDITON

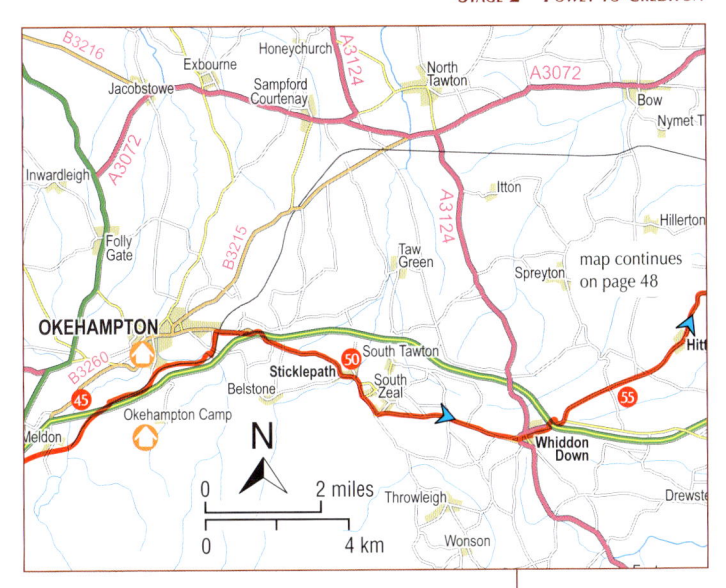

If you have no reason to stop in Okehampton, turn right after passing Okehampton Station and follow the track across the East Okement River and along Fatherford Lane to join the NCN 279 alongside the B3260 east of the town centre. Turn right and follow NCN 279 through **Sticklepath** (50/15 miles) and **Whiddon Down** (54/11 miles). Just before the A30, turn left and follow the A382 towards Hittisleigh. Cross the main road, turn left towards Hittisleigh and then after 200 metres turn left again still following signs for Hittisleigh, but finally abandoning the NCN 279 which continues eastwards to Exeter. Ride through **Hittisleigh** (57/8 miles) to **Yeoford** (61/4 miles). Turn left over the railway and ride into **Crediton** where the stage ends at the tourist fingerpost at the junction of High Street and Market Street.

> **Crediton** has a particularly magnificent parish church that is built on the site of what was the 'cathedral' of the Bishop of Crediton until the

CYCLING LAND'S END TO JOHN O' GROATS

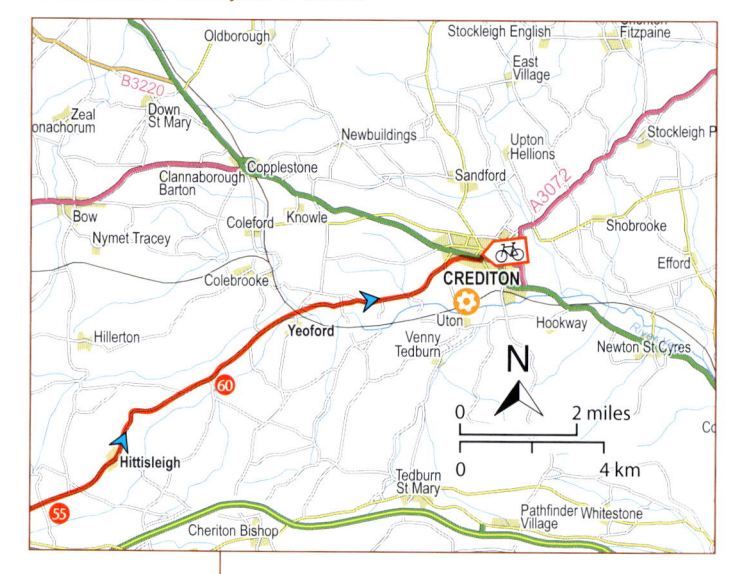

diocese transferred to Exeter in 1050. However, a college of canons remained in Crediton to administer the local interests of the diocese and they are responsible for most of the current building which dates from the 15th century.

There is another religious connection too. Records suggest Saint Boniface (c.675–754), a monk who played major part in spreading Christianity across Germany, was born here. German Catholics have venerated him as an important national figure for centuries, but it was not until 2019 that Devon County Council officially recognised him as the Patron Saint of Devon.

RIDING NORTH TO SOUTH – JOGLE

If you prefer to have a shorter final day so you can depart Land's End promptly consider continuing past Fowey to St Austell making this stage 75 miles (120km) and the final stage 55 miles (88km).

STAGE 3
Crediton to Clevedon

Start	Junction of High Street and Market Street, Crediton (SS 832 003)
Finish	Marine Parade, Clevedon (ST 403 720)
Distance	86 miles (138km)
Ascent	800m
Time	8–9hr
OS Maps	OS Landranger 191, 192, 181, 193, 182 and 172
Refreshments	Thorverton, Bradninch, Cullompton, Uffculme, Rockwell Green, Wellington, Bradford-on-Tone, Bishop's Hull, Taunton, Creech St Michael, Rooks Bridge, Winscombe, Sandford, Congresbury, Yatton and Clevedon
Accommodation	The only hostels along this stage are 5 miles off-route in Cheddar or 10 miles off route in Street, but there is good short-stay, self-catering accommodation at the end of the stage in Clevedon and plenty of B&Bs, budget hotels and other choices in the main towns along the route

The profile shows this is a stage of two halves; first through the remaining rolling hills of Devon and then out across the Somerset Levels where the going is noticeably easier. This is where you can make more rapid progress, covering a greater distance in a day.

Head up Market Street away from the shops and turn right along Parliament Street which soon becomes Belle Parade. Bear right at the mini roundabout along Blagdon Terrace and at its end turn left along the A3072 towards Tiverton. After 1 mile, turn right and cycle through **Shobrooke** (3/82 miles) to **Thorverton** (7/78 miles). Turn left, ride through the village, over the River Exe and through **Rudway Barton** (8/77miles). Turn left along the A396 towards Tiverton and then quickly right opposite The Ruffwell Inn. Go straight on at the next three

CYCLING LAND'S END TO JOHN O' GROATS

> Foreign weavers came to Cullompton during the 15th century establishing an industry which lasted until the 1970s when the last mill closed.

crossroads and then turn right towards Bradninch. After 800 metres, turn left still heading for Bradninch. Just over a mile further on, turn left and ride through **Bradninch** (12/73 miles) and over Cullompton Hill.

Cross the roundabout and ride through the centre of **Cullompton** (15/70 miles) and then turn right along Station Road heading towards Exeter. ◄

Continue to the outskirts of the town and then once over the M5 motorway, turn left towards Bradfield passing Bradfield House, a Grade I listed country house with an original mediaeval great hall hidden beneath a remodelled Victorian exterior. Ride through **Bradfield** (17/68 miles), Stenhill (18/67 miles) and Smithincott (19/66 miles) to **Uffculme** (20/65 miles) where the Coldharbour Mill Museum is housed in one of the oldest woollen mills

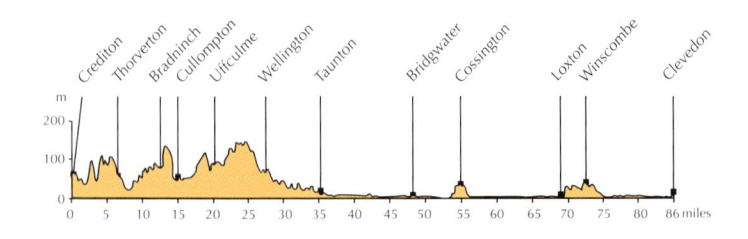

50

Stage 3 – Crediton to Clevedon

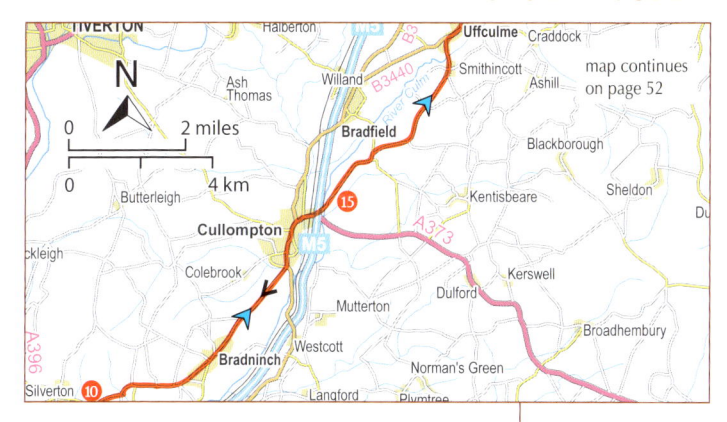

in the UK having been in continuous production since 1797. Turn right and then after 700 metres turn left at The Square in the centre of the village. Turn right along a narrow lane at an unsigned junction on the outskirts of the village. After 2 miles, turn right towards Nicolashayne, then 900 metres later, bear left at a fork, cross the B3391

Parked up outside St Giles' Church in Bradford-on-Tone

Cycling Land's End to John o' Groats

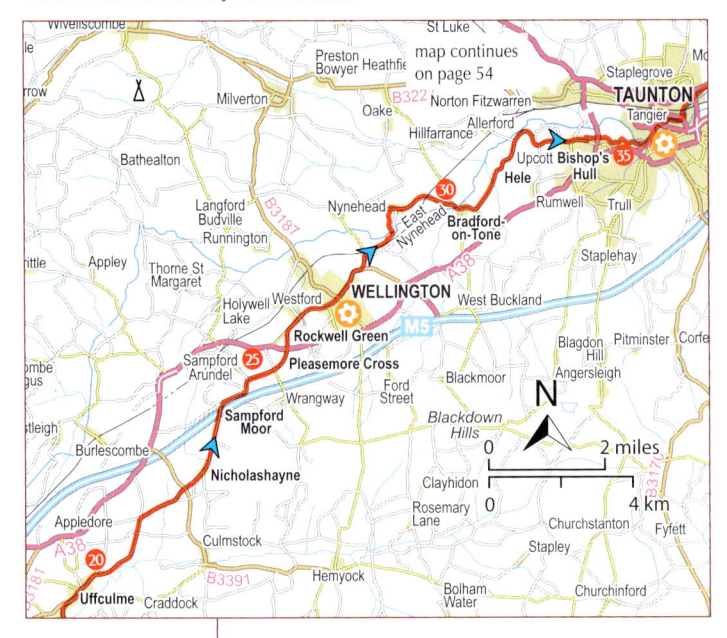

and ride through **Nicholashayne** (23/62 miles), which sits at the western end of the Blackdown Hills.

Continue over the M5, through **Sampford Moor** (24/61 miles) and **Pleasemoor Cross** (25/60 miles) to the A38. Turn right, then immediately left into Bagley Road. Turn right at the next junction and ride through **Rockwell Green** (26/59 miles) and then **Wellington** (27/58 miles). Once through the town centre, join a shared-use path and turn right towards Taunton at the first roundabout, then left at the next heading toward Nynehead. After 300 metres, turn right towards Bradford-on-Tone and then after 600 metres, turn left again still heading for Bradford-on-Tone. Cross the railway, then the River Tone, which gives its name to Taunton, turn right at the next junction, negotiate the unmanned level crossing and turn right where the road ends on the outskirts of **Bradford-on-Tone** (30/55 miles). Cross the River Tone and then turn left by

STAGE 3 – CREDITON TO CLEVEDON

the parish church in the centre of the village heading towards Hele.

After 400 metres, turn left and ride through **Hele** (32/53 miles). Soon after passing through the village our route joins NCN 3 and follows it for the next 23 miles making navigation much easier. After undulating terrain all the way from Land's End, the route is about to cross the Somerset Levels where it is rarely more than 10m above sea level. Having completed what many End-to-Enders consider to be the hardest part of the journey, allow yourself a minor celebration.

Follow NCN 3 through Upcott, **Bishop's Hull** and across an islet in the River Tone with the exotic name of Tangier into **Taunton** (35/50 miles) where the town centre is just off-route to the south. Continue past Somerset County Cricket Ground, along the riverbank and then the towpath of the Bridgwater and Taunton Canal for the next 12 miles to the outskirts of **Bridgwater** (47/83 miles).

> The 14-mile **Bridgwater and Taunton Canal**, which opened in 1827, was part of a grand but doomed plan to link the Bristol and English Channels saving wooden hulled ships the perilous journey around the Cornish peninsula. By the time it was extended to the Bridgwater Docks in 1841, it was effectively obsolete with metal-hulled ships able to safely sail around Cornwall and much of the canal traffic switching to the recently opened railways. By the early 1850s the canal company was bankrupt and the canal was abandoned for over a century before being restored and reopened to leisure craft in 1994.

Unless you wish to visit the town, which is home to an excellent bike shop that specialises in touring, leave the towpath soon after passing under the M5 motorway and follow NCN 3 along Somerset Bridge and across the River Parrett. Turn right; pass first under the railway and then the M5 and ride out across the Somerset Levels through **Chedzoy** (51/34 miles), Bawdrip (54/31 miles)

53

Cycling Land's End to John o' Groats

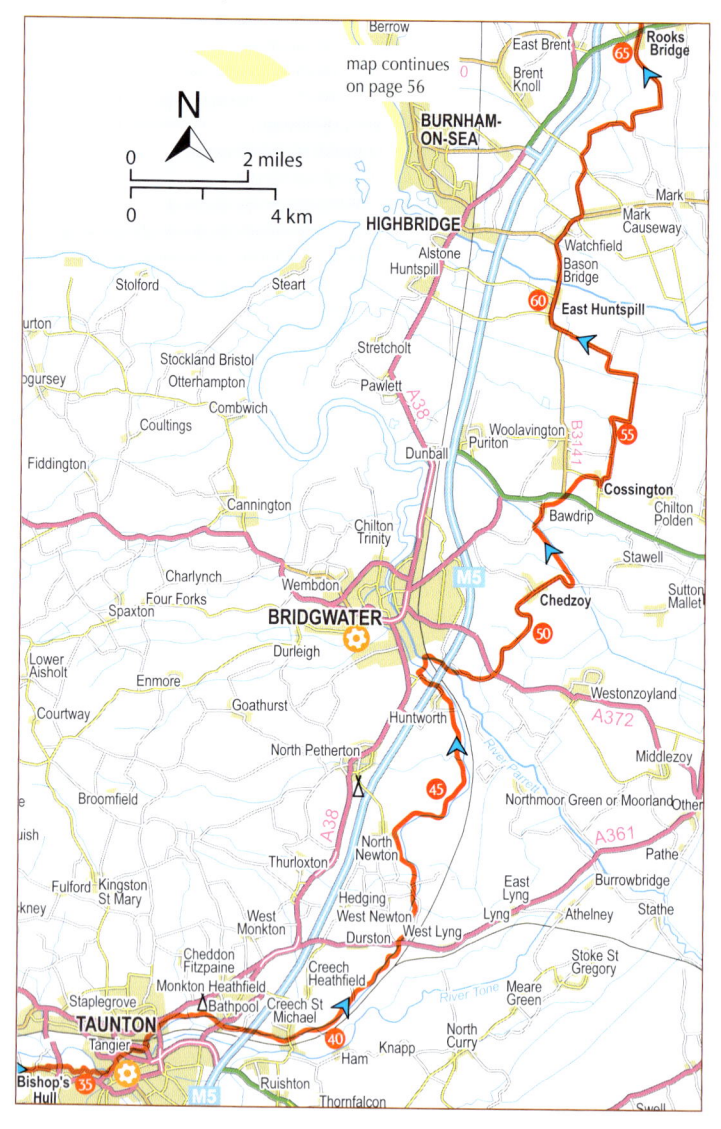

54

STAGE 3 – CREDITON TO CLEVEDON

and **Cossington** (55/33 miles) where NCN 3 turns east to Glastonbury, which is 11 miles away. ▶

Follow NCN 33 as far as **East Huntspill** (60/25 miles), then continue northwards through the village following signs for Wedmore. Turn right along the B3139 still heading towards Wedmore and then 450 metres after the junction signed for the M5, turn left along Dutch Road. Turn left at its end along Harp Road. After 300 metres turn right along Vole Road, then after a mile bear left and follow Pill Road to **Rooks Bridge** (65/20 miles). Cross the A38 following signs for Edingworth, turn right after a mile, cross the M5 and then turn right towards Loxton. After 1¾ miles, turn right and ride into **Loxton** (68/17 miles) and then right again towards Webbington, cross the M5 and ride into **Webbington** (69/16 miles). Turn left towards Winscombe, climbing through a gap in the Mendip Hills and ride through Barton to **Winscombe** (72/13 miles). Turn left as you enter the village, then turn right along The Lynch and loop around under the bridge over the disused railway. Follow NCN 26 or Strawberry Line as it has been designated, past **Sandford** (74/11 miles) and **Congresbury** (77/8 miles) and through **Yatton** (79/6 miles). ▶

Follow NCN 3 eastwards from Cossington to visit Glastonbury, Wells and Bristol re-joining the route by following NCN 4 from the city centre to Seven Beach in Stage 4.

The Strawberry Line follows the track-bed of the Cheddar Valley Line, which, until 1963 carried locally-grown strawberries to London markets.

Strollers on the pier at Clevedon look out across the Bristol Channel to South Wales

Cycling Land's End to John o' Groats

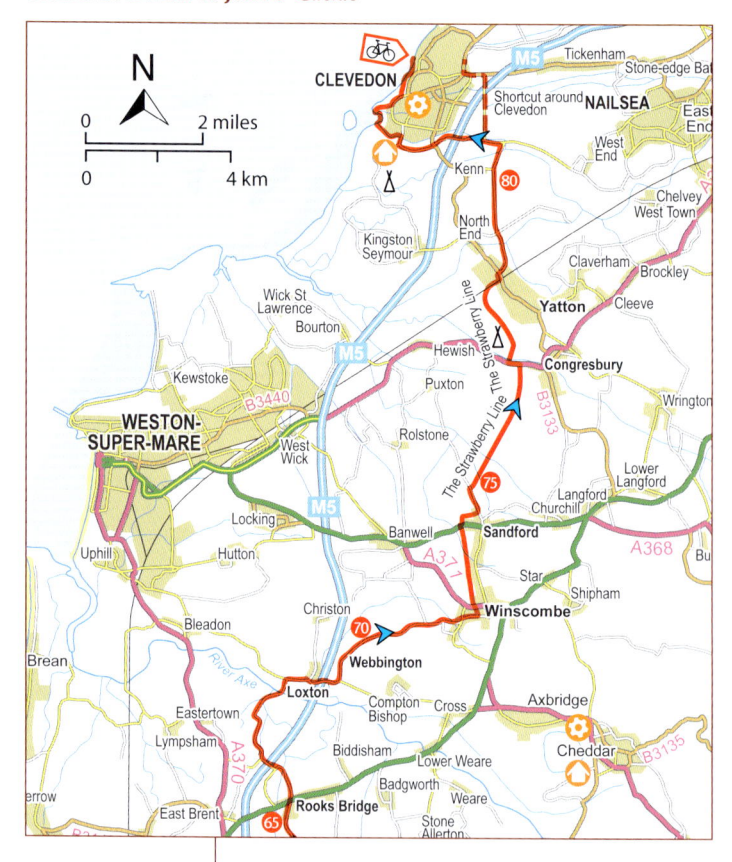

To by-pass Clevedon and save 4 miles, follow the NCN 410 northwards around the perimeter of the town and along the B3124 to join Stage 4 at the junction with Nortons Wood Lane.

At its end, turn left towards **Clevedon** briefly following NCN 410, cross the M5, then turn left and immediately right along Colehouse Lane. ◄

Turn right after passing the radio mast, cross a drainage ditch and turn left along a gravel track and follow it around to Old Church Road. At what might appear to be its end turn left into another stretch of Old Church Road and then turn left along Elton Road. Follow this road around the front with the sea on your left and then turn left along The Beach past Clevedon's famous pier and into Marine Parade where this stage ends.

Clevedon gets its name from two Old English words; *cleve* meaning 'cleft' and *don* meaning 'hill', which is a fitting as it is set among seven low hills. It remained an agricultural village until the Victorian era when it grew as a seaside resort. The town's famous pier dates from 1869 and is one of the earliest examples still in existence in the United Kingdom. Part of it collapsed in 1970 and it fell into disrepair until 1985, when it was restored and rebuilt. It is a now a Grade 1 listed building and an important attraction for day trippers.

Clevedon's pier which dates from 1869 is one of the few remaining Victorian piers in the United Kingdom

RIDING NORTH TO SOUTH – JOGLE

If you ride this stage from north to south you will encounter 80 per cent of the climbing in the last 35 miles so try to cover the first 50 miles across the Somerset Levels to Taunton before lunch leaving plenty of time for the more challenging riding to come.

CYCLING LAND'S END TO JOHN O' GROATS

STAGE 4
Clevedon to Worcester

Start	Marine Parade, Clevedon (ST 403 720)
Finish	The Beach, Croft Road, Worcester (SO 845 550)
Distance	91 miles (146km)
Ascent	700m
Time	8–9hr
OS Maps	OS Landranger 172, 162 and 150
Refreshments	Eastern-in-Gordano, just off-route in Severn Beach, Northwick, Littleton-upon-Severn, Berkeley, Shepherd's Patch, Gloucester, Tewkesbury and the garden centre at Norton near the end of the stage
Accommodation	The only hostel directly on the route is at Slimbridge, but there are plenty of other types of accommodation, including budget hotels, towards the end of the stage

A stage with easy route finding that follows the National Cycle Network up the Severn Estuary and Severn Valley. The route only once gets over 80m (262ft) above sea level so if you have a good following wind from the south west, it could be your easiest stage.

Ride northwards along Marine Parade and then Wellington Terrace with the sea on your left. Continue

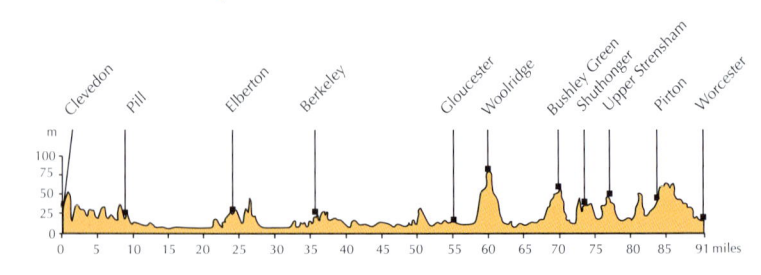

Stage 4 – Clevedon to Worcester

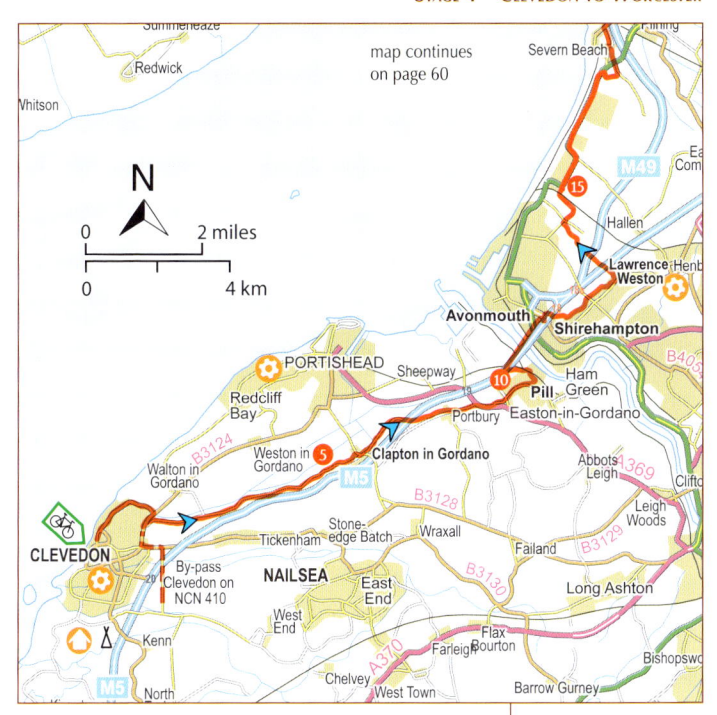

along this road as it swings inland, then after 1½ miles turn right along the B3124 back towards Clevedon. After 400 metres turn left along Nortons Wood Lane and follow NCN 410 through **Clapton in Gordano** (5/85miles), where Clapton Court, a Grade II listed manor dating from the 15th century that was once owned by the Wills tobacco family of Bristol sits on the hillside below the M5 motorway. ▸

Continue through Portbury to **Pill** (9/81miles) following NCN 410 and 41, which briefly follow the same route, back towards the motorway, across the River Avon on the shared-use path alongside the southbound carriageway and then down to meet the B4054 in **Shirehampton** (11/79 miles). After 100 metres, turn

---

Clapton in Gordano and other nearby villages get their name from the Old English word 'gorden' meaning muddy valley.

Cycling Land's End to John o' Groats

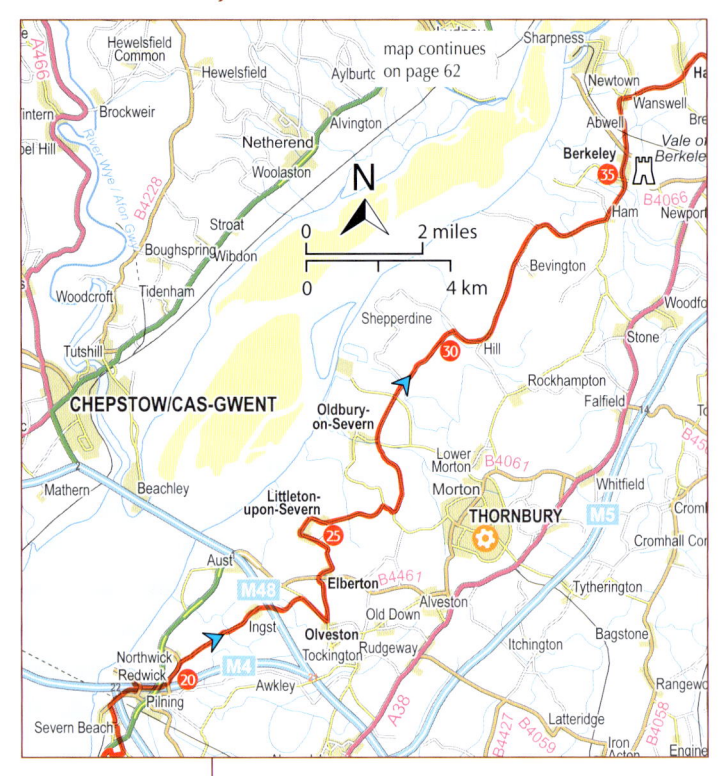

In the 1920s, entrepreneur Robert Stride established Severn Beach as a resort. It remained popular until the 1970s despite lacking a real beach.

left along Barrack Lane, bear right across some wasteland and follow NCN 410/41 through **Lawrence Weston**. Continue over the M5 and then the M49 and through the logistic parks of **Avonmouth** (14/76 miles) where we temporarily part company with NCN 410 and stick solely to NCN 41. It may not be the nicest cycling, but it is shared-use path for the next 3 miles.

Follow NCN 41 past Seven Beach, over the M49, M4 and M48 motorways, and then continue along meandering country lanes through **Olveston** (23/67 miles), **Elberton** (24/66 miles) and **Littleton-upon-Severn** (25/65 miles) by now briefly reunited with NCN 410. ◄

60

The largely 12th Berkeley Castle location of a murder most foul – or not

Ride on through **Oldbury-on-Severn** (28/62 miles), Hill and Ham to **Berkeley** (35/55 miles), a delightful place to break and investigate Berkeley Castle. ▶

Except for a period when it was controlled by the Tudors, **Berkeley Castle** has been in the Berkeley family since they built it around an earlier motte and bailey in the 12th century. In 1327, Edward II (1284–1327), who had been deposed by his wife Queen Isabella and her ally Roger Mortimer, died here in mysterious circumstances. Some contemporary sources say he was brutally murdered and subsequently buried by the high altar in Gloucester Cathedral where there is a magnificent tomb. But other sources suggest Edward escaped to Europe and that the body in the tomb is that of a porter of Berkeley Castle. The only thing for certain is that you should not investigate Edward's death if you are of a sensitive disposition.

Continue through Abwell, Wanswell and **Halmore** (38/52 miles) to Slimbridge with views of the western edge of The Cotswolds to the east and the Forest of Dean across the Severn Estuary to the west. At Shepherd's Patch (42 /48 miles), whose position near

Berkeley was the birthplace of physician and scientist Edward Jenner (1749–1823) who pioneered the smallpox vaccine.

Cycling Land's End to John o' Groats

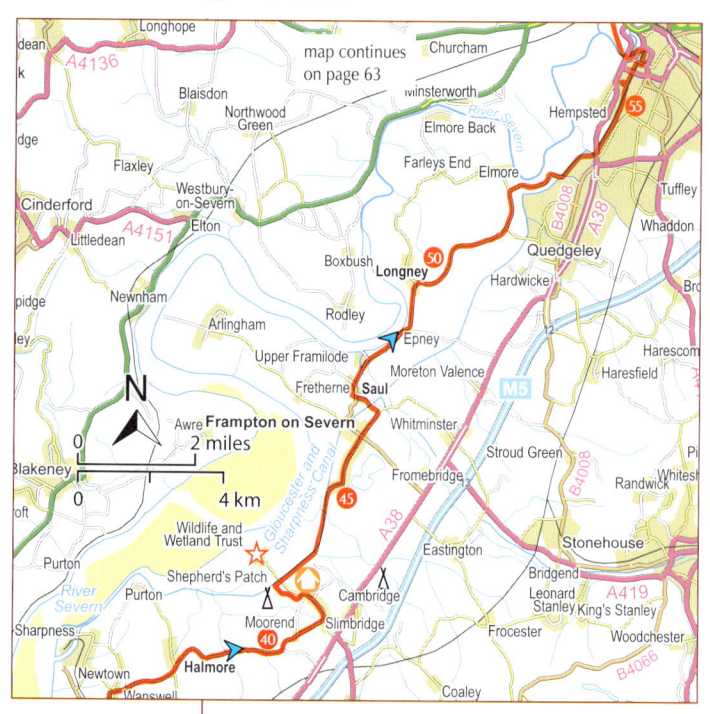

The Gloucester and Sharpness Canal at Shepherd's Patch

STAGE 4 – CLEVEDON TO WORCESTER

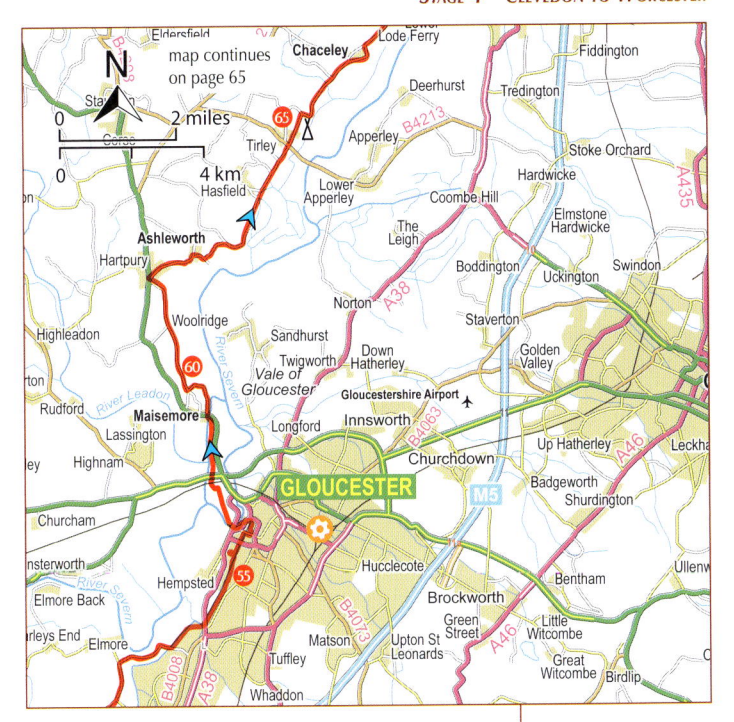

the ever popular Wildlife and Wetland Trust bird reserve at Slimbridge means it has a busy pub, a café, a hostel and camping, turn right along the Gloucester and Sharpness Canal for 2 miles before returning to country lanes to **Frampton on Severn** (45/45 miles) which has a long wide village green that is no doubt due to the Clifford family who, except for one minor hiatus in the early 20th century, have owned nearby Frampton Court since the 11th century.

Once through the village, our route joins NCN 45 and follows it, (with only one short cut), right to the end of the stage. Ride on through **Saul** (46/44 miles), Epney (48/42 miles) and **Longney** (49/41 miles) and then re-join the Gloucester and Sharpness Canal which provides a direct route into **Gloucester** (55/35 miles).

> **Gloucester**, which has Roman origins, thrived during the medieval era when the main trade was wool from the nearby Cotswolds. It has continued to be an important city in modern times when engineering and financial services dominate the local economy.
>
> The city is the country's most inland port. Ships always had difficulty coming up the River Severn so during the first quarter of the 19th century local businessmen set about raising funds to construct a canal to link the city to the Bristol Channel. Completed in 1827, the Gloucester and Sharpness Canal was once the broadest and deepest canal in the world, capable of being used by smaller oil tankers. Today the traffic on the canal is predominantly pleasure boats and the fine warehouses and buildings surrounding the city's historic docks have found new uses.

Follow NCN 45 around the city's rejuvenated docks, across the River Severn, under the ring road and A40 and northwards alongside the river to **Maisemore** (58/32 miles). Climb Spring Hill, admire the views, then descend to Hartpury and follow NCN 454 through **Ashleworth** (61/29 miles), Tirley (64/26 miles) and **Chaceley** (66/24 miles). ◂

Turn right 1 mile north of Chaceley to Lower Lode Inn where a small ferry sometimes operates across the River Severn to Tewkesbury between Easter and mid-September. Phone 07856 792 463 for bookings.

Continue through **Forthampton** (68/22 miles) which has some interesting timbered farm buildings, then cross the A438, turning right into Green Street by a house with a Dutch gable and climb gently up through Bushley Green, where the cricket pitch is on one side of the road and the pavilion on the other. Then enjoy the fine view across to Tewkesbury on the descent to **Bushley** where the route meets the A438 again. Turn left towards Tewkesbury and then after crossing the River Severn at **The Mythe** (72/18 miles), turn left towards Worcester and follow the A38 for a mile up to **Shuthonger**. Turn right in the centre of the village and follow the NCN 45 through the pretty villages

Stage 4 – Clevedon to Worcester

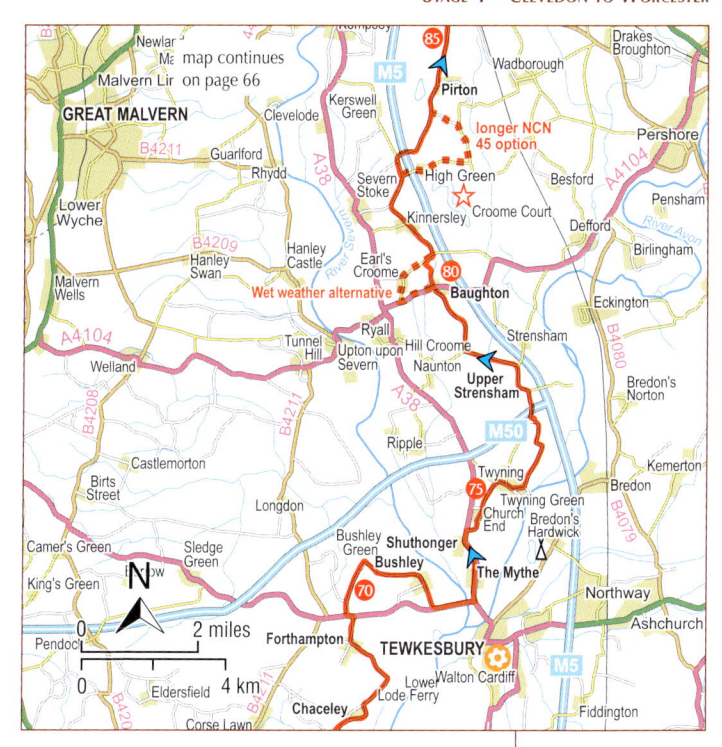

of Church End and Twyning (75/15 miles), where there are many traditional crook-framed cottages, and over the M50. ▶

From here to Worcester, the NCN 45 weaves through some pretty villages alongside the M5. Ride through **Upper Strensham** (77/13 miles), where you could easily cross over the motorway and nip into the services, and descend to Hill Croome (79/11 miles) with a fine view of the Malvern Hills to the west. Continue to **Baughton** (80/10 miles), but leave the NCN 45, which briefly follows a muddy bridleway. Instead turn left along the A4104 and after 900 metres turn right and ride through Earl's Croome, re-joining the NCN 45 just beyond the village.

> Turn right along the A438 in The Mythe to visit Tewkesbury, which floods frequently due to its position on low lying land at the confluence of the River Severn and the River Avon.

Cycling Land's End to John o' Groats

'Capability' Brown (c.1715–1783) landscaped the gardens surrounding Croome Court for the 6th Earl of Coventry. The property, which has a restaurant, is open daily.

After Kinnersley (81/9 miles), NCN 45 gives two options. Follow the first turning if you want to go around a longer loop that passes Croome Landscape Park. ◄ For a more direct route, which is a mile shorter, follow the second turning towards **Pirton** (84/6miles), where the options reunite. Continue over the M5, pick up a shared-use path on the outskirts of **Worcester** and cross the A4440 by the shared-use bridge. By now the NCN 45 has been joined by NCN 442 which we follow through the southern suburbs to the River Severn. After a mile of pleasant cycling along the riverbank, the stage ends at The Beach on Croft Road, just before the railway viaduct.

> **Worcester** is famous for being the location of last battle of the English Civil War, when Cromwell's forces defeated the Royalists on the western bank of the River Severn on 3 September 1651. It is also famed for its Royal Worcester porcelain which was manufactured here for over 250 years until the final factory closed in 2009; for gloves, and for Worcester Sauce, of which more later.

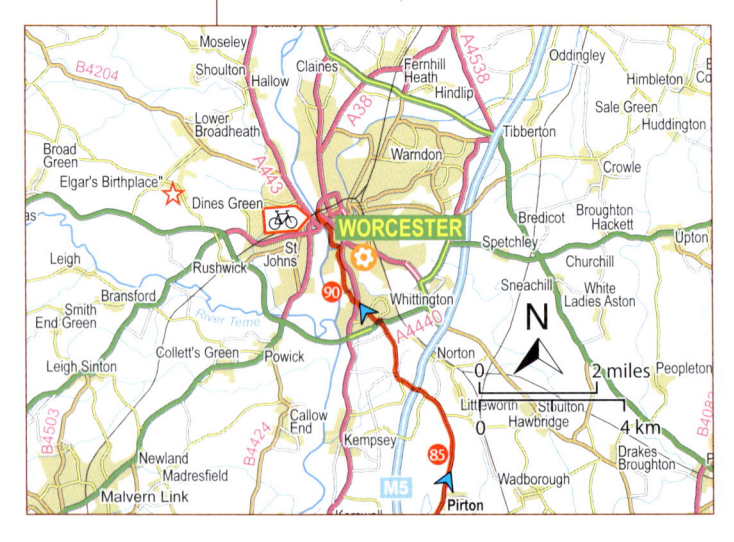

STAGE 4 – CLEVEDON TO WORCESTER

The glove industry reached its peak during the early years of the 19th century when 150 manufacturers in and around Worcester made nearly half the country's gloves, employing over 30,000 people. Things changed radically in the 19th century when more fashionable French gloves flooded the market and mechanisation replaced hand-sewing. Consequently the number of people employed in the trade dwindled. Today there are no glove manufacturers in the city.

RIDING NORTH TO SOUTH – JOGLE

If you fancy an evening in Bristol or visiting Wells or Glastonbury, leave the route at Severn Bridge and follow NCN 4 to Queen Square in central Bristol, where there is plenty of accommodation. Leave by following NCN 3 from Queen Square through Wells and Glastonbury and re-join the route in Cossington. It adds a couple of miles and an extra 500m of climbing to the journey.

ELGAR AND HIS SUNBEAMS

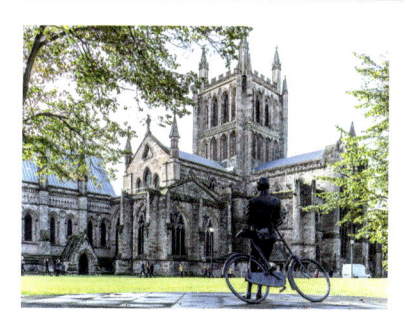

There is a statue of Sir Edward Elgar just off route in the centre of Worcester, but this one in Hereford shows him contemplating the cathedral tower while leaning against one of his beloved Sunbeams

During 1903, while living in Malvern, the composer Sir Edward Elgar (1857–1934) purchased the first of two Royal Sunbeam bicycles manufactured in Wolverhampton by John Marston Ltd., a long-established company that only diversified into bicycles, after their tinplate and enamel ware business started to decline.

Many of Elgar's friends, including some portrayed in the Enigma Variations, started cycling and he was happy to pay £21–10s-0d for what at the time was the Rolls-Royce of bicycles, complete with an oil-bath chain case designed to continuously lubricate the chain.

Elgar cycled all over Worcestershire and Herefordshire and sometimes into Wales, mostly with friends but sometimes with his wife Alice or his daughter Clarice. Perhaps the ride that meant the most to him though was the 48-mile round trip he made from Malvern to Stoke Prior on 23rd June 1904 to tell his 83-year old father that he had been knighted by the Prime Minister Arthur Balfour, who was another avid cyclist.

Alice Elgar made an entry in her diary in June 1908 that 'E is depressed about bicycling on account of motors' and by the end of the decade 'E' had stopped cycling for good. Neither of the two Sunbeams he owned survive but his well-used cycling maps are on show at his Birthplace Museum in Lower Broadheath, 3 miles off-route to the west of Worcester.

A statue of Sir Edward Elgar in the cathedral close in Hereford

STAGE 5
Worcester to Nantwich

Start	The Beach, Croft Road, Worcester (SO 845 550)
Finish	Junction of High Street and Water Lode in Nantwich (SJ 650 524)
Distance	83 miles (134km)
Ascent	900m
Time	8–9hrs
OS Maps	OS Landranger 150, 138, 127 and 118
Refreshments	On or near the route at Droitwich, Hartlebury, Stourport, Kidderminster, Kinver, Cosford, Newport, Market Drayton, Audlem, Overwater Marina, Nantwich and isolated pubs along the stage
Accommodation	There are no hostels along this stage but plenty of hotels and B&Bs in the towns towards the end of the stage

This stage goes up the basin of the Severn Valley and across its watershed between Market Drayton and Audlem after which rivers drain northwards into the Irish Sea. Although it's invisible, it is an important tipping point on the journey where you transition into Northern England. The first 25 miles of the stage go through a string of towns that were once economically important but are now predominantly commuter towns. But after that it is mostly agricultural country with fields of crops separated by red sandy knolls topped with pine trees.

Follow NCN 46 northwards under the railway viaduct, through Pitchfork Park alongside Worcester Racecourse and along Waterworks Lane before turning left through Gheluvelt Park. Continue following waymarker signs for NCN 46 through the pleasant residential streets, across the A449 and along Cornmeadow Lane to the northern suburb of **Fearnhill Heath** (4/79 miles). ▶

After a mile, cross the Droitwich Canal, turn right and briefly follow the towpath and then turn right and

Gheluvelt Park commemorates the Worcestershire Regiment's role in the Battle of Gheluvelt, or the First Battle of Ypres, as it is also known, in 1914.

CYCLING LAND'S END TO JOHN O' GROATS

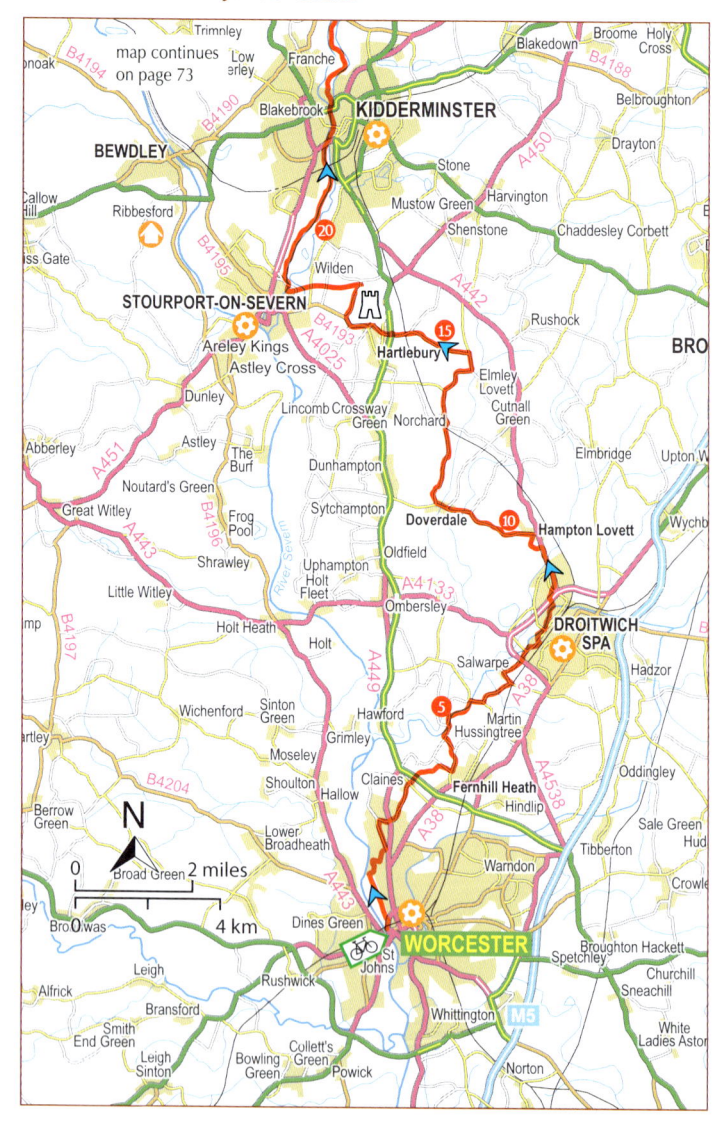

70

STAGE 5 – WORCESTER TO NANTWICH

follow NCN 46 through the narrow lanes, under the A38 by-pass and through the outer suburbs of **Droitwich Spa** (8/75 miles). After another short stretch along the canal towpath, leave NCN 46 and follow NCN 45 over the canal, across the playing fields and under the A38. Turn right and follow NCN 45 through the northern suburbs of Droitwich Spa and around the industrial units of **Hampton Lovett** (10/73 miles).

> The Romans called **Droitwich**, '*Salinae*', indicating a place where salt could be found. In the 18th and 19th centuries it was extracted in vast quantities and transported along the Droitwich Canal to Birmingham and the industrial towns to the east. During the 19th century, Droitwich developed as a spa town with the supposed benefits derived from bathing in the waters rather than drinking them. By the 20th century, its proximity to Birmingham gave it a new future as a dormitory town.

The next 9 miles through **Doverdale** (12/71 miles) and **Hartlebury** (16/67 miles) are much more rural and all the better for it. ▶

Turn right along Charlton Lane on the outskirts of Hartlebury and then turn left along a disused railway and follow NCN 45 into **Stourport-on-Severn** (19/64 miles). After just over a mile of pleasant cycling mostly at the bottom of a sandstone cutting, bear right at a waymarker and drop down to meet the Staffordshire and Worcestershire Canal. Turn right along the towpath. ▶

The NCN 45 soon heads west into Shropshire, but we follow the canal towpath and NCN 54 for the next 6½ miles through the centre of **Kidderminster** (22/61 miles), passing Slingfield Mill, a former Victorian worsted mill that subsequently became a carpet factory and eventually a retail outlet. ▶

Be prepared for a steep ramp, where you will have to dismount to cross a narrow footbridge to the towpath on the opposite bank of the canal. Continue to **Cookley**

Hartlebury Castle was once the residence of the Bishop of Worcester, but today it houses the County Museum with a café.

Turn left along the canal for the historic centre of Stourport-on-Severn, which sprung up when the local canal network was developed during the 18th century.

Since 1785 Kidderminster has been a centre for carpet making, which at its peak in the early 20th century employed about 15,000 people.

CYCLING LAND'S END TO JOHN O' GROATS

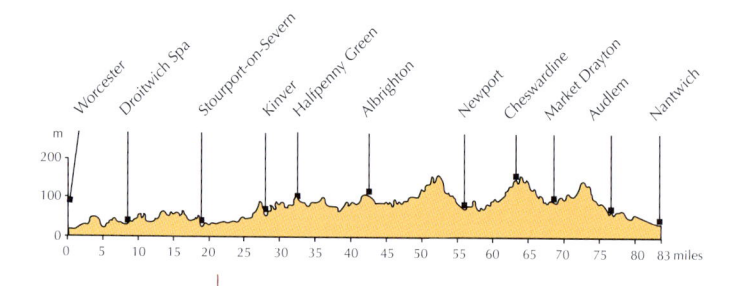

(26/57 miles) then leave the towpath just before Cookley Tunnel, dismount and push up to Bridge Road.

Turn left, cross the River Stour and then turn left towards Kinver. ◄ Ride through **Kinver** (28/55 miles) which is a pretty village at the end of a narrow finger of Staffordshire that is surrounded by the counties of Shropshire, Worcestershire and the West Midlands.

Turn right towards Enville at the mini-roundabout in the centre of the village and then right along Chester Road once you reach the outskirts. Turn left along the A458 towards Bridgenorth and then, 500 metres further on, turn right following a brown tourist sign for Halfpenny Green Vineyard. Cross the junction by the pub in **Halfpenny Green** (33/50 miles) and the next staggered crossroads following signs for Upper Aston and Ludstone. After passing through Upper Aston (35/48 miles) turn left along the B4176 and then ½ mile further on turn right towards Highgate. This is easy riding through pleasant sandstone country with occasional stands of Scots pine and plenty of mixed woodland.

Turn right by the pub in **Upper Ludstone** (36/47 miles), weaving your way through the outdoor seating, go straight ahead at the next crossroads and cross the A454 following a brown tourist sign for Patsull. Go straight ahead at the next two crossroads and then turn right towards Albrighton. Ride through **Burnhill Green** (40/43 miles), turn right along the A464 and then turn quickly left into Green Lane and follow it into **Albrighton** (42/41 miles). Turn left along Elm Road and then right at the

> Carved into the red sandstone edge above Kinver are the famous Rock Houses which were inhabited until the 1960s.

Stage 5 – Worcester to Nantwich

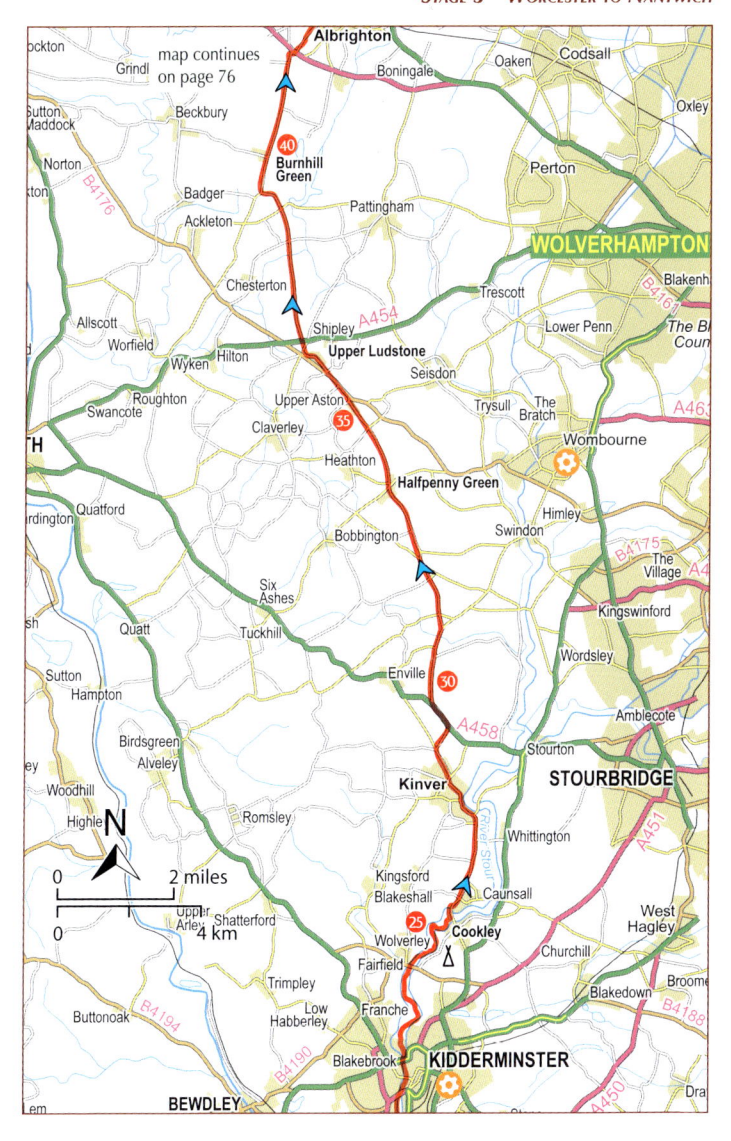

Parked up by a Hawker Hunter at RAF Cosford Museum

RAF Museum Cosford houses the archives and collections of the Royal Air Force including many iconic planes. Admission is free and there is a café.

Along Marsh Lane look out for the flowers (July) or seed-heads (August) of opium poppies mostly grown to produce opiates for pharmaceuticals.

roundabout and follow Bowling Green Road to its end. Turn left along Newport Road, joining NCN 81 which the route follows for the next 3 miles. As you approach the busy A41 bear left onto a shared use path and follow the NCN 81 left along Worcester Road towards RAF Cosford. Follow NCN 81 under the railway bridge, along the perimeter of the aerodrome and round the bend into wooded Neachley Lane at the entrance to the RAF Museum Cosford (44/39 miles). ◄

The route follows the NCN 81 for 2 miles before it swings left towards Telford and we turn right under the M54 and then quickly left along Lizard Lane which gets its name from the low wooded hill on left where some locals say there was once a leper colony. After 2 miles, turn right at the crossroads, cross the busy A5 and then a shallow ford and ride into the hamlet of Burlington (49/34 miles). Turn left along Marsh Lane opposite a large agricultural shed and at its end turn right along the B4379 towards Heath Hill. Ride through **Sherrifhales** (50/33 miles) gently climbing the southern slope of Heath Hill and then turn left into Lilyhurst Road towards Lilleshall. ◄

Stage 5 – Worcester to Nantwich

Turn right after 600 metres heading towards Lilleshall Hall Golf Club and follow this quiet lane past Lilleshall Hall National Sports Centre.

Lilleshall Hall National Sports Centre is set in the grounds of a 12th century abbey, which escaped the wrath of Henry VIII by going into voluntary dissolution in 1538. The estate then became the home of the Leveson family for nearly four centuries, until World War I. One subsequent owner was Herbert Ford (1893–1963), a shrewd Ironbridge businessman who married the wealthy Anne Perrins of the famous Lea and Perrins Worcestershire Sauce family. During the 1930s Ford developed the estate into an amusement park.

At the outbreak of World War II the amusement park closed and the house was commissioned for other uses. By the end of the war it needed extensive renovation far in excess of what Ford could manage so he sold it to the Central Council of Physical Recreation. It has been a centre of excellence for over 70 years and many famous sports stars have passed through its doors including the England football team who trained here for two weeks prior to their success in the 1966 World Cup. When it is not full of aspiring medal winners, it offers overnight accommodation.

Enjoy riding down the broad avenue of conifers that is the main approach to the Centre, turn left at the crossroads at its end and then quickly right along Littlehales Road. Turn left at its end in Chetwynd Aston, cross the A518 at 'Sheep roundabout' as it is known locally for obvious reasons and continue into **Newport** (55/28 miles) where the route joins the NCN 552. Continue through the town and past Chetwynd Deer Park then join a shared-use path to cross the A41. ▶

Fallow deer still run in Chetwynd Deer Park which is hidden behind a sandstone wall just outside town.

The fine Regency and Georgian houses that line the generously proportioned main street in **Newport**

Cycling Land's End to John o' Groats

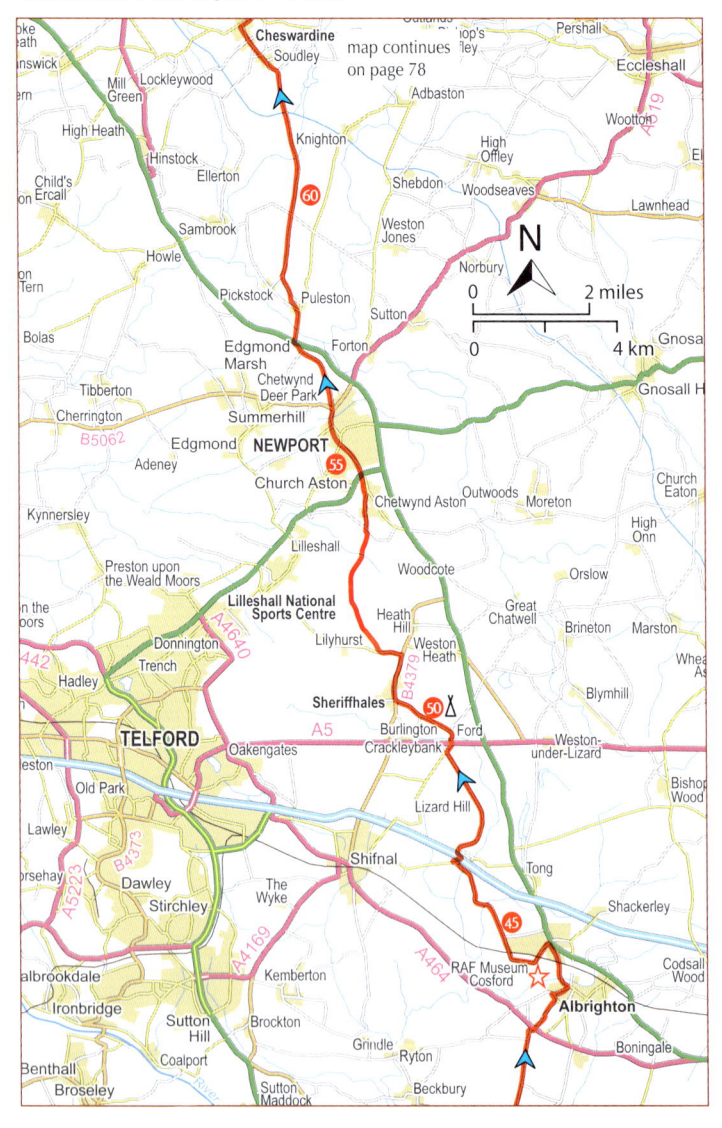

were constructed after the 'Great Fire of Newport' destroyed many of the tightly packed medieval buildings in 1665. It seems to have been a common hazard in Shropshire during the 17th century with major fires in Market Drayton in 1651 and Wem in 1677.

An interesting group of buildings that pre-date the fire are the alms houses and grammar school opposite the parish church. Both were founded by locally-born William Adams (1585–1661), a London merchant who left his wealth to his place of birth stipulating that there should be 'Two Almeshouses adjoining to ye Street for 4 single people 2 whereof to be Men & 2 Women to inhabit in successively forever'; his wishes restated on the plaques on their gables.

After passing through Puleston (58/25 miles) turn left following NCN 552 towards Cheswardine. Continue through the hamlet of Soudley and then turn right towards Chipnall in front of the church in **Cheswardine** (63/20 miles) and follow NCN 552 towards Market Drayton. After 500 metres turn left by the entrance to Cheswardine

The Guildhall in Newport is one of the few timber buildings to have escaped the Great Fire of 1665 that left 162 families homeless

The plaque in Cheswardine with some somewhat questionable distances to Land's End and John o' Groats

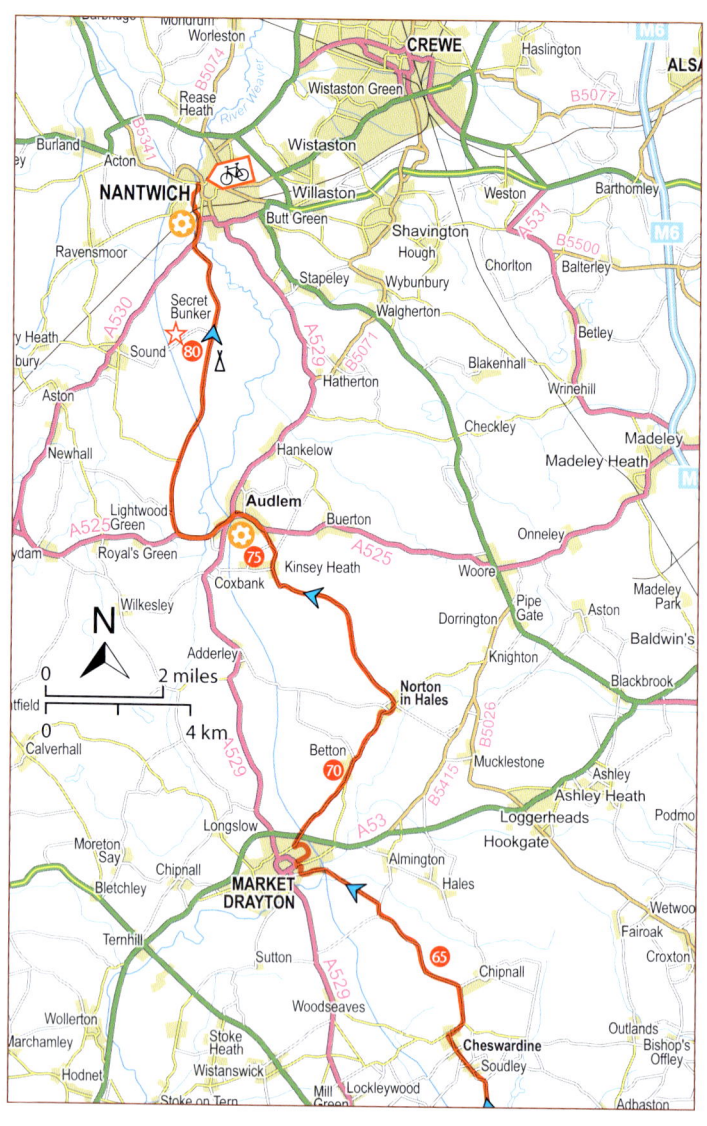

Cycling Land's End to John o' Groats

STAGE 5 – WORCESTER TO NANTWICH

Hall, a grand house that is now a care home; and left again after ¾ mile. ▶

Continue into **Market Drayton** (68/15 miles) and follow NCN 552 on a winding route around the periphery of town centre in the direction of Audlem. Once outside the town, ride over the A53 and the Shropshire Union Canal and through Betton to **Norton in Hales** (71/12 miles), a very pretty village that has had repeated success in the annual Britain in Bloom competition. Turn left in the village centre and follow the NCN 552 towards Audlem. Along the way you cross the county boundary between Shropshire and Cheshire, pass the parish of Buerton and get some fine views northwards across the Cheshire Plain. As you get towards the end of this pleasant lane, follow waymarkers for NCN 552 left along Paddock Lane and then turn left along Woore Road and ride into **Audlem** (76/7 miles).

> Edward I granted **Audlem** a charter to hold a market in 1296, but the sandstone Buttermarket that stands below the 13th century Church of St James is thought to have been erected in 1733. It is a simple structure but elegant enough to warrant a Grade II listing. Next to it is a granite boulder with an inset for a metal ring that was used for bear-baiting – a practice that was popular throughout the 17th and 18th centuries until it was prohibited in 1835. The monument opposite the Buttermarket also has a connection with practices that are now seen as abhorrent. It commemorates Doctor Richard Baker Bellyse (1809–1877) who practiced in the village for over 40 years. His grandfather, John Bellyse (1738–1829), bred both racing greyhounds and game birds for cockfighting which resulted in him gaining the nickname 'Cockfighter Bellyse'. Cockfighting was also banned by the same Cruelty to Animals Act in 1835.

Leave the village by following the A525 towards Whitchurch. After a mile turn right into Coole Lane and

A milestone below an old signpost in Cheswardine reminds you how far they have come and how far you have to go – with both distances seemingly understated.

CYCLING LAND'S END TO JOHN O' GROATS

Previously used as a decoy site to lure German bombers away from Crewe, Hack Green was redeveloped during the Cold War as a refuge for government personnel in the event of a nuclear attack.

follow it for 5 miles to its end leaving NCN 551 for this more direct route into Nantwich. Along the way the route passes Overwater Marina which has a popular café and a turning that after a mile brings you to Hack Green Secret Nuclear Bunker (www.hackgreen.co.uk), which is now a tourist attraction. ◄

At the end of Coole Lane, turn right along the A530 towards **Nantwich** and then left along Shrewbridge Road just after passing Nantwich Lake. Turn left along a shared-use path opposite Brookfield Park, soon re-joining NCN 551 which the route follows to the end of this stage at the junction of High Street and Water Lode in Nantwich town centre. An Ice Age glacier carried the granite boulder on display there from Scotland to Cheshire. At an estimated 10 inches per day, it will have taken 3000 years or more, whereas you should reach Scotland in just a few days.

> During the medieval period **Nantwich** was the most important of the Cheshire salt towns and an important centre for tanning. The last salt house closed in the mid-19th century and the last tannery in the 1970s. However, its previous prosperity means the town has a large collection of historic buildings.

RIDING NORTH TO SOUTH – JOGLE

Once across the A5, which marks the watershed between rivers that drain northwards into the Irish Sea and southwards into the Bristol Channel, riding becomes easier as you descend into the Severn Valley.

STAGE 6
Nantwich to Garstang

Start	Nantwich – junction of High Street and Water Lode (SJ 650 524)
Finish	Garstang – junction of Park Hill Road and Moss Lane (SD 491 452)
Distance	85 miles (136km)
Ascent	600m
Time	8–9hrs
OS Maps	OS Landranger 118, 109, 108 and 102
Refreshments	Venetian Marina before Cholmondeston, Winsford, Northwich, Higher Walton, Newton-le-Willows, beside the Leeds and Liverpool Canal near Chorley, Avenham and Miller Park in Preston and Preston Marina
Accommodation	There are no hostels and relatively few campsites along this stage but plenty of hotels and B&Bs in the towns along the route

This stage starts next to the River Weaver and then re-joins it 12 miles further on by which time it has become the Weaver Navigation. After providing 5 miles of traffic-free cycling, it swings northwest to the Mersey Estuary while the route heads north across first the Mersey Ship Canal and then the River Mersey and through a string of industrial towns in Merseyside, Greater Manchester and Lancashire using over 30 miles of well-surfaced canal towpaths and shared-use paths. Once across the River Ribble, the route skirts Preston into more rural North Lancashire although the busy M6, which is repeatedly crossed during this stage, is never far away.

From the start at the junction of High Street and Water Lode, follow a shared-use path northwards along Water Lode towards Chester crossing to a path alongside the opposite carriage first at the junction with Well Lane and then again at the junction with Fairfax Drive. After ¾ mile, turn right along Welshmans Lane and at its end,

Cycling Land's End to John o' Groats

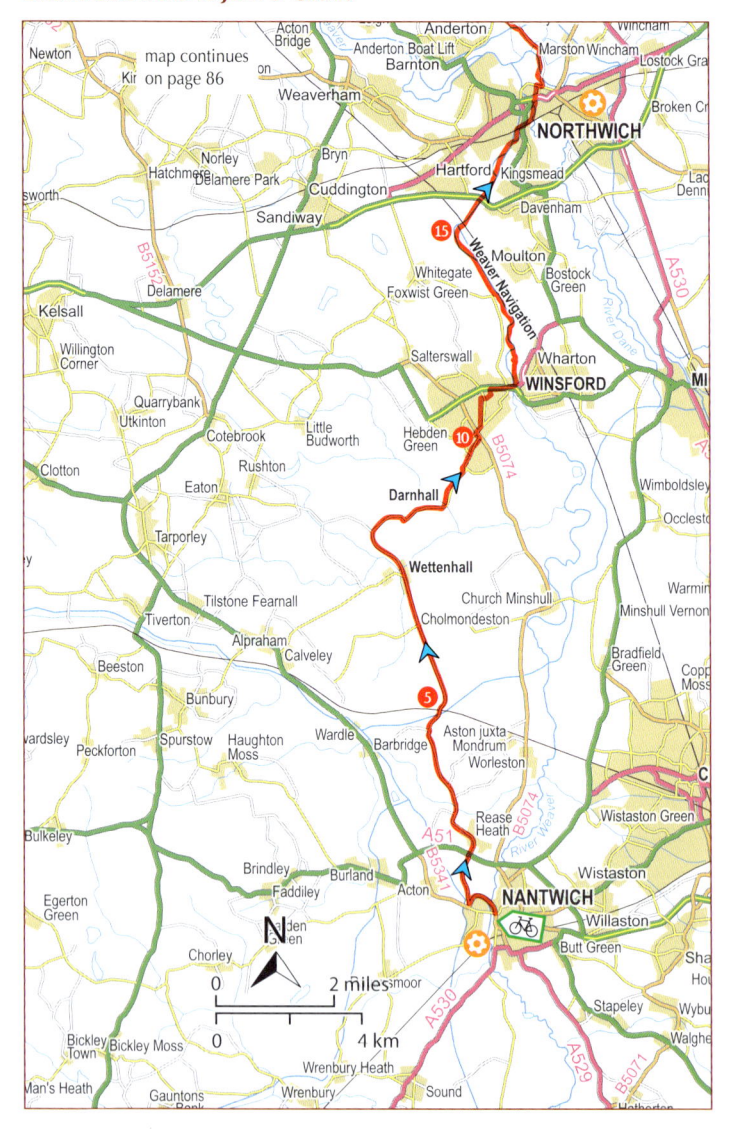

STAGE 6 – NANTWICH TO GARSTANG

cross the A51 into Wettenhall Road re-joining NCN 551 which the route follows for the first 12 miles until past Winsford.

Follow this remarkably quiet road northwards first through the unnamed hamlet of Poole where there is a wonderfully maintained Wesleyan Methodist Chapel dating from 1834. Continue over a branch of the Shropshire Union Canal, where there is café that is a favourite of local cyclists, and through Cholmondeston (6/80 miles), **Wettenhall** (7/79 miles) and **Darnhall** (9/77 miles). The Peckforton Hills, where the River Weaver rises, are visible 7 miles away to the west but this road has barely an incline making for rapid progress past fields of dairy cows and the occasional arable crop.

At its end, turn left following signs for NCN 551 towards **Winsford** (10/76 miles) and once around the bend, turn left again and follow Green Glebe Road around and across a staggered junction into Townfield Drive. Go straight across into Townsfield Road at the traffic lights and then follow signs for NCN 551 left down Dene Drive. Turn right into The Drumber and ride around the perimeter of Winsford Cross Shopping Centre to meet the busy A54. Cross both carriageways and then turn right into High Street. Follow the shared-use path around the roundabout, uphill beside Wharton Road and then turn left beside the A5018 following signs for Northwich. After 500 metres, turn left into Weaver Valley Road opposite the entrance to Wharton Road Retail Park, where there is both a supermarket and a fast-food restaurant, and then

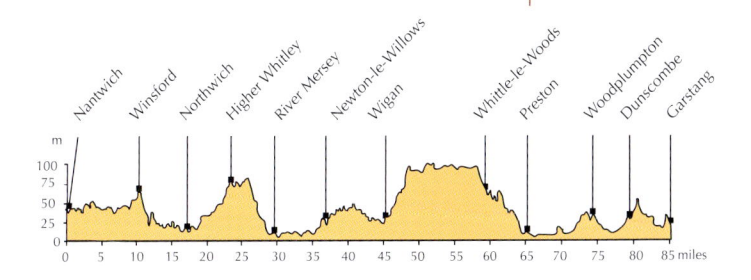

83

Passing the UK's largest and oldest working salt mine alongside the Weaver Navigation in Winsford

immediately right through a generously wide kissing gate and follow NCN5 alongside the Weaver Navigation.

Widening, deepening and the construction of locks during the early decades of the 18th century turned the River Weaver into **Weaver Navigation**. Other canals were connected to the Weaver Navigation including the Trent and Mersey Canal which necessitated building the Anderton Boat Lift which provides a 50-foot (15.2 m) vertical link between the two waterways. Completed in 1875 and used for over a century, it is now restored to full working order. It is 1km off route and you can visit it by turning left after Marbury Country Park (19/64 miles).

The compacted aggregate path alongside the Weaver Navigation is generally well-drained and makes for pleasant cycling with plenty to see including cormorants and a number of locks and heritage buildings along its bank. Just after passing the boatyard on the opposite bank, turn right under the railway viaduct, leaving the NCN 5 and ride through Chinkers Field alongside the River Danc. As the park starts to narrow, bear right along a narrow path, cross Whalley Road and ride along Percy Street. Cross the busy Chester Way at the pelican crossing and ride

Stage 6 – Nantwich to Garstang

up Venables Road and through the centre of **Northwich** (17/69 miles). ▶

Turn right at the roundabout at the end of Venables Way, then after 150 metres turn left into Old Warrington Road which soon becomes Marbury Lane. Continue through Marbury Country Park, which were once the grounds of Marbury Hall, a grand house in the style of a French château, which was demolished in 1968. Turn right at the end and follow Marbury Road into **Comberbach** (21/65 miles). Turn left into Senna Lane following signs towards Whitley. After a mile, turn left towards Little Leigh and then immediately right into Goosebrook Lane, which soon becomes Old Mill Lane.

Turn sharply left into an unsigned lane and then left again at the junction with Bentley's Farm Lane. Turn right into Dark Lane by the pond in **Higher Whitley** (23/63 miles) and then bear left at the next unmarked junction. Turn left at the right-hand bend and follow the gated and generally well-surfaced bridleway that eventually becomes Limes Lane to its end at the A49. Cross into Pillmoss Lane, which soon runs adjacent the busy M56 and turn right over the motorway. Turn left at the next junction following signs for Walton and ride through Hatton (26/60) to **Higher Walton** (28/58 miles).

It is said that timber-framed houses became popular in Northwich as they were better able to withstand subsidence from collapsing salt mines.

A small selection of the many bikes and cycling paraphernalia at Walton Hall

85

Cycling Land's End to John o' Groats

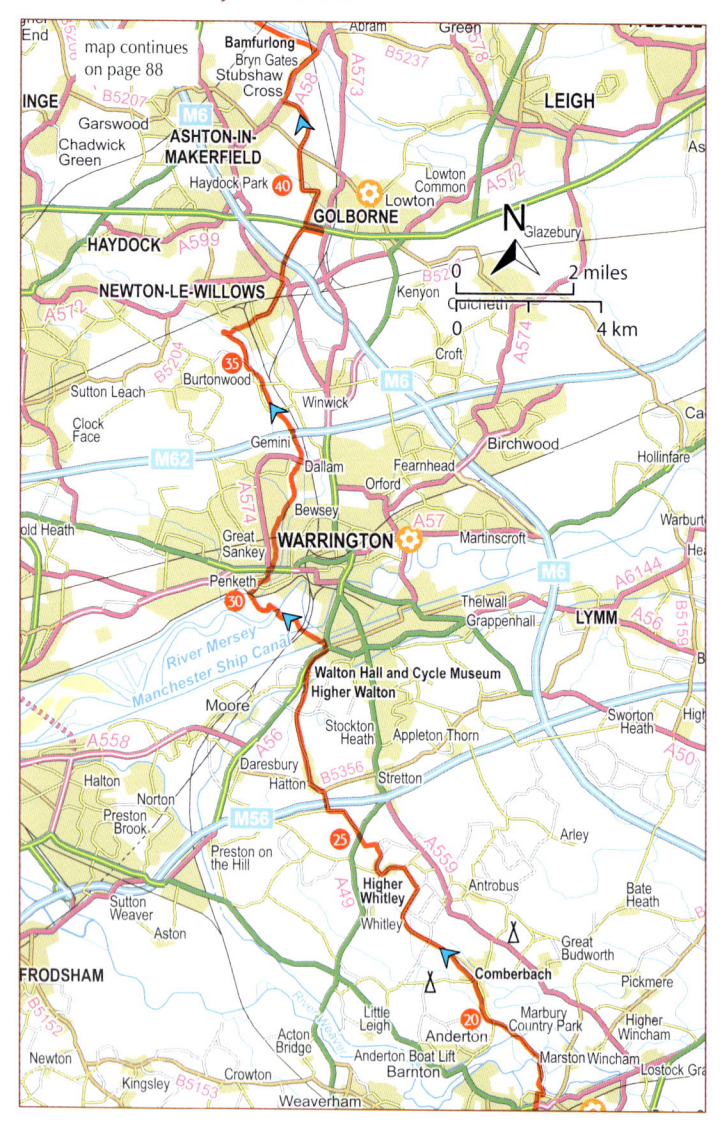

STAGE 6 – NANTWICH TO GARSTANG

Housed in the outbuildings of **Walton Hall** (walton-hallgardens.co.uk) is a collection of historic bicycles and cycling paraphernalia collected by local man Paul Adams. The Cycle Museum is only open at weekends, but Walton Hall and its café are open every day and entrance is free.

Turn right along the Old Chester Road, cross the A56 to pick up the shared-use path alongside the opposite carriage way. Once over the **Manchester Ship Canal**, take the second left into Taylor Street and follow the Trans Pennine Trail (NCN 62) along Eastford Road and over the **River Mersey**. Immediately after crossing Sankey Brook, turn right onto a shared-use path and follow it through Sankey Valley Park. Here the Sankey Canal and the Sankey Brook run parallel for over 4 miles through a green corridor that effectively cuts through **Warrington** (31/55 miles) without seeing much of it. ▶

Keep heading northwards first on one bank, then on the other, following signs for Bewsey and then Gemini, a massive retail park where the home retailer Ikea opened its first UK store in 1987. After 4½ miles turn right by a white metal footbridge, ride through Sankey Canal Car Park and along Branlegh Road. Skirt the barrier and then bear left at the T-junction into what is still Branlegh Road. At its end, turn left and then immediately right around the roundabout into Park Road South, which becomes Park Road North once through the railway tunnel, which was constructed in the 1830s to carry the track of the Liverpool to Manchester railway, which was the world's first inter-city railway. At the end of Park Road North in **Newton-le-Willows** (37/49 miles), turn left along the High Street, then right and follow Rob Lane, which becomes Newton Lane once under the M6.

The route crosses the busy East Lancashire Road and there is a dip in the central barrier and an ample central reservation so you could cross with care. If you are not so adventurous, turn right along the cycle path towards Golborne. After 700 metres, cross to the opposite carriageway and turn into Warrington Road. After 100

Flat-bottomed sailing barges called Mersey Flats once carried coal from collieries at Haydock along the Sankey Canal to the then flourishing chemical factories around St Helens.

87

Cycling Land's End to John o' Groats

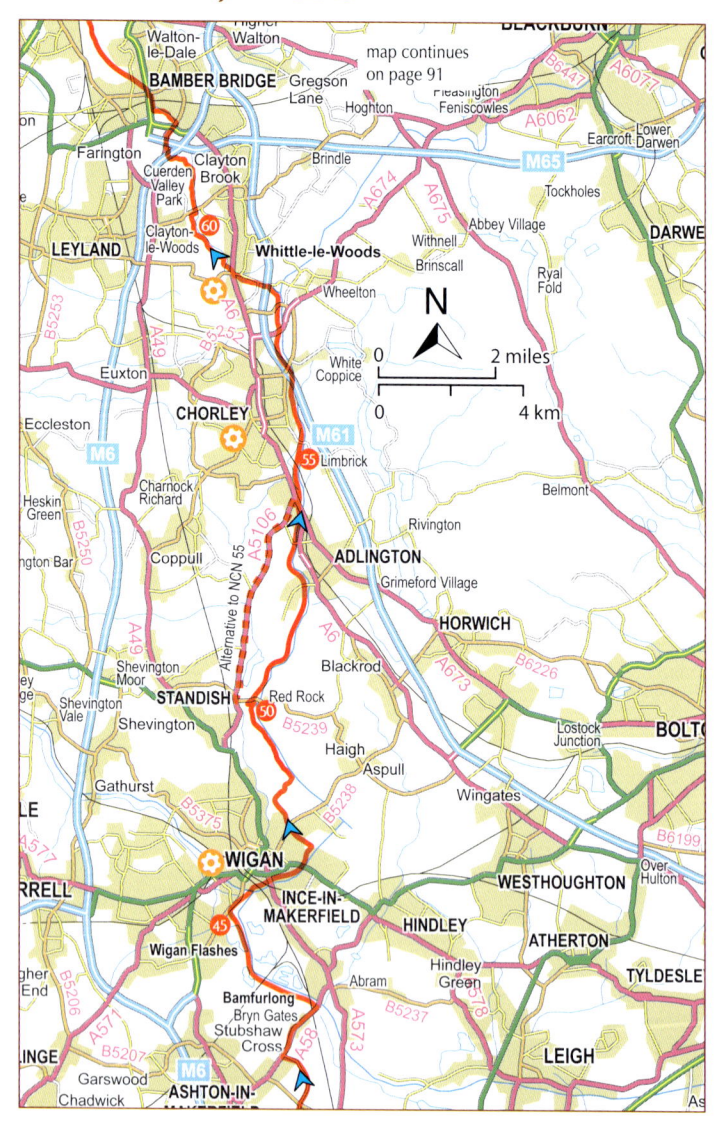

STAGE 6 – NANTWICH TO GARSTANG

metres, turn left into Park Road and then right through the barrier into Sandy Lane. This lane follows the boundary of Haydock Park Racecourse and is normally quiet except on race days as it leads directly to the main entrance. As you approach you may wish to dismount and walk as loose sand is often scattered on the tarmac where the course cross the road. ▸

Turn right into Harvey Lane by the main gate and then left along Helen Street. At its end, turn left along Edge Green Road. After 400 metres turn left along Golborne Road. Then turn quickly right into another bit of Edge Green Road which soon becomes Riding Lane.

Turn right along Bolton Road and ride through Bryn Gates and **Bamfurlong** (42/44 miles) with Rivington Pike and its neighbouring hills visible 10 miles away to the northeast. Leave the road immediately after crossing the Leeds and Liverpool Canal (Leigh Branch), cross the carriageway, drop down to join the towpath and loop back under the bridge heading northwards through the **Wigan Flashes**. ▸

This stretch of towpath is block-paved making for smooth and fast riding. It's truly excellent, which is more than can be said for the barriers, which will begin to get annoying for anyone riding with panniers. After 1½ miles, cross the bridge and continue northwards riding along the top of a causeway between the Leeds and Liverpool Canal and Scotman's or Scotsman's Flash, which is thought to be named after local Scots who used it for curling during the Victorian era.

After 3 miles, cross the footbridge and turn right following the towpath under the main west coast railway line heading towards Haigh Hall. It starts flat enough, but the going gets harder as you climb up the towpath alongside a string of locks. There are 21 in all, but the route only passes nine of them. After 1½ miles, leave the towpath at bridge 58 and turn left following NCN 55 along a stretch of disused railway track before bearing right to re-join the canal near Haigh Hall Country Park.

Leave the towpath at Bridge 63 where there are prominent traffic lights. Turn left along the B5239, then

Racing first took place on Golborne Heath (as it was then known) in 1752. The course was renamed Haydock Park in 1898.

Formed as a result of mining subsidence, the Wigan Flashes provide a habitat for rare plant species, willow tits and the elusive bittern.

Cycling Land's End to John o' Groats

turn sharply right after 200 metres still following signs for NCN 55. Ride through the car park and out along what it ought to be a perfectly serviceable stretch of disused railway. However, after being churned up by off-road drivers, the first few hundred yards can be muddy. You could persist but if you want an alternative continue along the B5239 for another 400 metres and then turn right along the A5106. After 1½ miles, turn right into Rawlinson Lane following signs for the Lancashire Cycleway and to re-join the route, turn left onto the towpath of the Leeds and Liverpool Canal. ◀

> Use the nearby bridges to get to the White Bear Marina Café and the Boatyard Bus Café on the opposite bank of the Leeds and Liverpool Canal.

If you persist you will soon be past the worst of it especially when the track narrows. After 2 miles, slow for a twisting descent that takes you underneath a viaduct and then climb the steps to join the canal towpath for the next 6 miles around the eastern perimeter of **Chorley** (55/31 miles), ignoring waymarkers to NCN 55 which loops off into the town of which we see very little.

The towpath is in good condition and progress is fast. Pass under the noisy M61 and then 2 miles further on bear at a set of locks and follow a narrower path along a dead end branch of the canal to join Town Lane. Turn left briefly following local route 91 along Town Lane and under the M61. Turn left at the next junction and then sharply right before The Roebuck Inn into School Lane. Cross the A6 into Kem Mill Lane in **Whittle-le-Woods** (58/28 miles) and turn left at its end soon re-joining NCN 55 which the route follows into Preston.

Ride through Cuerden Valley Park, which is crossed by the B5256, and head for the Wigan Road Car Park which is just beyond the bridge across the M6. Turn right along the shared-use path alongside that A49 and follow it under the M65 and over the A6 to the outskirts of **Bamber Bridge** (62/24miles). Turn left into Havelock Road following signs for NCN 55. Turn left through the tunnel beneath the busy A6 expressway that now splits Brownedge Road in two. At the next junction turn right and follow the NCN 55 into the trees and along the track of a disused tramway that once linked canals on either side of **Preston** (65/21 miles). Once across the River

Stage 6 – Nantwich to Garstang

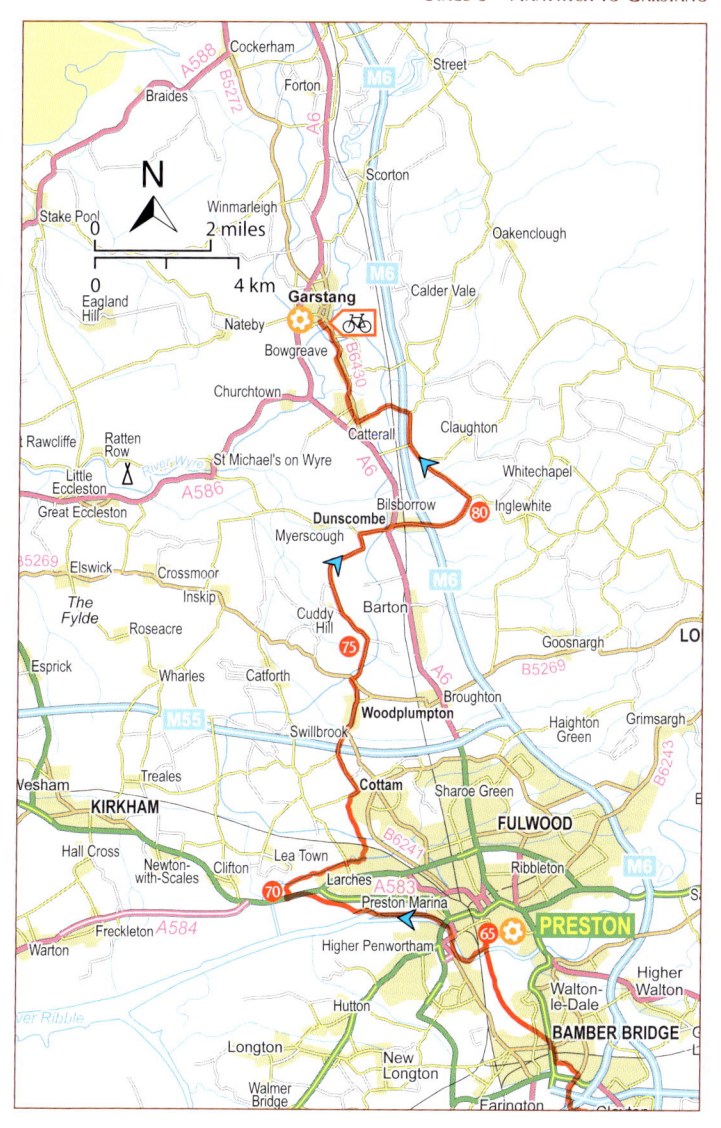

CYCLING LAND'S END TO JOHN O' GROATS

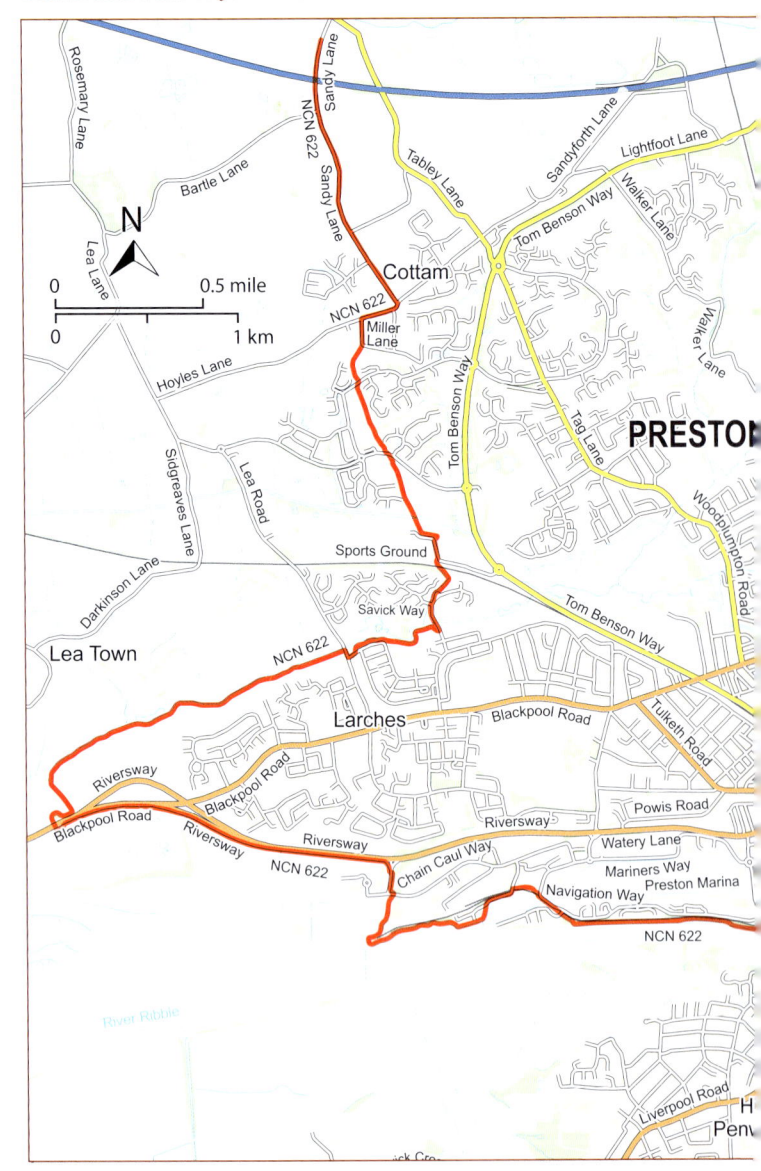

STAGE 6 – NANTWICH TO GARSTANG

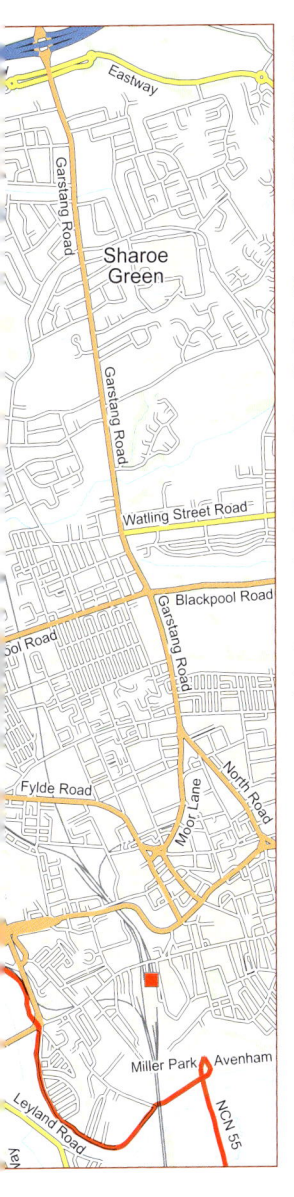

Ribble, turn right following signs for Kirkham and ride into the well-kept Avenham and Miller Parks, where there is a café. Loop around below the bridge and follow NCN 622 downstream. ▶

Cross the swing bridge at Preston Marina and continue following the NCN 622 westwards turning inland alongside Riversway and then the busy A583 Blackpool Road. Turn sharply left immediately before a footbridge, cross the A583 and then swing back eastwards towards the city still following waymarkers for NCN 622. It may seem a circuitous route but it is easy off-road cycling and there are no traffic lights to delay you.

Preston Marina is built around **Albert Edward Dock** which was the largest dock in the country when it opened in 1892. Initially cotton and wood pulp were the most important cargoes landed here but by the 1960s it had transformed itself into a container port and roll-on-roll-off ferry

Preston is circumnavigated by following NC622, or the Preston Guild Wheel as it is known locally, a 21-mile shared-use, hub-and-spoke path around the city.

93

Boat lifting gear at the now residential Preston Dock

port. Traffic peaked in 1968, when 500 dockers were employed by the port. But as the size of ships increased, fewer could use the dock and it quickly fell into decline before closing in 1979, only making a profit in 17 years of the 90 years it was used.

The NCN 622 finally swings north along Savick Way and passes through the University of Central Lancaster Sports Ground on its way to **Cottam** (73/13 miles) where we leave it and continue straight on along Miller Lane. Turn right along Hoyles Lane and then left 200 metres further on and follow Sandy Lane into **Woodplumpton** (74/12 miles) where our route follows the Lancashire Cycleway. Stick to it for the next 6 miles crossing the A6 at **Dunscombe** (79/7miles) where a stretch of shared-use path keeps cyclists separate from the traffic. A mile beyond the M6, turn left into Lydiate Lane which becomes Ducketts Lane, Lodge Road and eventually Stubbins Lane for the final few miles into **Garstang**.

For a few miles our route briefly follows NCN 6 which you should continue to follow if you are not staying overnight in Garstang. Otherwise turn right along the

The ruins of Greenhalgh Castle, Garstang (Image by Chris Andrews, used under Creative Commons Licence)

B6430 when you reach Catterall and ride the final two miles to Garstang where the stage ends. ▶

RIDING NORTH TO SOUTH – JOGLE

In sunny conditions wearing sunglasses and a peaked cap beneath your helmet will give you better visibility of pedestrians and dogs on the many stretches of traffic-free, shared-use path on this stage.

Garstang is a peaceful market town bypassed by the A6, M6 and much of history; the exception being in 1645 when Royalists in Greenhalgh Castle surrendered to Cromwell's forces.

Cycling Land's End to John o' Groats

STAGE 7
Garstang to Penrith

Start	Garstang – junction of Park Hill Road and Moss Lane (SD 491 452)
Finish	Cornmarket, Penrith NY 516 301
Distance	70 miles (112km)
Ascent	1400m
Time	8–9hrs
OS Maps	OS Landranger 102, 97 and 90
Refreshments	Scorton, Caton, Crook of Lune (Wed-Sun during summer), Kirkby Lonsdale, Barbon, Sedbergh, Shap and Askham
Accommodation	Penrith has a busy bike-orientated hostel that is frequently packed with cyclists riding the Coast-to-Coast route as well as plenty of other choices of accommodation

While this stage has the most climbing, it is kept to a minimum by sticking to the lowest ground over the watershed between the Lune Valley and the Eden Valley. There is spectacular scenery throughout: first the route skirts along the western moorland of the Forest of Bowland which is an Area of Outstanding Natural Beauty; then comes a long stretch from Kirkby Lonsdale to the Howgill Fells within the Yorkshire Dales National Park; and finally there are a few miles between Shap and Penrith within the Lake District National Park.

Decorated bicycles and wheelbarrows are on display in Scorton during its Bikes & Barrows Festival held over May Day bank holiday.

Ride up Park Hill Road towards Lancaster, turn right along Croston Road at the roundabout and then turn left towards Lancaster at the next roundabout. After 700 metres turn right along Green Lane East and then bear left by The Hawthorns into what is still Green Lane. Turn right along Gubberford Lane and ride through **Scorton** (2/67 miles) by now following NCN 6. ◄

Ride out of the village, over the M6 and then turn left along Clevely Bank Lane, crossing back over the M6.

Stage 7 – Garstang to Penrith

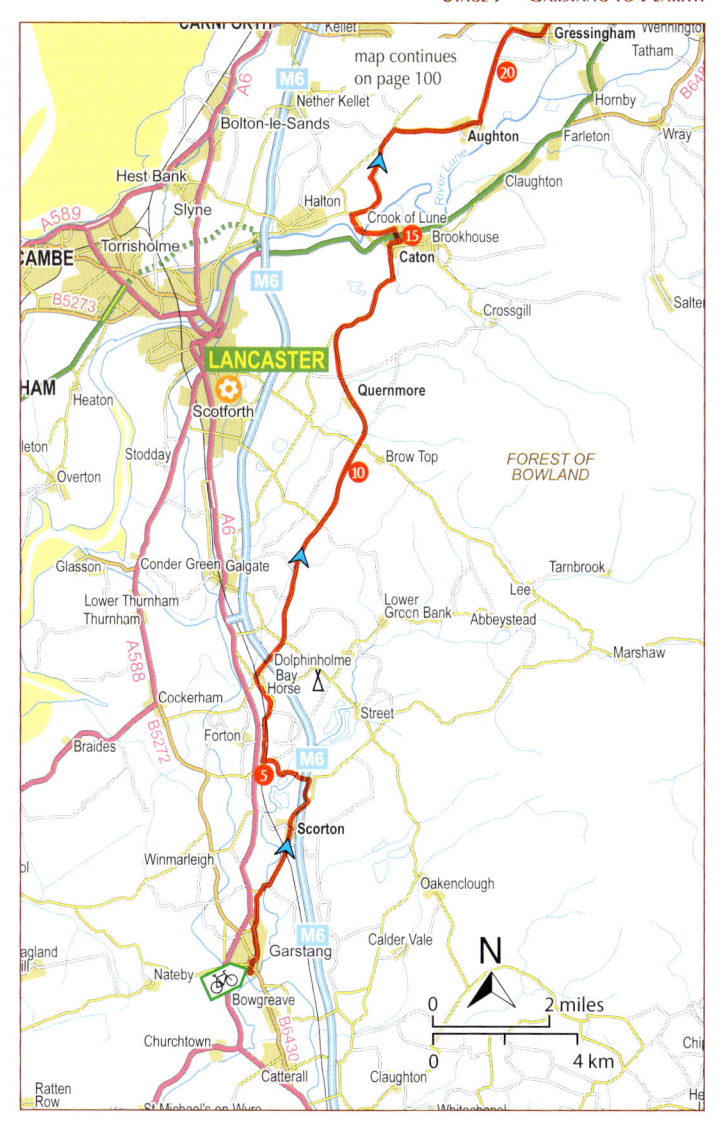

CYCLING LAND'S END TO JOHN O' GROATS

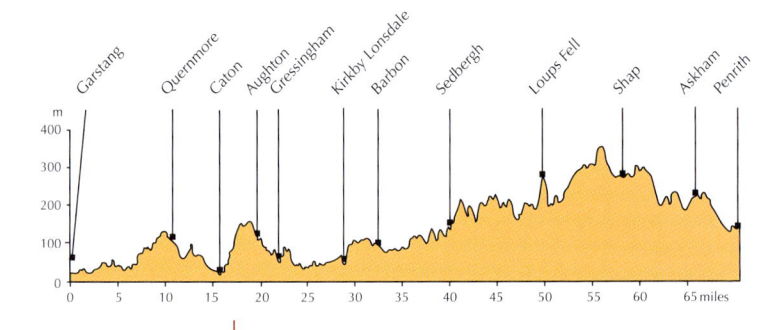

After passing the country store, where there is a café, and crossing over the west-coast mainline railway, turn right and ride through Hollins Lane and Bay Horse (6/63 miles). Turn right along Whams Lane heading towards Quernmore and Caton and cross over the M6, which we meet yet again in another 40 miles. Cross the next crossroads, where the NCN 5 turns left to Lancaster, and follow regional route 90 through **Quernmore** (11/58 miles) to **Caton** (15/54 miles). As the route gains height on the western boundary of the Forest of Bowland there are excellent views across Morecombe Bay and the flatlands of The Fylde to Blackpool and its famous tower.

As you enter Caton follow signs for local route 90 right and then left into the village centre and cross the A683 at the roundabout. Follow local route 90 left along the track bed of an old railway line towards Crook O' Lune where the café may or may not be open. Turn right out of the carpark and right again after 500 metres and climb up around Halton Hill following signs for NCN 69. As you ascend you get some fine views across the Lune Valley to the Forest of Bowland beyond. ◄

> After touring the district in 1816, J. M. W. Turner did an oil painting of the Crook o' Lune, which gets its name because the meandering River Lune forms the shape of a shepherd's crook.

Turn right at the top of the climb and then turn right again after 600 metres and enjoy a long descent past **Aughton** (19/50 miles), pronounced 'aeftuhn' rather than 'awrtuhn'. to **Gressingham** (21/48 miles). It was here that the Gressingham Duck, a cross between mallard and Pekin ducks, was first produced in 1980. But you are

STAGE 7 – GARSTANG TO PENRITH

unlikely to see any as they are now only reared in East Anglia.

Turn left on the edge of the village and follow local route 90 uphill to meet the B6254. Turn right towards Arkholme (23/46 miles), where route 90 goes left and ride through the village briefly following the Cumbria Cycleway through Whittington (26/43 miles) to the outskirts of **Kirkby Lonsdale** (28/41 miles).

Kirkby Lonsdale sprung up at a crossing point over the River Lune where several drovers' and packhorse routes converged. It is mentioned in the Domesday Book as *Cherchibi* (village with a church) and gained a charter to hold a Thursday market and an annual fair in 1227. At one time town had 29 inns and ale houses to cater for thirsty travellers and market goers and eight of them still function as licensed premises, which is quite remarkable for a town with fewer than 2000 inhabitants.

Its location between the Lake District and the Yorkshire Dales National Park has helped Kirkby Lonsdale remain relatively unspoilt with its most famous visitor, the poet and critic poet John Ruskin

A local cyclist heading out of Kirkby Lonsdale

Cycling Land's End to John o' Groats

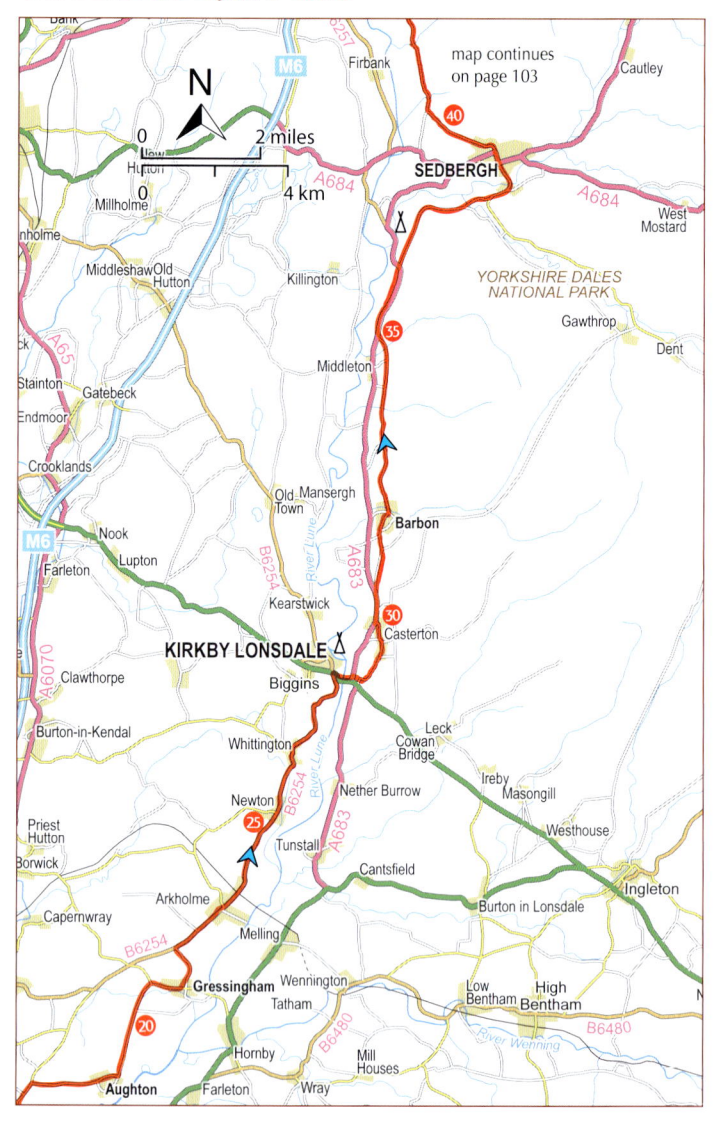

100

who has a view named after him, to declare 'I do not know in all my country, still less in France or Italy, a place more naturally divine.'

Today the town centre is an eclectic mix of elegant 18th century buildings and what were once artisan's cottages tightly packed around cobbled courtyards separated by narrow alleyways with names such as Salt Pie Lane and Jingling Lane. But left largely untroubled by tourists, the town has developed at its own pace, gaining an envied reputation for the quality and variety of its shops, eateries and bars.

Cross the 14th century Devil's Bridge and A683 and ride up the narrow path beyond the parking area which eventually widens into a lane. Continue through High Casterton to Casterton (30/39 miles). Bear left in front of the parish church and then turn right along the A683. After ½ mile, turn right towards **Barbon** (32/37 miles) which is a pretty limestone village. Turn left at the war memorial and then right opposite the Wesleyan Chapel and ride for 3 miles along this quiet lane, with the first hills of the Yorkshire Dales National Park immediately to the east. When you meet the A683 again at Middleton Hall, turn right and then after a mile, turn right again following a brown tourist sign for Holme Open Farm. Pass through the gate at the end of the bridge over the disused railway and then bear left through another gate and ride into **Sedbergh** (40/29 miles) now following NCN 68.

Sedbergh is officially England's 'book town'. However, its ambition to rival the more famous Hay-on-Wye in Wales never took off and today there are only a few booksellers in the town. More successful is Sedbergh School, which was established in 1525. In recent times it has been famed for its sporting prowess, having produced a number of famous rugby players. No doubt their fitness is helped by the annual Wilson Run, reputed to be the toughest school run in the country, which since 1881 has

Heading into Sedbergh which is tucked in below the Howgills Fells

covered the same 10-mile course around the lower slopes of the nearby Howgill and Baugh Fells.

Leave the town up Howgill Lane next to The Dalesman Inn following NCN 68/70, which follow the same route here, and ride around the lower slopes of the voluptuously rounded Howgill Fells. Meet the River Lune where the main west-coast railway and the M6 motorway run alongside each other. After passing beneath the railway and motorway, turn right along the A685 towards Tebay. After a mile, turn left towards Roundthwaite. Ride up and over **Loups Fell**, from where Blenthcathra (or Saddleback), the most distinct of the Northern Fells of the Lake District, is visible 20 miles away to the northwest. Turn left in Greenholme towards Shap following waymarkers for NCN 68/70. Two miles further on at a spot between the northbound and southbound carriageways of the M6, turn left again. After 1½ miles of slightly bizarre cycling surrounded by speeding traffic, turn left along the B6261 towards Shap. Turn left again at the next junction and then right along the A6 to **Shap** (57/12 miles). Note the turning on the left to Wet Sleddale, which fans of the cult movie *Withnail & I* will know is the location of Crow Crag, Uncle Monty's ramshackle farmhouse where the

Stage 7 – Garstang to Penrith

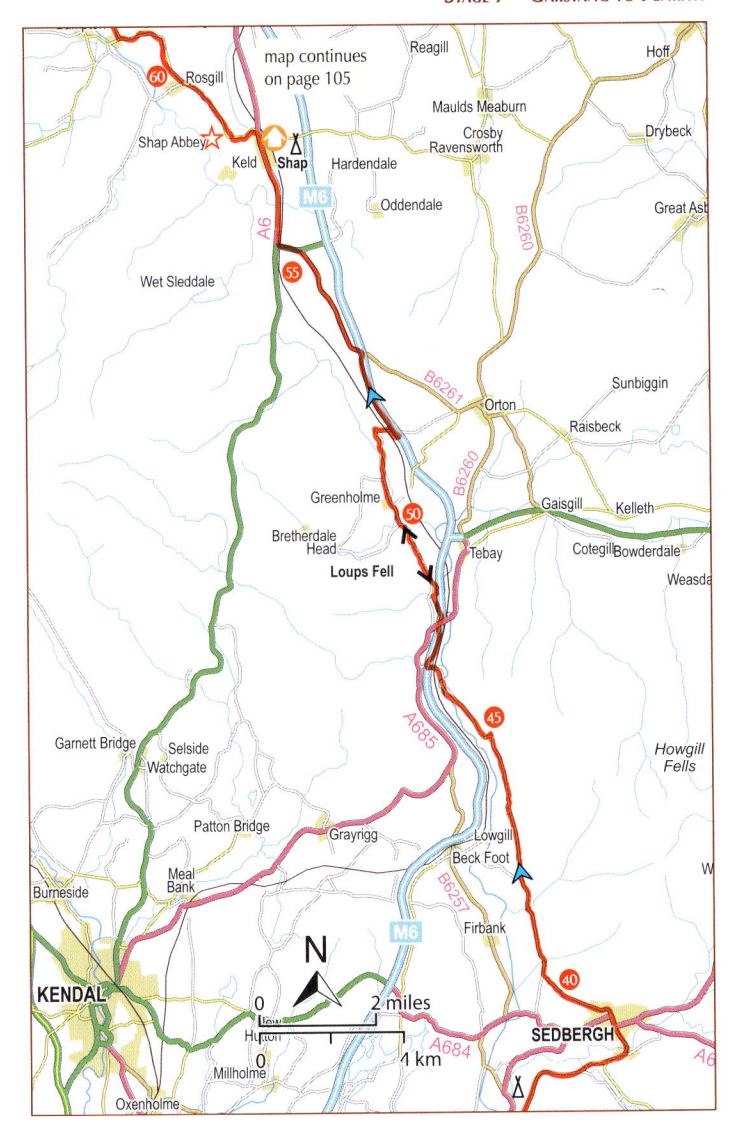

two friends lament that 'We've gone on holiday by mistake'. At this point of your journey you may be thinking 'I'm riding LEJOG by mistake' too.

At the top of the village, turn left towards Haweswater. Although you are technically in the Lake District National Park, it feels more like the Yorkshire Dales National Park with sturdy limestone walls, verges packs with the blue flowers of scabious, harebells and cranesbills and an occasional limekiln. Continue past the entrance to Shap Abbey and then once you get to the edge of Bampton Grange (61/8 miles), turn right towards Knipe and Whale and enjoy the views across the valley to Haweswater Reservoir and the Far Eastern Fells of the Lake District. ◂

After a mile turn right through a gate by a telephone box and ride past Whale and ride through **Askham** (65/4 miles), which is a particularly attractive village with solid sandstone houses set around two village greens. To the east is the flat-topped Cross Fell, (2,930 ft /893m), which is the highest summit of the Pennines and the highest point in England outside the Lake District. Two miles

Henry VIII closed the 12th century Shap Abbey in 1540 and much of the stone was incorporated into local buildings so all that remains today is an impressive 15th century tower.

A field of wildflowers that is part of a larger rewilding programme on the Lowther Estate near Askham

Stage 7 – Garstang to Penrith

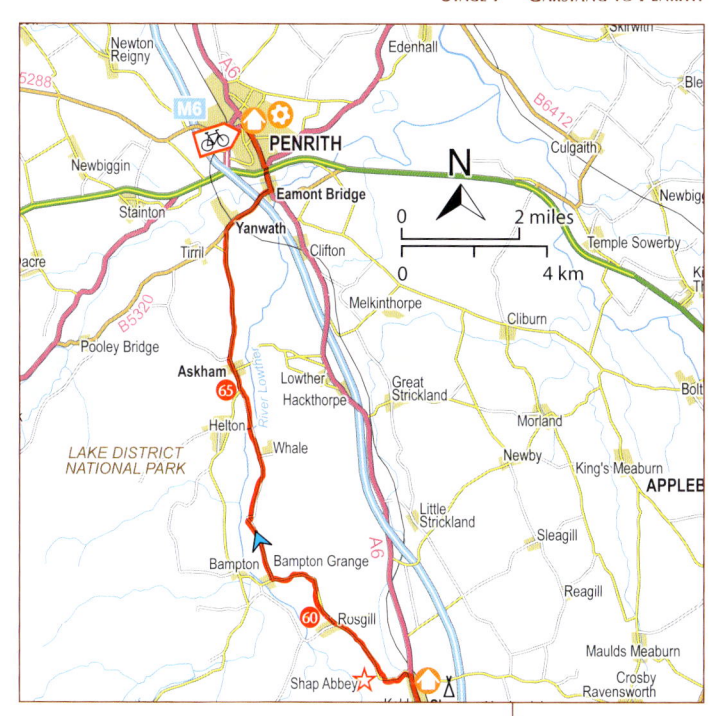

further on turn right along the B5320 and ride through **Yanwath** (67/2 miles) and over the M6 motorway to its end at a T junction with the A6 in Eamont Bridge. ▶

Turn left and ride through **Eamont Bridge** (68/1 mile) before joining a shared-use path to cross the roundabout on the busy A66. Continue into the centre of **Penrith** where this stage ends by the Victorian clock tower on Cornmarket that was erected in 1861 by the wealthy Musgrave family in memory of their son Philip, who died of an illness contracted while fighting in the Crimean War.

Known as the 'old red town' because of its sandstone buildings, **Penrith** is very much the heart of

Now a farm, Yanwath Hall, consists of a small 14th century pele tower and a 15th century manorial hall, which is reputed to be the finest in England.

Cumbria, despite its position outside of the Lake District National Park. Unlike its more commercial neighbours to the west, this is a working town serving the needs of the local community. Henry III granted a market charter to Penrith was in 1223 and it has been a busy trading centre ever since.

Traditionally farmers brought their produce in from the country by cart, which is why there are old stable buildings tucked away behind many of the town's inns which today house delightful restaurants and specialist shops. The inns and streets were where produce was bought and sold with grain traded outside the inns along Cornmarket, rye at The Black Bull and wheat at The Black Lion. And once trading was done no doubt the farmers retreated indoors to celebrate their profit or commiserate their loss.

RIDING NORTH TO SOUTH – JOGLE

Riding this stage north to south gives 200m less climbing, but does little to alleviate the short, sharp climb over Loups Fell which is equally fierce in either direction.

Looking west towards Haweswater Reservoir and the Western Fells from near Knipe

STAGE 8
Penrith to Moffat

Start	Cornmarket, Penrith (NY 516 301)
Finish	War memorial in the centre of Moffat (NT 085 053)
Distance	70 miles (112km)
Ascent	700m
Time	7–8hrs
OS Maps	OS Landranger 90, 85 and 78
Refreshments	Carlisle, Gretna, Annan, Lochmaben and isolated pubs along the stage
Accommodation	No campsites for tents before you get into Scotland, but a good selection of B&Bs and hotels in the main towns all along the stage

After a gentle climb out of Penrith comes 15 miles of easy pedalling to Carlisle and another 10 miles of flat terrain around the Solway Estuary to Annan. Then comes a long but almost imperceptible climb inland. Once you reach Beattock the climbing is done and all that's left are the final couple of miles into Moffat. While many End-to-Enders follow NCN 74 along the B7076, which runs adjacent to the busy A74M for 25 miles, our route follows the B7020 a few miles to the west which is both quieter and better surfaced.

From the clock tower on Cornmarket, walk your bike along Devonshire Street to the George Hotel and then bear right into a narrow alley which widens after The Woolpack Inn. Remount and keep bearing right along Burrowgate, past The Grey Goat Inn and into Sandgate. Turn left at the min-roundabout and follow NCN 7 along Meeting House Lane, across the next roundabout, and along Drovers Lane. At the next roundabout, turn right and then after 100 metres turn left along Robinson Street and follow NCN 7 under the main west coast railway line and the M6 Motorway and through the campus of Newton Rigg College (2/68 miles). ▶

A part of Askham Bryan College in York, Newton Rigg College is one of the leading land-based colleges in the UK.

Cycling Land's End to John o' Groats

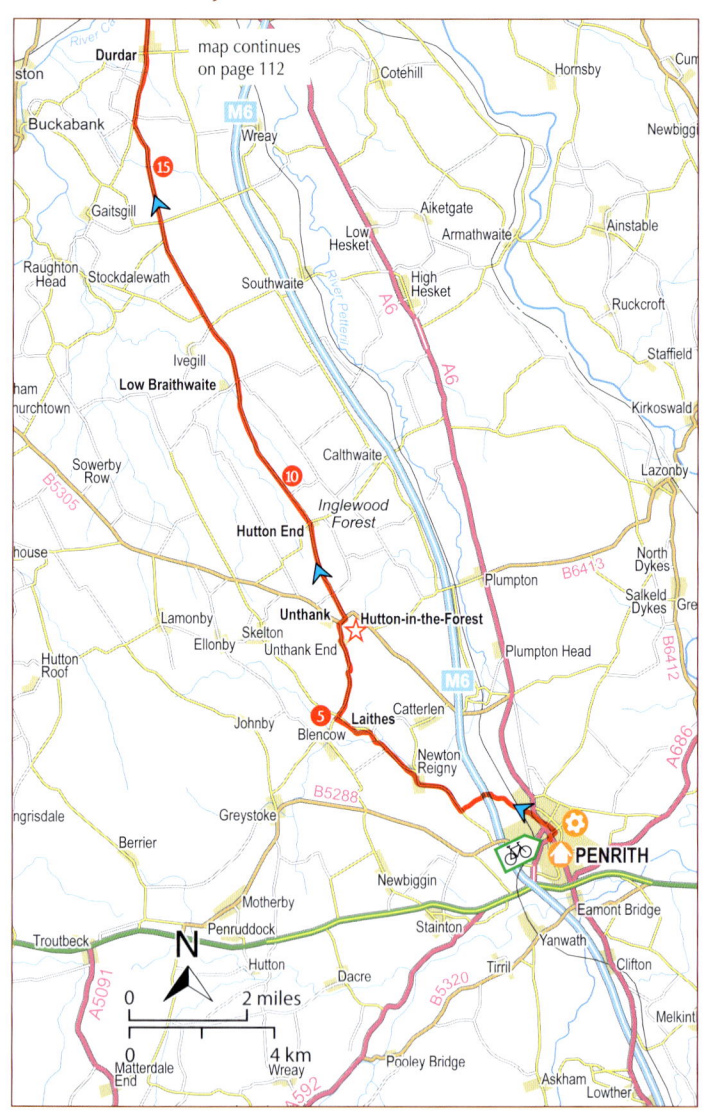

108

STAGE 8 – PENRITH TO MOFFAT

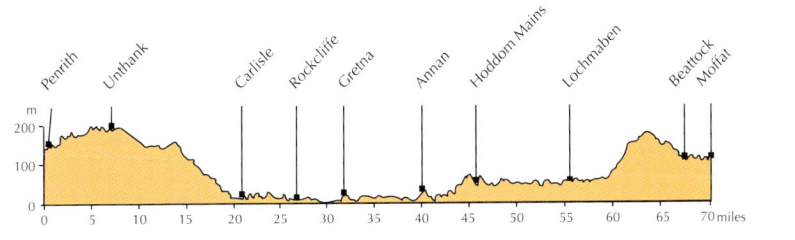

Turn right along Newton Road and ride through Newton Reigny, where Catterlen Hall – a large house constructed around a 15th century pele tower – can be glimpsed from the road. Ride though **Laithes** (4/66 miles) and then turn right at the next crossroads, leaving NCN 7 and NCN71, and ride into **Unthank** (7/63 miles). Turn right along the B5305 towards the M6 and then after 200 metres turn left towards Carlisle, passing the parish church which is partially hidden behind pine trees on the right. A mile to the west is Skelton Transmitting Station where the 365-metre (1,198 foot) very low frequency transmitter is the tallest structure in the UK.

Hutton-in-the-Forest on the edge of Unthank is a Grade I listed country house that since 1605 has belonged to the Fletcher-Vane family. The current house, which dates from the 17th century, is built around an earlier Pele tower which still survives. Much extended and remodelled in subsequent centuries, the house is an eclectic mix of styles including some early Arts and Crafts wallpapers and furniture. It is open from April to October. See www.hutton-in-the-forest.co.uk for further information.

Ride through **Hutton End** (8/62 miles), past **Low Braithwaite** (11/59 miles) and through **Durdar** (17/53 miles) enjoying the flat terrain and the views of the

Cycling Land's End to John o' Groats

The prominent 'Dixons Chimney' on the boundary of Denton Holme was the tallest in the UK when it was built alongside what was England's largest cotton mill in 1836.

Pennines to the east, the last of the Northern Fells of the Lake District to the west and eventually the first glimpse of Scotland straight ahead. Continue straight on past the racecourse and into the outer suburbs of Carlisle. Immediately after St Herbert Church (19/51 miles), which has a distinctive semi-circular end wall, turn left along Jubilee Road. Turn right into Lund Crescent and then after 300 metres, turn left along a path and cross over the west coast main line railway and then the River Caldew to Denton Holme. ◄

Turn immediately right through Denton Street Playground and follow NCN 7 along the riverbank into the centre of **Carlisle** (21/49 miles).

> Its position on the flatlands of the Solway Estuary near the Scottish border meant **Carlisle** was always going to be an important settlement. The Romans used it as an important base for supplying the forts along Hadrian's Wall; the Normans as a strategic military stronghold; and the Victorian railway engineers as the last staging post before a difficult push through the Southern Uplands to the commercially vibrant cities and towns in Scotland's central belt. As a result, Carlisle has a rich and interesting history which can be seen all over the city.

The largely 12th-century Carlisle Castle was built by the Normans to defend the border

STAGE 8 – PENRITH TO MOFFAT

But being the last major centre of population before the Scottish border far removed from Westminster and out of sight of much of the UK's population has meant that Carlisle has also been used to try things out. None is stranger than the Carlisle & District State Management Scheme of 1916, when the government nationalised the brewing, distribution and sale of alcohol in Carlisle because drunkenness among munitions workers in the area was compromising the UK's ability to supply sufficient armaments during World War I. Mangers of the government-owned public houses were incentivised to sell food and soft drinks rather than alcohol and between 1916 and 1919 customers could not buy drinks for others.

Many public houses were closed, others refurbished and new ones built to a standard design called the 'New Model Inn'. This was the creation

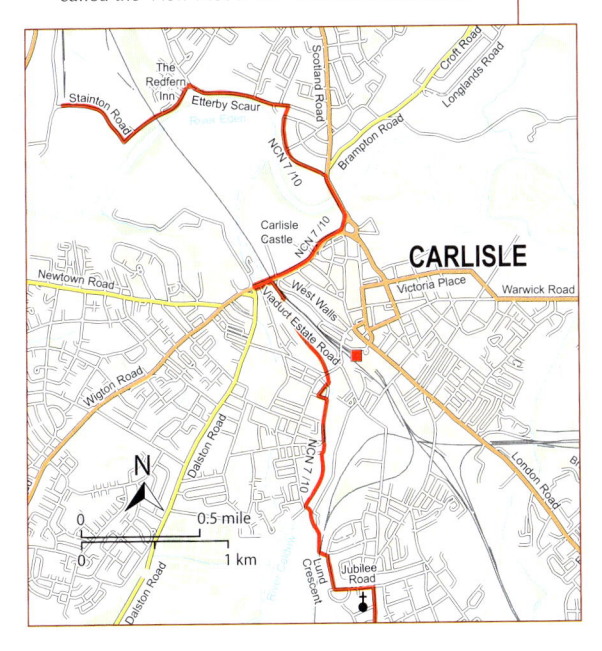

Cycling Land's End to John o' Groats

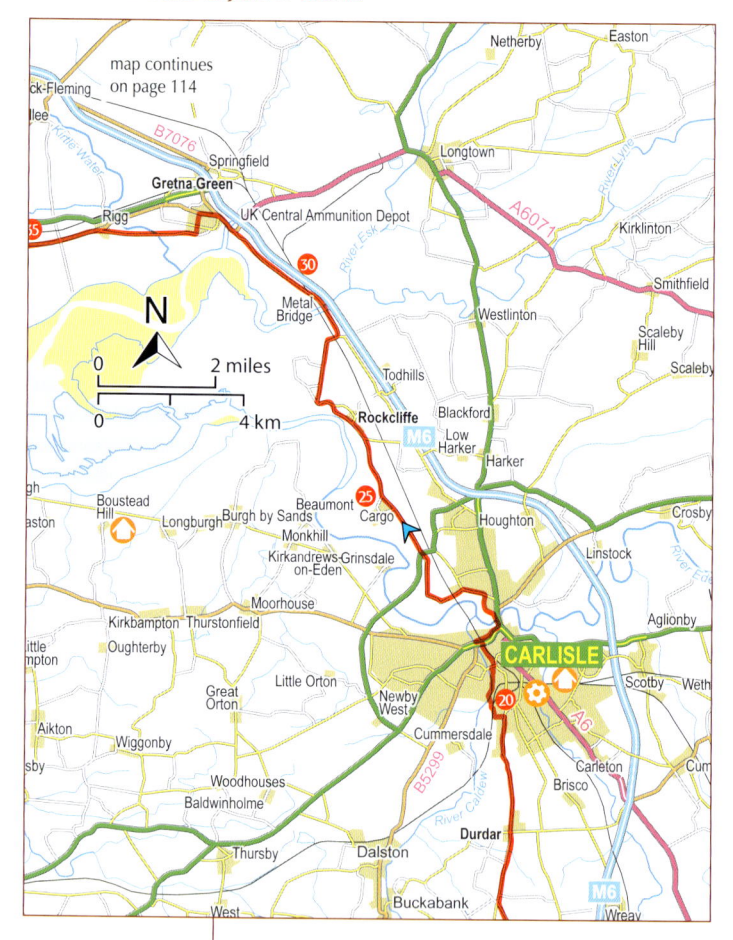

of the scheme's chief architect, Harry Redfern. You can see a fine example of his work at The Redfern Inn which bears his name just off route in Kingmoor Road, Etterby. There are 48 other pubs still trading today within the city's boundary that were once part of the State Management Scheme which only

STAGE 8 – PENRITH TO MOFFAT

ended in 1973, when the government finally sold off the pubs. See www.thestatemanagementstory.org for further information.

Follow NCN 7 west to cross the A565, back alongside the opposite carriageway past Carlisle Castle and then left over the River Eden and along its north bank through the well-preserved Victorian suburbs of Stanwix and Etterby (23/47 miles). Use the shared-use path the cross the roundabout at Kingmoor and ride past Cargo and through **Rockcliffe** (26/44 miles) before swinging north towards the M6. Turn left towards Gretna, abandoning NCN 7 and ride past Metal Bridge Inn and one of the UK's Central Ammunition Depots, which is hidden away in underground bunkers in the trees between the motorway and the wind turbines. ▶

Turn left towards Gretna at a junction with the B7076 and ride across the Scottish border stopping for the obligatory photograph and perhaps a well-earned coffee in the Old Toll Bar, which was one of eight toll houses built to Telford's standard design along the road between Carlisle and Glasgow in the 1820s. Turn left at the next

Long replaced with a concrete structure, the original iron bridge at Metal Bridge was designed by Thomas Telford (1757–1834) when he improved the road to Glasgow in the 1820s.

Parked up opposite the Old Toll Bar on the Scottish border

CYCLING LAND'S END TO JOHN O' GROATS

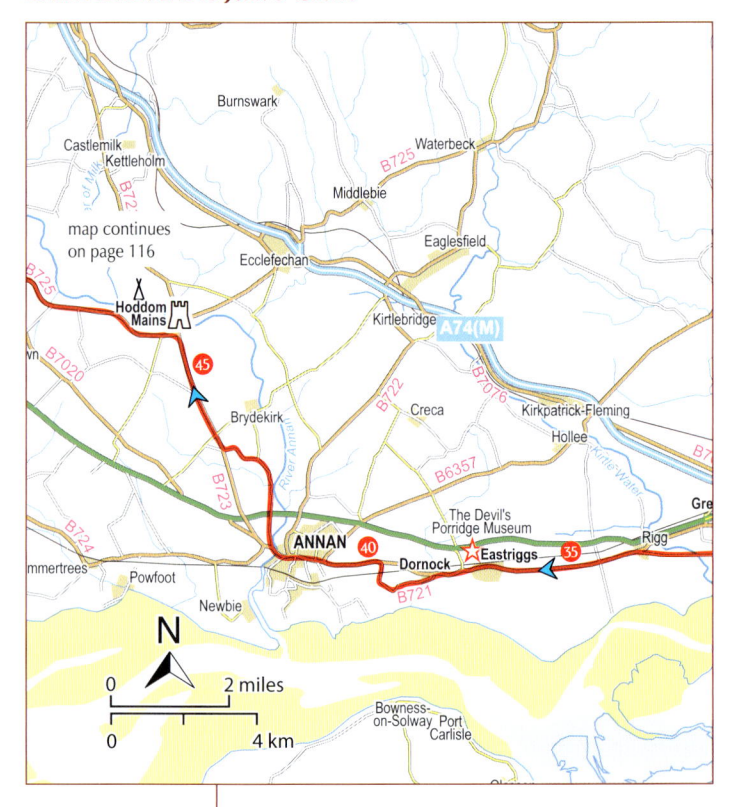

roundabout and ride into **Gretna** (32/38 miles). Turn left at the traffic lights in the centre of the village, following NCN 7 along Central Avenue and out along the north bank of the Solway through **Eastriggs** (36/34 miles) and **Dornock** (38/32 miles), where you get good views south back to the hills of the Lake District.

> The munitions factory built at **Gretna** during World War I employed 12,000 mainly female workers on a site that stretched for 9 miles from Eastriggs to Longtown. Workers kneaded nitro-glycerine

Stage 8 – Penrith to Moffat

and guncotton into a paste they called the 'Devil's Porridge' with their skin turning yellow from contact with sulphur. This led to them being called the 'Canary Girls', but it was nothing to sing about as many of them would make the ultimate sacrifice. Their story is told in The Devil's Porridge Museum in Eastriggs. See www.devilsporridge.org.uk for further information.

Follow the B721 through the centre of **Annan** (40/30 miles) and over the River Annan, leaving NCN 7 which continues westwards along the Solway coast and close by Merrick (843m/2766ft) which is the prominent hill that is occasionally visible 40 miles away to the west. ▶

Turn right towards Brydekirk and then after 1½ miles turn left along an unsigned road that leads to the B723. Turn right and then 2 miles further on turn left and ride through **Hoddom Mains** (46/24) where the 16th century castle has the largest tower of any in the Border country. Continue through Dalton (49/21 miles), a pleasant village of tidy cottages, where the road becomes the B7020.

Continue northwards first looking out for a pyramidal monument on the summit of Almagill Hill, which was erected in memory a 19th century huntsman called Joe Graham who found the Dumfriesshire hunt, and then the fine red sandstone mansion of Rammerscales peeking out above the woods to the west of the road.

Now decommissioned, the futuristic structure to the north of Annan is Chapelcross nuclear plant which produced both electricity and weapons-grade plutonium.

In 1758 **Rammerscales** was purchaséd by Dr James Mounsey (1710–1773), a local man who had studied medicine in Edinburgh and travelled extensively in Russia before returning home. It was hardly a stress-free retirement; Mounsey always slept with a loaded firearm by his bed and arranged for all the rooms in Rammerscales to have two doors so as provide a ready escape as he was constantly in fear for his life.

During his time in Russia, Mounsey became Royal Physician to the Empress Elizabeth on a

Cycling Land's End to John o' Groats

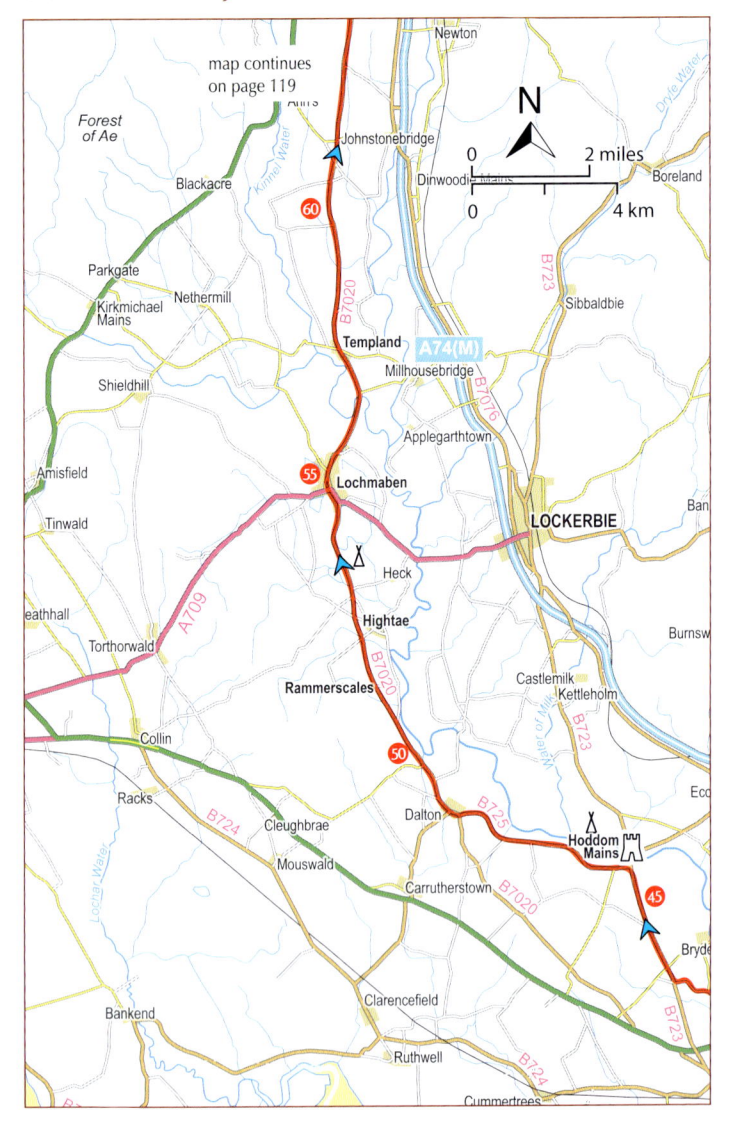

STAGE 8 – PENRITH TO MOFFAT

grand salary of 4,000 roubles a year. On 25th December 1761 she died while in his care. Six months later her successor, the 34 year old Tsar Peter III, also died in Mounsey's care, his death presumed to have been due to poisoning organised by his wife and subsequent successor, Catherine the Great.

The rapid and untimely death of two rulers put Mounsey in a dangerous position as traditionally when an emperor died their close associates were exiled to Siberia. However, Catherine allowed Mounsey to retire on the grounds of ill health and he returned to Scotland with a considerable fortune and several pounds of rhubarb seeds hidden in his luggage.

At the time rhubarb, which was widely used as a laxative, was expensive and its supply was tightly controlled by the Russian state. But this frightened man, who was constantly on the look-out for strangers who might be Russian agents sent to kill him for his supposed involvement in the death of two tsars, put himself further at risk by smuggling rhubarb into the UK and then promoting its wider adoption for which he was awarded the gold medal of the Royal Society of Arts in 1770. Mounsey died of natural causes in 1773 and is buried in Lochmaben Churchyard beneath an imposing 30 feet tall granite memorial.

Continue past **Hightae** (51/19 miles). Turn left when you reach **Lochmaben** (55/15 miles) and ride along its broad High Street and then bear right at the statue of Robert the Bruce in front of the town hall and continue through **Templand** (57/13 miles). The next 5 miles are all ascent, but it is barely noticeable as the gradient is very easy. Where this road ends at the junction with the A701 (65/5 miles), turn right towards the motorway and after 600 metres, turn left and ride through the outskirts of Beattock. After ½ mile turn right at the end of a copse and ride through 'Jessie's Tunnel' beneath the main west-coast

Riding through Jessie's Tunnel near Beattock

Some say 'Jessie's Tunnel' is named after a girl who was hit by a train; some that it is named after boys scared of crossing the track; and others that a certain Jessie plied her trade there.

railway and then turn left through the centre of **Beattock** (67/3miles). ◀

As you approach the motorway join the shared-use path and follow it alongside the A701, under the A74(M) and into **Moffat** where the stage ends at the war memorial in the centre of the town.

During the 18th and 19th centuries **Moffat** was a popular spa town on a par with Harrogate and Bath in England with throngs of visitors staying to take the sulphurous waters which were said to cure everything from skin conditions to rheumatism.

Many of the town's impressive buildings were built to cater for this burgeoning tourist trade including the Town Hall, which was originally built as the 'Baths Hall', and Scotland's oldest pharmacy which was established by Thomas Hetherington in 1844 and still trades under his name despite now being part of a national chain.

118

Stage 8 – Penrith to Moffat

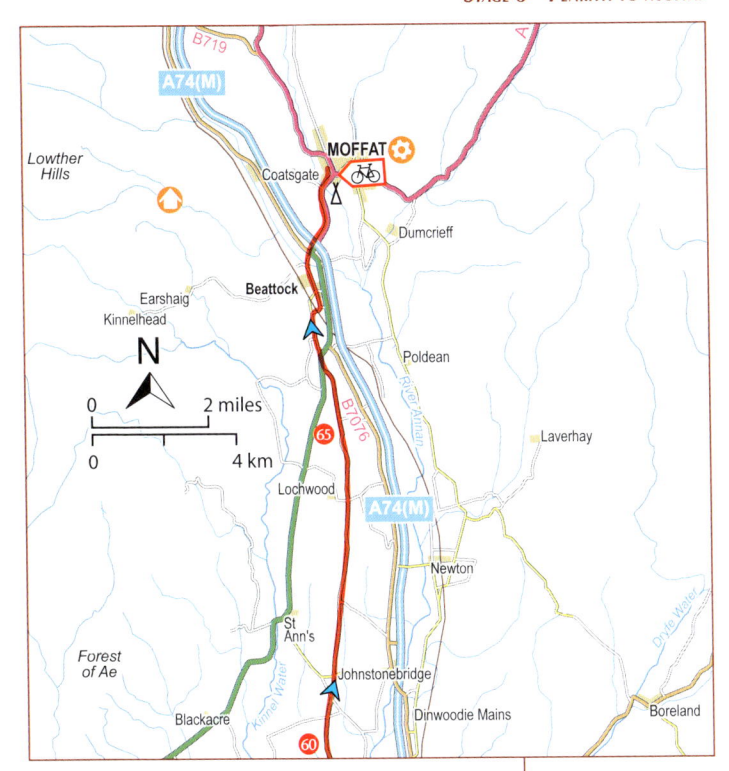

RIDING NORTH TO SOUTH – JOGLE

Should there be strong winds from the south west driving up from the Solway Firth, you may wish to shorten this stage by following the more sheltered NCN 74 through Lockerbie to Gretna saving 4½ miles.

CYCLING LAND'S END TO JOHN O' GROATS

STAGE 9
Moffat to South Queensferry

Start	War memorial in the centre of Moffat (NT 085 053)
Finish	High Street, Queensferry (NT 129 784)
Distance	64 miles (102km)
Ascent	900m
Time	7–8hrs
OS Maps	OS Landranger 78, 72 and 65
Refreshments	Thankerton, Carnwath, Mid Calder and Kirkliston
Accommodation	You will have to go off route for hostels and campsites, but there are plenty of B&Bs and budget hotels near the end of this stage

Cycling through cities tends to be slower than less urban areas, if only because you can spend an inordinate amount of time waiting for lights to cross main roads and dog walkers to reel in their pooches. So this stage bypasses the wonderful city of Edinburgh by sticking to the quieter roads to the west of the Pentland Hills before dropping down to South Queensferry. Should you wish to visit the centre of Edinburgh leave the stage at East Calder, follow NCN 75 into the city and return to South Queensferry along NCN 1 adding 16 miles to the journey.

Ensure you have enough energy-giving snacks to get you through this stage as cafés are scarce and may not be open. Start by heading south away from the centre of Moffat following the A701 to the A74(M). Pass under the motorway then take the third exit at roundabout following NCN 74 along the B7076 towards Abington. It is uphill for the next 10 miles, but it only marginally raises the heartrate as the gradient rarely goes above 2 per cent. You may still hear your pulse though as, other than the occasional lumber wagon and local resident, the road is rarely busy even when it becomes the A702 just before Crawford.

Stage 9 – Moffat to South Queensferry

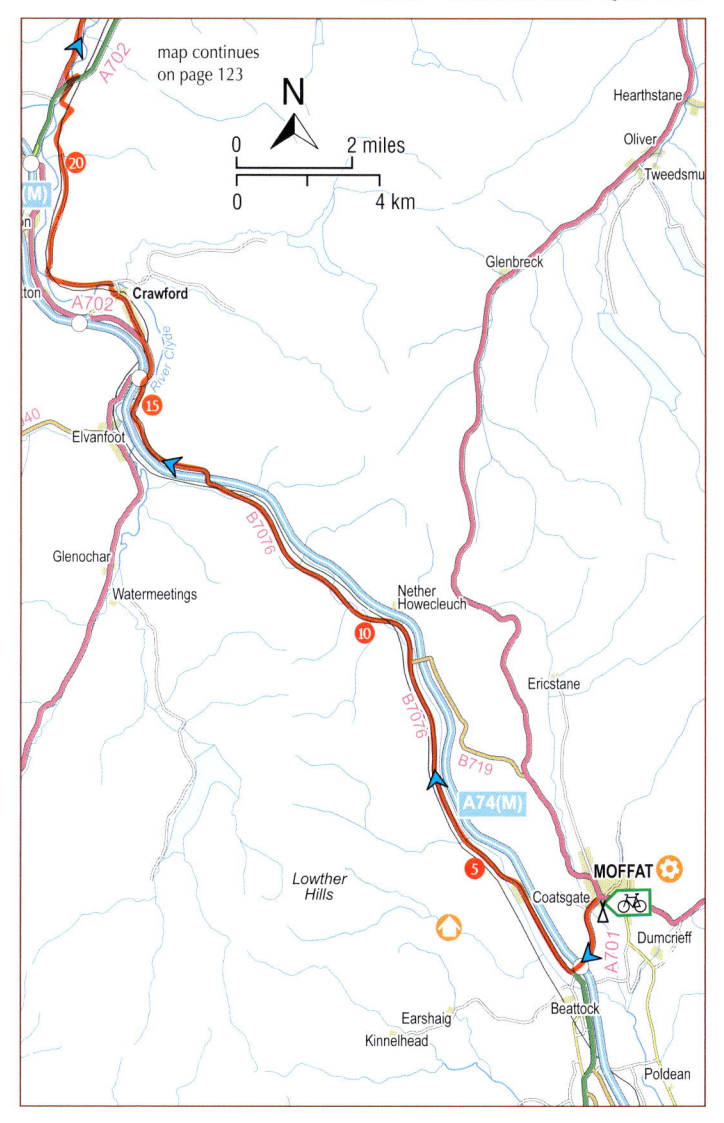

Hillside grazing for sheep and electricity from the Clyde Wind Farm make up much of the economy of the Southern Uplands

After 16 miles, turn right into **Crawford** (17/47 miles) and turn right towards Camps Reservoir in the centre of the village. Cross over the west coast mainline railway and the River Clyde, which is formed by the confluence of two streams, the Daer Water and the Potrail Water, which rise in the Lowther Hills 10 miles to the south and then turn left along an unsigned road that runs northwards alongside the railway.

Crawford is perhaps so quiet because of its claim to be one the most haunted villages in Scotland.

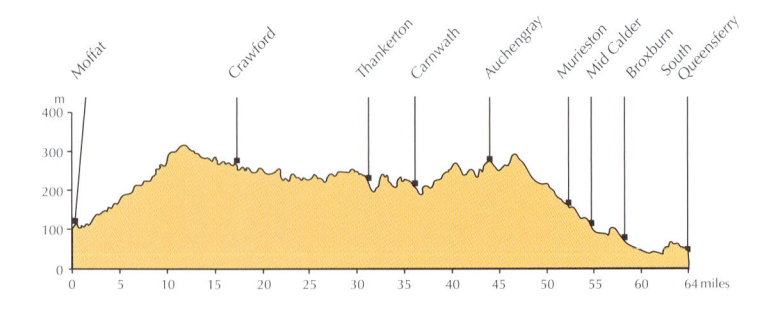

Stage 9 – Moffat to South Queensferry

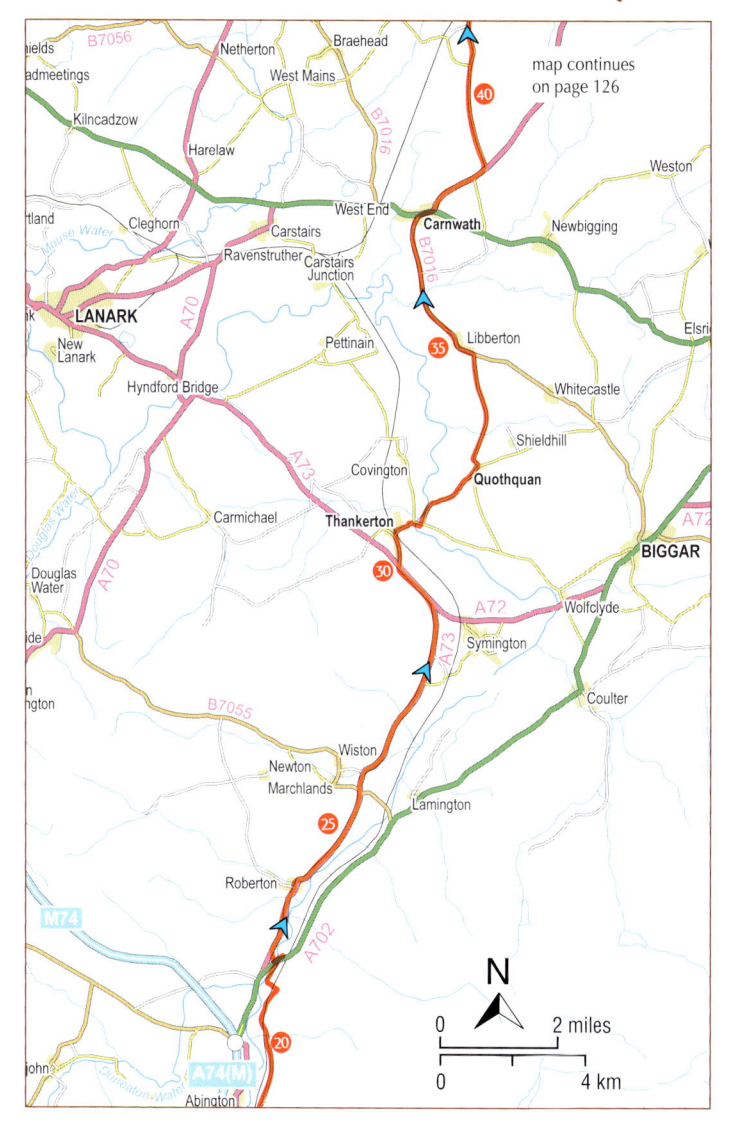

The now-closed Post Horn Inn is said to have three ghosts: an inn-keeper's daughter who was accidentally killed by a stagecoach; a coachman wearing a dark cloak; and a five-year-old girl who was hanged for stealing bread in 1805. Ghostly Roman legionnaires only visible from the knees up are also said to have been seen marching up the Main Street which is built above a Roman road.

After 5 miles, turn left along the A702, cross the River Clyde and turn right by a pair of semi-detached houses. At the end of this short road, turn right along the A73 which is a generously wide road with good visibility and limited traffic. After 7½ miles, turn right towards **Thankerton** (30/34 miles) and once at the village green turn right again towards Carnwath. Cross the railway and then turn right following signs for Carnwath. Cross the narrow bridge over the River Clyde and then at the bottom of the hill turn left still following signs for Carnwath.

Once through the centre of **Quothquan** (33/31 miles), turn left towards Carnwath. Follow the road for 2 miles and then turn left along the B7016 towards Carnwath. Ride through Libberton (35/29 miles) into **Carnwath** (36/28 miles).

The Apple Pie Café and Bakery in the moorland village of **Carnwath** is a popular cake-stop for local cyclists and is often a control point on the 1500km London-Edinburgh-London, self-supported, cycle ride that participants aim to complete in 125 hours. See www.londonedinburghlondon.com for details.

But if you don't fancy that you could try The Red Hose Race. Except for wars and outbreaks of Foot & Mouth Disease, it has been run every year since 1508, making it what is believed to be the oldest footrace in Britain and possibly Europe. It started when James IV of Scotland granted lands around Carnwath to John Lord Somerville specifying that he should present '... one pair of hose containing half an ell of English cloth at the feast of St. John the Baptist, called Midsummer, to the man running most quickly from Carnwath to 'Calla Cross', the rationale being that a fast runner could quickly bring news of any approaching invasion to Edinburgh and the red hose would make the messenger instantly recognisable. Today there are cash prizes but only winners from Carnwath or neighbouring parishes are entitled to wear the red socks.

Ride through the village along the A70 towards Edinburgh and then turn left at the mini-roundabout by the war memorial. After 1½ miles, turn left and ride across the open moorland landscape through the tiny villages of **Auchengray** (43/21 miles) and **Woolfords** (45/19 miles). There are good views eastwards across the Cobbinshaw Reservoir to the Pentland Hills and northwards across the more densely populated Central Lowlands to the Ochil Hills, which our route crosses on Stage 10. ▶

Cobbinshaw Reservoir was built to feed the Edinburgh and Glasgow Union Canal which flourished for a mere 20 years between 1822 and 1842.

One and a half miles after Woolfords, turn right at a junction surrounded by conifer plantations and enjoy 15 miles of gradual descent. Cross the B7008 towards **Murieston** and then 1½ miles further on immediately after crossing over a railway bridge just before the beginnings of Brucefield Industrial Estate, turn right along a shared-use path. At its end, turn right along Murieston South District Road and after 200 metres turn left along Bellsquarry Road South. After ½ mile, turn right into Dunvegan Gardens, then immediately left along the shared-use path and follow past Williamston Primary School to the end of Bankton Lane. Turn left along Murieston East Road and ride across the bridge over the A71 into Dedridge East Road. Turn left into Dedridge East Industrial Estate, follow Abbotford Rise around to the left, and then turn left along the shared-use path at its end.

Bear right after passing through the tunnel under Dedridge East Road and then turn right alongside St Ninian's Primary School. Ride through another tunnel, across a foot bridge over the A899 and then turn right and follow the path around to the B8046. Cross the junction towards Kirk of Calder and follow the road into

Cycling Land's End to John o' Groats

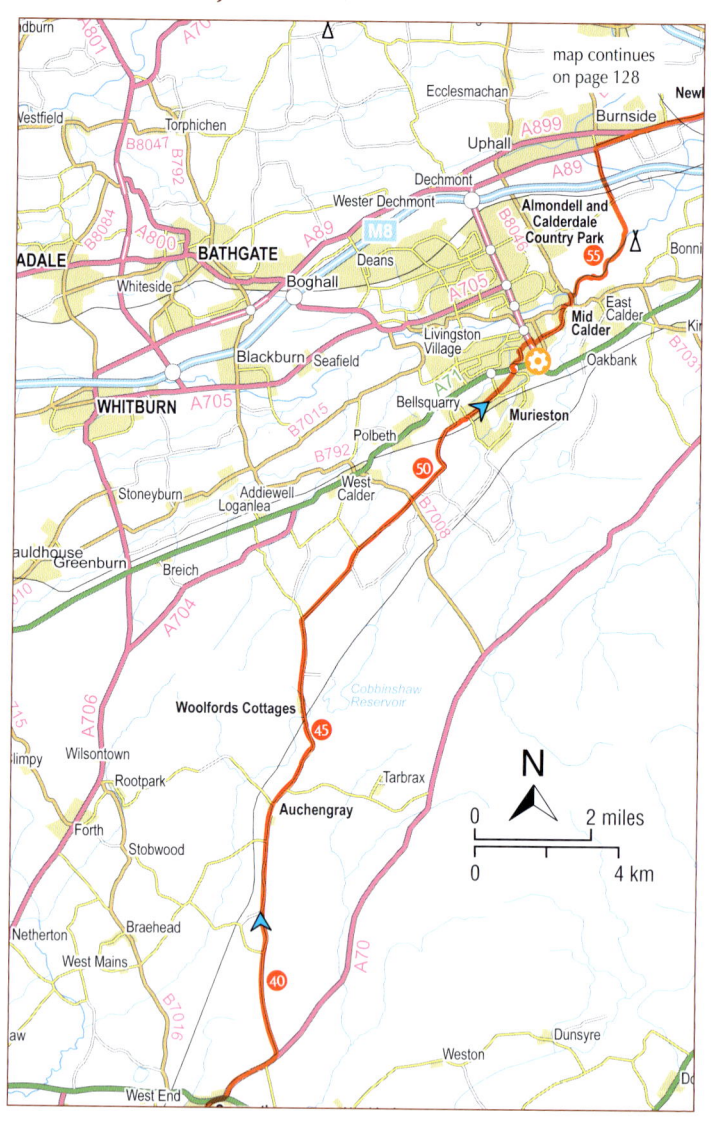

STAGE 9 – MOFFAT TO SOUTH QUEENSFERRY

Mid Calder (54/10 miles). Turn right along the B7015 towards East Calder and 220 metres later, turn left along Pumpherston Road. Turn right immediately after the car park and recycling area and follow NCN 75 up particularly steep ramp into Almondell and Calderwood Country Park.

Ride past the sewage works, cross the footbridge over the River Almond and then stick to paths along this bank leaving NCN 75 which re-crosses the river and heads east into Edinburgh.

> The **Almondell & Calderwood Country Park** was formed from two ancient estates. Almondell House was the historic seat of the Earls of Buchan and Calderwood. It was built in the 1790s by Henry Erskine, the younger son of the 10th Earl of Buchan and was occupied by his descendents before being abandoned and finally 'blown up' by the Territorial Army in June 1969 as a training exercise.
>
> Calderwood is an area of woodland that was owned by the Sandilands Family, the Barons of Torphichen, who still live at nearby Calder House. Following the Wildlife and Countryside Act of 1967, Almondell and Calderwood were combined to form West Lothian's first Country Park in 1969 with the old stable block of Almondell being converted into the visitor centre in 1981.

Continue through the Country Park to the North Car Park and then follow Roman Camp Road under the railway and M8 to meet the A89 by Station Road Neighbourhood Park at on the southern outskirts of **Broxburn** (57/7 miles). Turn right and follow the shared-use path along the eastbound carriageway for 2 miles to **Newbridge** (60/4 miles) past the pretentiously labelled Edinburgh's Luxury Car Village. Follow the shared-use path across the blue footbridge over the M9 and once off the ramp, turn right and follow the course of a disused railway track northwards to **Kirkliston** (61/3 miles) crossing the River Almond just before entering the village. Turn

Cycling Land's End to John o' Groats

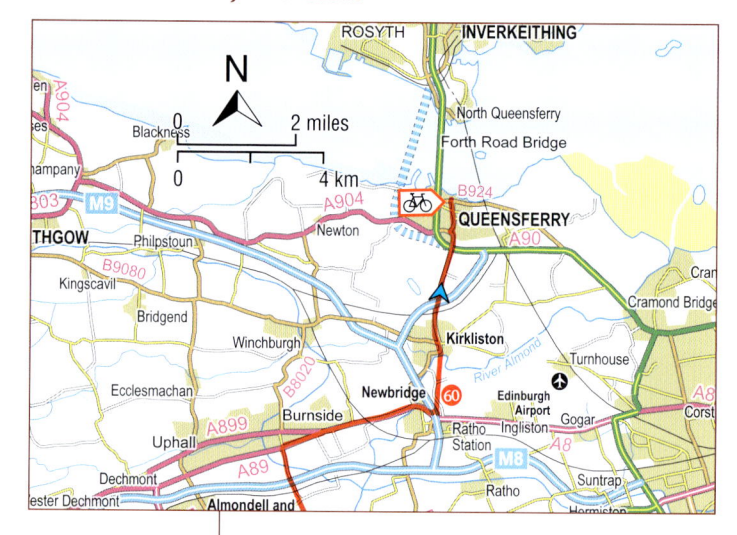

left along Wellflatts Road and left again along Station Terrace. Once you reach the High Street, turn right follow this road, (the B800), northwards under the M90, then over the A90 and A9000 making use of the shared-use path alongside the northbound carriageway for most of the way to the end in **South Queensferry**. Use the shared-use path around the roundabout on the southern edge of the town, take the third exit signed for the Historic Town and ride down Kirkliston Road and then The Loan to the western end of the High Street where the stage ends by The Jubilee Clock Tower.

THE FORTH ROAD BRIDGE

South Queensferry is named after Queen Margaret of Scotland (1045–1093) who is thought to have established a ferry service here to help pilgrims on their way north to St Andrews. At the end of the 19th century pilgrims could have taken a train over the Forth Bridge which, when it was opened in 1880, had the longest single cantilever bridge span in the world. During its construction 73 men lost their lives.

STAGE 9 – MOFFAT TO SOUTH QUEENSFERRY

The ferry only stopped when the Forth Road Bridge was opened in 1964 when it was the largest suspension bridge in the world outside the USA. During it construction only seven lives were lost. By 2000 the bridge was carrying more traffic than it was designed for so once the Queensferry Crossing was completed in 2017, with the loss of just a single life, all traffic was transferred to the new bridge leaving the older road crossing as a 'public transport corridor' carrying only buses, taxis, cyclists and pedestrians.

The Forth Road Bridge, which is now reserved for cyclists and public transport, and the older Forth Bridge, which is a milestone in the history of modern railway engineering and remains the longest cantilever bridge in the world

RIDING NORTH TO SOUTH – JOGLE

As 60 per cent of this stage is 250m/820ft or more above sea level where there is little shelter, it would be particularly hard work if there is a strong wind from the south. So ensure you are well stocked up on energy-giving snacks before you set out as there are few places to re-fuel along the way.

Cycling Land's End to John o' Groats

STAGE 10
South Queensferry to Pitlochry

Start	High Street, Queensferry (NT 129 784)
Finish	Junction of Atholl Road and West Moulin Road, Pitlochry (NN 939 582)
Distance	66 miles (106km)
Ascent	1300m
Time	8–9hrs
OS Maps	OS Landranger 65, 58 and 52
Refreshments	Inverkeithing, Townhill, Kinross, Bridge of Earn, Perth, Dunkeld and Pitlochry
Accommodation	Lots of accommodation of all types in and around Perth and Pitlochry

The decreasing number of roads north of the Firth of Forth means choices are increasing limited and our 'optimal' route sticks to the tried and trusted National Cycle Network across Fife and then through the passes between the Grampian Mountains and the Cairngorm Mountains. Following National Routes means there are lots of shared-use paths that separate you from traffic in urban areas and you will probably meet plenty of fellow End-to-Enders to share experiences with.

Head west along Hopetoun Road, then turn left into Stewart Terrace immediately before the **Forth Road Bridge** and follow a shared-use path that weaves around the concrete supports before turning back on itself onto the bridge. On a calm day with good visibility, the next mile riding 44m above the Firth of Forth offers good views upstream to the dockyards at Rosyth and downstream to the islands of Inchcolm off the Fife shore, which has a former Augustinian abbey that is Scotland's most complete surviving monastic house, and the larger Inchkeith, 10 miles away at the mouth of the estuary. On a blustery day, keeping a heavily laden bike upright

Stage 10 – South Queensferry to Pitlochry

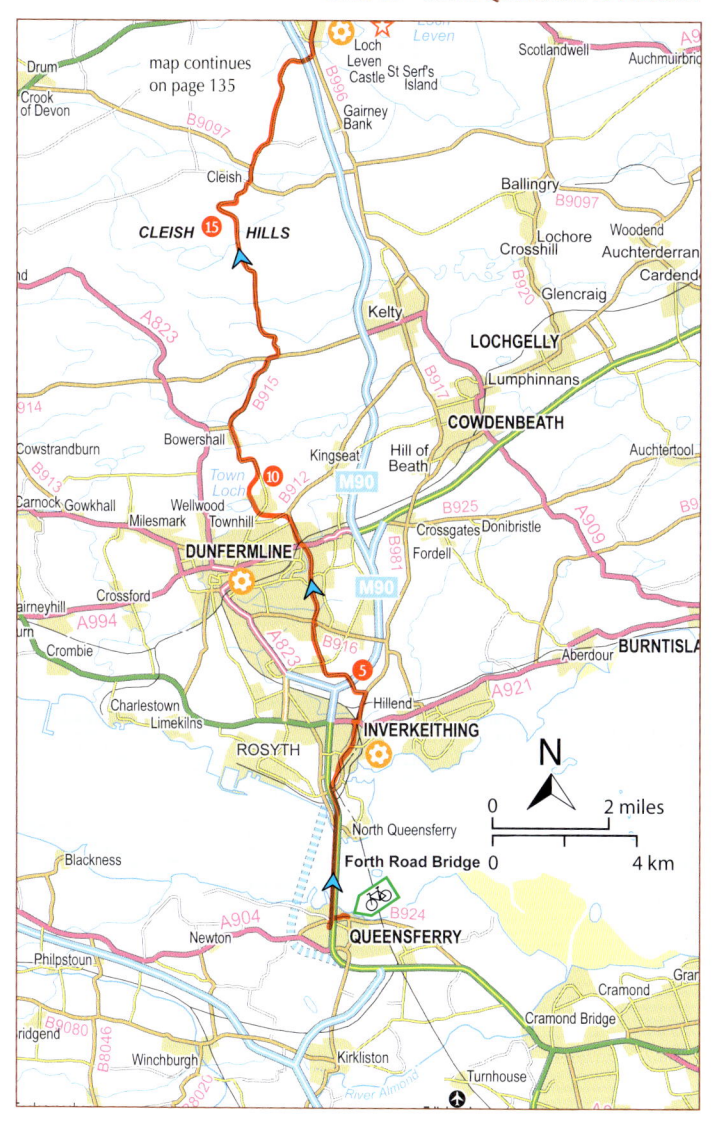

CYCLING LAND'S END TO JOHN O' GROATS

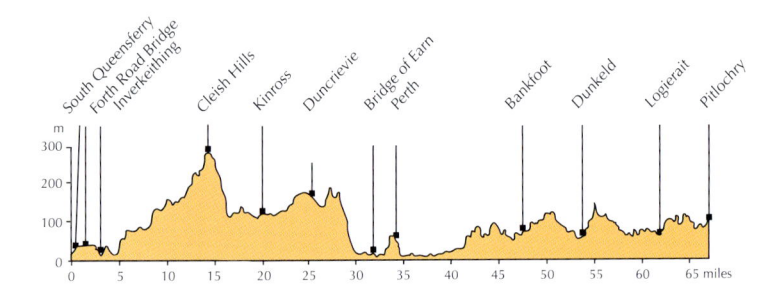

may prove too much of a challenge and it may be safer to walk.

> In 1497 Edinburgh city council passed an act that made **Inchkeith** and some other islands in the Firth of Forth a place of 'compulsory retirement' for people suffering from syphilis. They were instructed to board a ship at Leith and once there, 'to remain till God provide for their health' which in all probability meant a slow and agonising death.

Once across on the Fife shore, follow the shared-use path across to the southbound carriageway and follow NCN 1 around the Ferrytoll Gyratory, which maintains its name despite the Scottish Parliament voting to scrap tolls on the bridge after February 2008, through **Inverkeithing** (3/63 miles) and across the A921 using a shared-use path. After ½ mile turn left following NCN1 towards Kinross, cross the M90 and then join a shared-use path and ride for 4 miles through the modern and easily forgettable eastern suburbs of the ancient town of Dunfermline. Three hundred metres after passing the town's Queen Margaret Hospital, follow NCN 1 left towards Townhill Park along a stretch of disused railway track. Cycle past Town Loch (9/57 miles), where there is a café that opens every day except for Mondays. Turn left when you emerge back on the road at the northern boundary of Townhill

Stage 10 – South Queensferry to Pitlochry

and then 1½ miles further on turn right along the B915 still following NCN1.

Continue for 1½ miles and then turn left towards Cleish and climb up and over the **Cleish Hills**, which at an altitude of 284m (932 ft) give good views of the surrounding countryside. Turn right at the bottom of the twisting descent, turn left towards Crook of Devon at the next junction and then ½ mile further on turn right towards Kinross, all the time following waymarkers for NCN1. After 2 miles, pass under the M90 and then turn left along the B996 and ride into **Kinross** (20/46 miles).

KINROSS

Kinross, which until 1930 was the county town of Kinross-shire, is surrounded by fertile agricultural land and until the construction of the M90 made it an attractive dormitory town for commuters, most of the inhabitants were originally employed in farming. Loch Leven, which can easily be visited by following NCN1 along the Loch Leven Heritage Trail and returning to the town along Sandport Close or Kirkgate, is a large freshwater loch that was a third larger before it was partially drained between 1826 and 1836. The drop in the water level exposed several small islands, as well as greatly increasing the size of the existing ones including the largest St Serf's Inch and Castle Island where Mary, Queen of Scots, was held captive in the imposing Loch Leven Castle from 17 June 1567 until her escape on 2 May 1568. Soon after her arrival she fell ill due to suspected poisoning, but survived and sometime before 24 July she miscarried twins that she had conceived with the Earl of Bothwell who had fled to Scandinavia just before Mary's incarceration. The corpses of the twins were hastily buried in the grounds of Loch Leven Castle and a few days later Mary was forced to abdicate in favour of her

Looking south across Loch Leven to the Lomond Hills of Fife

infant son James who subsequently became James VI of Scotland and James I of England.

On 2 May 1568, Mary escaped from Loch Leven Castle with the aid of George Douglas, brother of Sir William Douglas, the castle's owner. She fled south hoping for protection from her cousin Queen Elizabeth I. However, she was soon recaptured and spent nearly two decades being moved between strongholds in England before being executed on the morning of 8 February 1587 at Fotheringhay Castle in Northamptonshire. Bothwell fared no better. He was held prisoner by the Danish court and spent the last ten years of his life chained to a pillar in Dragsholm Castle.

Bridge of Earn has always been an important crossing place with King Robert I of Scotland (1306–1329) ordering an older bridge to be repaired during his reign.

Follow NCN 775 northwards along the A922 to **Milnathort** (21/45 miles), turn right along the B996 towards Glenrothes and then turn left on the edge of the town following NCN 775 towards Perth. Cross the M90, climb gently up through **Duncrievie** and **Glenfarg** (25/41 miles) at the eastern end of the Ochil Hills, and then enjoy a 2 mile long descent down the lower slopes of Balmanno Hill before turning left along the A912 to **Bridge of Earn** (31/35 miles). ◄

Cross the River Earn and then ½ mile further on join a shared-use path that weaves under the M90 interchange. Turn right on the outskirts of **Perth** (34/22 miles) and follow Friarton Road over the railway and through the industrial units alongside the River Tay. Continue northwards with the river to your right and join a shared-use path through the eastern edge of the city centre where the route joins NCN 77. Follow NCN 77 around the north eastern suburbs and then westwards alongside the River Almond to **Almondbank** (41/25 miles).

PERTH

Although its population is less than 50,000, Perth, which is often called the 'Gateway to the Highlands', has always been an important city. Scottish kings were crowned at Scone Abbey 3 miles to the northeast and extended stays by the royal court soon lead to Perth becoming known as a 'capital'

Stage 10 – South Queensferry to Pitlochry

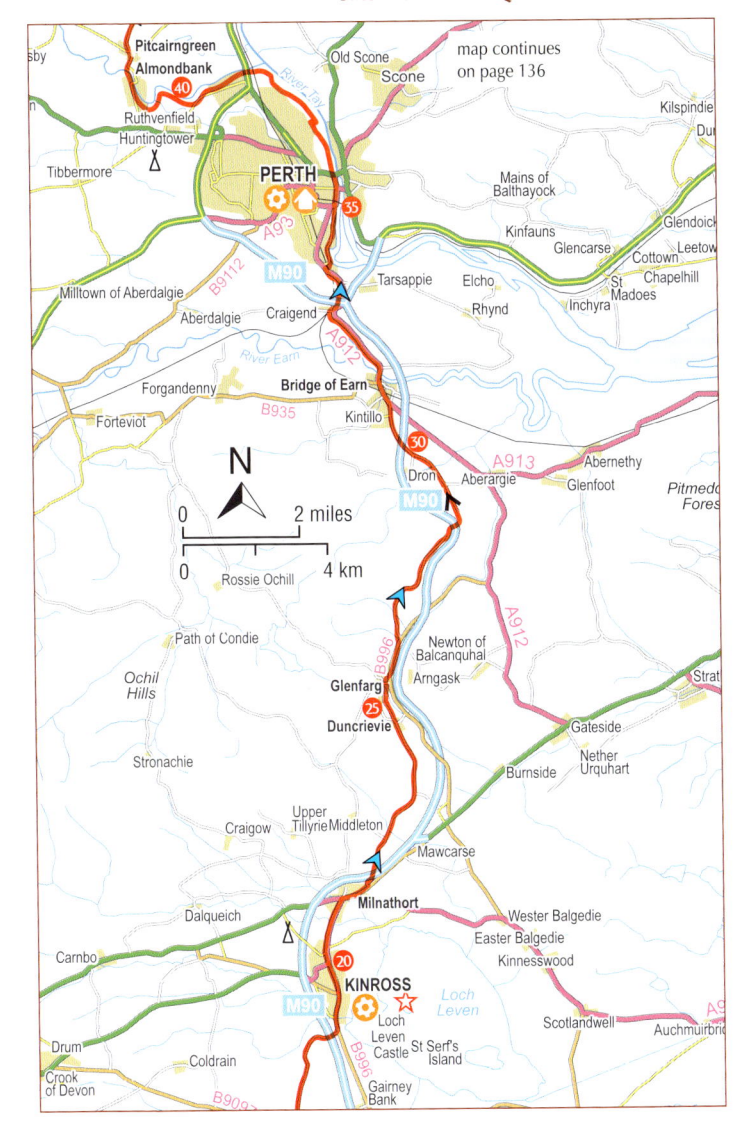

Cycling Land's End to John o' Groats

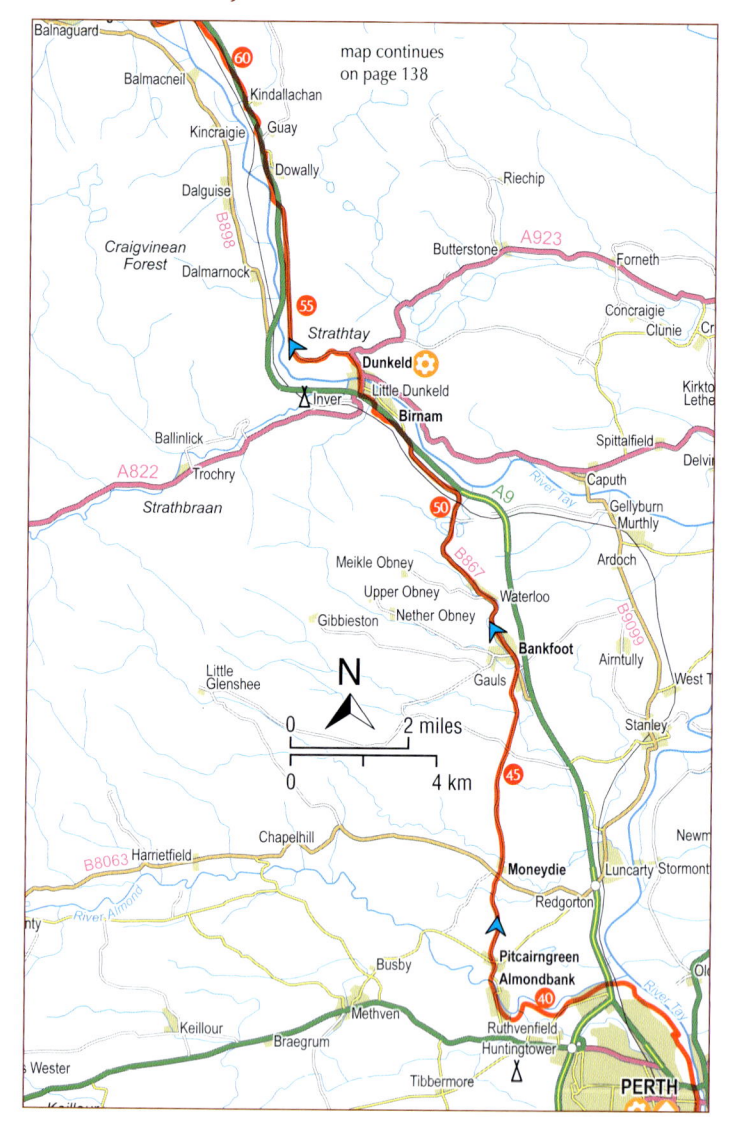

STAGE 10 – SOUTH QUEENSFERRY TO PITLOCHRY

of Scotland. During the Middle Ages, the city became one of the richest burghs in the country, doing trade with France, the Low Countries and Baltic Countries for goods such as Spanish silk and French wine.

However not everyone respected its long history as Scotland's second city. During the local government shake-up in the 1970s, Perth lost its city status. Despite this road signs around the perimeter continued to use the term 'The City of Perth' and gave directions to the 'City Centre' showing the dogged determination of the city's leaders to retain its former status. Persistence paid off and Perth once again became a city after winning a UK-wide competition during the Queen's Diamond Jubilee in 2012.

Continue northwards following NCN 77 through **Pitcairngreen** and **Moneydie** (43/23 miles) to **Bankfoot** (47/19 miles) and then turn left along the B867. Ride through Waterloo (48/18 miles), a hamlet that was either settled by soldiers returning from the eponymous battle or built for the widows of soldiers who did not return, to **Birnam** (52/14 miles). ▶

Cross the River Tay into **Dunkeld** (53/13 miles) and ride through the town centre, leaving the NCN 77 which takes the slightly longer route to the west side of the River Tay, to follow regional route 83 along a pleasant road with light traffic that runs parallel to the busy A9. After 7 miles, join a shared-use path alongside the A827, cross the A9 and the River Tummel to **Logierait** (61/5 miles) and then follow NCN7 northwards along a quiet road above the west bank of the River Tummel. Cross the river by the suspension footbridge and follow NCN7 into **Pitlochry** where this stage ends at the junction of Atholl Road and West Moulin Road.

> James Stobie, a factor to the 4th Duke of Atholl, designed Pitcairngreen as a landscaped manufacturing village for the textile magnate Thomas Graham in 1786.

Pitlochry developed as a tourist resort after Queen Victoria and Prince Albert visited the area in 1842. Its growth was helped by the arrival of the railway in 1863 and it remains a bustling tourist resort used as a base by hillwalkers attracted to nearby summits such as Ben Vrackie (841m/2759ft) and Schiehallion (1,083m/3,553ft) and by those who

Cycling Land's End to John o' Groats

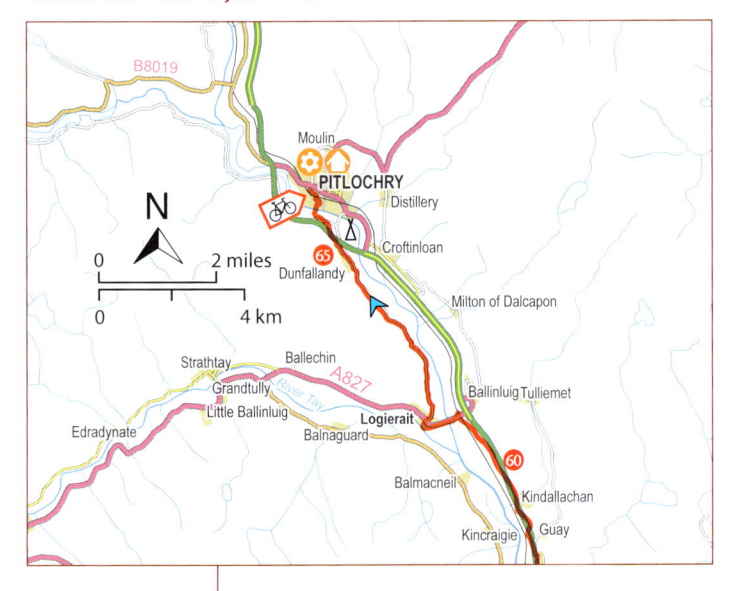

prefer to absorb the Highland scenery through the car or coach window.

RIDING NORTH TO SOUTH – JOGLE

Although riding this stage north to south results in 100m less climbing, be prepared to two short sharp climbs where gradients briefly get into the double figures. The first is the climb up across the eastern end of the Ochil Hills, which comes after 37 miles; and the second is the climb through the Cleish Hills at 51 miles.

STAGE 9A
Moffat to Balloch

Start	War memorial in the centre of Moffat (NT 085 053)
Finish	Bridge of the River Leven in Balloch (NS 391 819)
Distance	83 miles (133 km)
Ascent	1000m
Time	8–9hrs
OS Maps	OS Landranger 78, 72, 71, 64, 63 and 56
Refreshments	Abington, Abington Services, Red Moss Truck Stop, Happendon Services and then frequently all the way to the end of the stage
Accommodation	For hostels you will need to stay over in Glasgow or ride further into Stage 10a, but otherwise there is ample accommodation of all types near the end of the route

Although Stages 9a and 10a provide a more scenic alternative through Central Scotland than Stages 9 and 10, they do add an additional 44 miles (71km) and 900m of ascent. Stage 9a is fairly benign with the last 25 miles being almost entirely flat, but Stage 10a is long and has a considerable amount of climbing making for a hard day. Because of this you may wish to continue Stage 9a into Stage 10a by finishing your day at Drymen or Aberfolyle giving yourself an easier next stage. Alternatively, if you have the time, you may decide to split Stages 9a and 10a over 3 days, perhaps enjoying a night out in the vibrant city of Glasgow.

Check you have enough energy giving snacks to get you through the first 35 miles where there are few cafés. Then ride south away from the centre of Moffat following the A701 to the A74(M). Pass under the motorway then take the third exit at the roundabout heading towards Abington along the B7076. The route is now following NCN 74 and will stick with it all the way to Glasgow making navigation easy. The next 10 miles are uphill but it is barely noticeable as the gradient rarely goes above

Cycling Land's End to John o' Groats

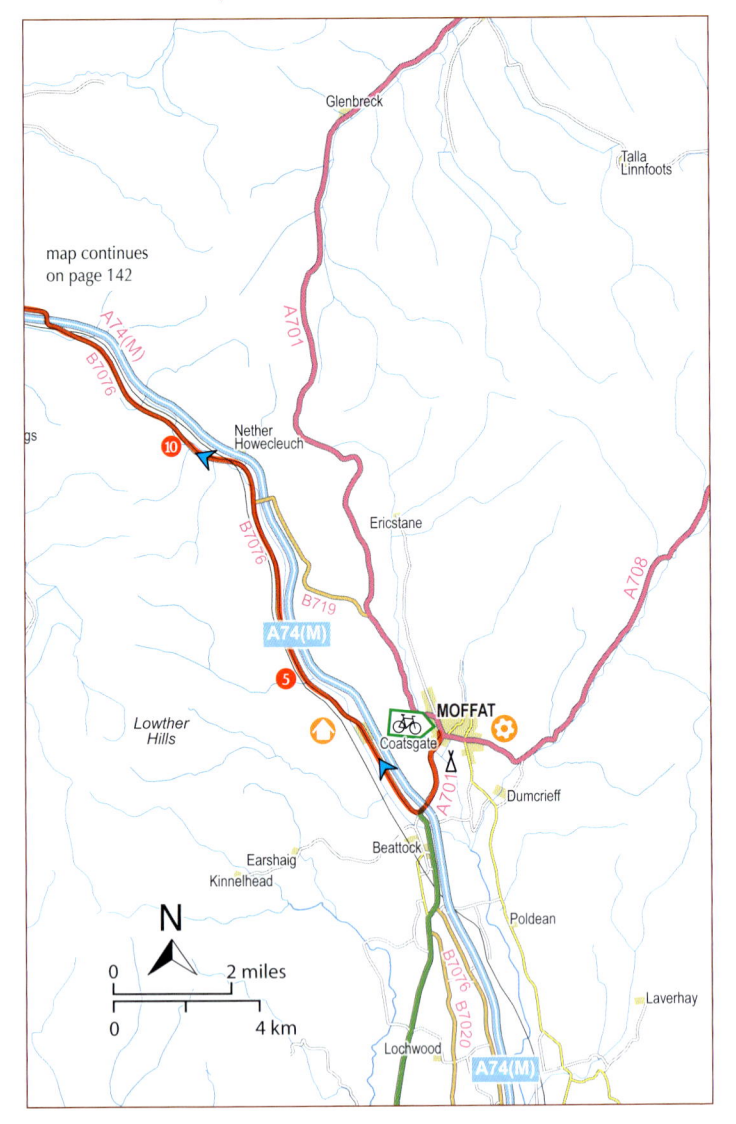

STAGE 9A – MOFFAT TO BALLOCH

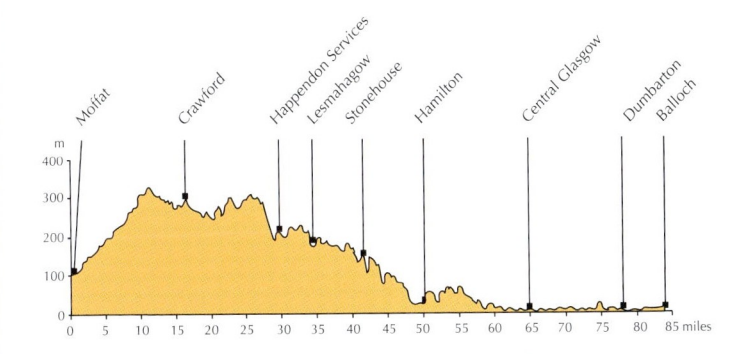

two per cent. Just before **Crawford** the road becomes the A702 but remains quiet as most of the traffic uses the nearby A74(M).

The first opportunity for a cake stop is at **Abington** (20/63 miles) or shortly afterwards at Abington Services at junction 13 of the M74 (21/62 miles), which is easily accessible from the route. Otherwise continue following NCN 74 along the quieter roads alongside the busy A74(M). It is generously provisioned with stretches of shared-use path around busy roundabouts and alongside lengths of roads where the traffic tends to be fast moving, which is just as well because this area of high moorland reaches altitudes in excess of 300m (984ft) and can be shrouded in mists and low-cloud even during the summer months. There are further opportunities for a break at the isolated Red Moss Truck Stop (24/59 miles) and **Happendon Services** (29/54 miles). ▶

> There is gold in the isolated hills south of Red Moss and in 2015 someone panning in a local stream discovered a nugget estimated to be worth £10,000

Otherwise the unchanging landscape and easy terrain means the miles pass by unnoticed. Things change once you get to Lesmahagow though as the rest of stage is almost entirely urban and you will have to stay alert to ensure you don't inadvertently go off-route even though navigation is fairly simple as the route follows NCN 74 all the way into Glasgow's inner suburbs.

Follow NCN 74 across both carriageways of the B7078, along Balgray Road and then turn right along

Cycling Land's End to John o' Groats

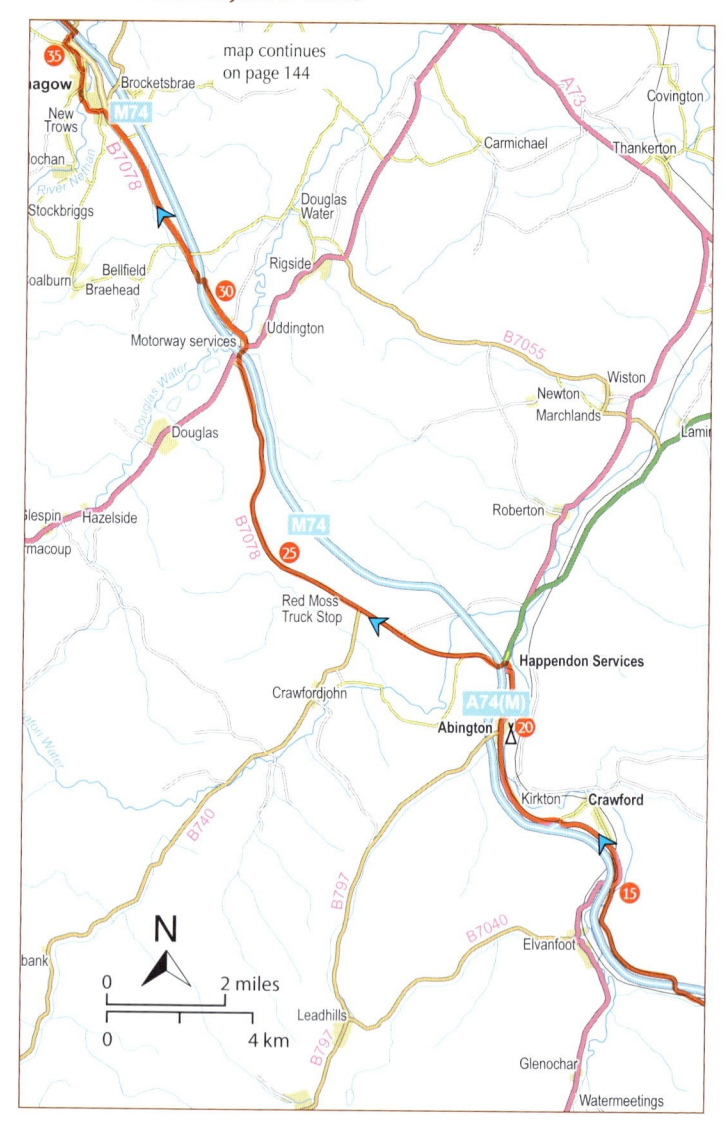

Stage 9a – Moffat to Balloch

Abbeygreen Road and follow it through the centre of **Lesmahagow** (34/49 miles). ▶

Just after passing the football pitch in Glebe Park, turn left up School Road. After ½ mile of steady climbing, turn right along Teiglum Road, join the shared-use path the negotiate the access roundabouts either side of the M74 and re-join the B7078 all the time following marker signs for NCN 74. Continue through Kirkmuirhill and **Blackwood** (37/46 miles), two villages that now merge into each other, cross over the M74 and the ½ mile further on turn left and follow this quiet road out into the country, past Tanhill Farm (39/44 miles) and down to **Stonehouse** (41/42 miles). Ride through the village, under the bypass and down to Avon Water, a 24-mile-long tributary of the River Clyde that the route crosses repeatedly in the next few miles.

Climb away from the river and then fork right following NCN 74 towards Larkhall. Descend into **Larkhall** (44/39 miles), cross the Avon Water and ride uphill along Millheugh Brae and into McNeill Street. Turn left into Raploch Street and follow NCN 74 left along Watson Street, right along Burnbrae Street and out through the sports pitches to join a shared-use path once again alongside the B7078.

After 2 miles, turn left into Chatelherault Country Park and follow signs for NCN 74 across Avon Water and then along its bank, under the M74 and down to the River Clyde. Follow the path beneath the A723, back under the M74 and into Strathclyde Park, bypassing the centre of **Hamilton** (50/33 miles) which is just ½ mile to the south.

> The hunting lodge cum banqueting house in Chatelherault Country Park was designed to be viewed along a 5km tree-lined avenue from the now demolished **Hamilton Palace**, which until 1921, stood just to the south of the **Hamilton Mausoleum** under what is now a retail park. With much of the parkland now built over, it is difficult to envisage the splendour of what was widely acknowledged to have been one of the grandest estates in Britain

---

Once a bustling mining community, Lesmahagow is now a quiet town – so quiet that the International Society for Krishna Consciousness chose it as their base in Scotland (see www.iskconscotland.org).

Cycling Land's End to John o' Groats

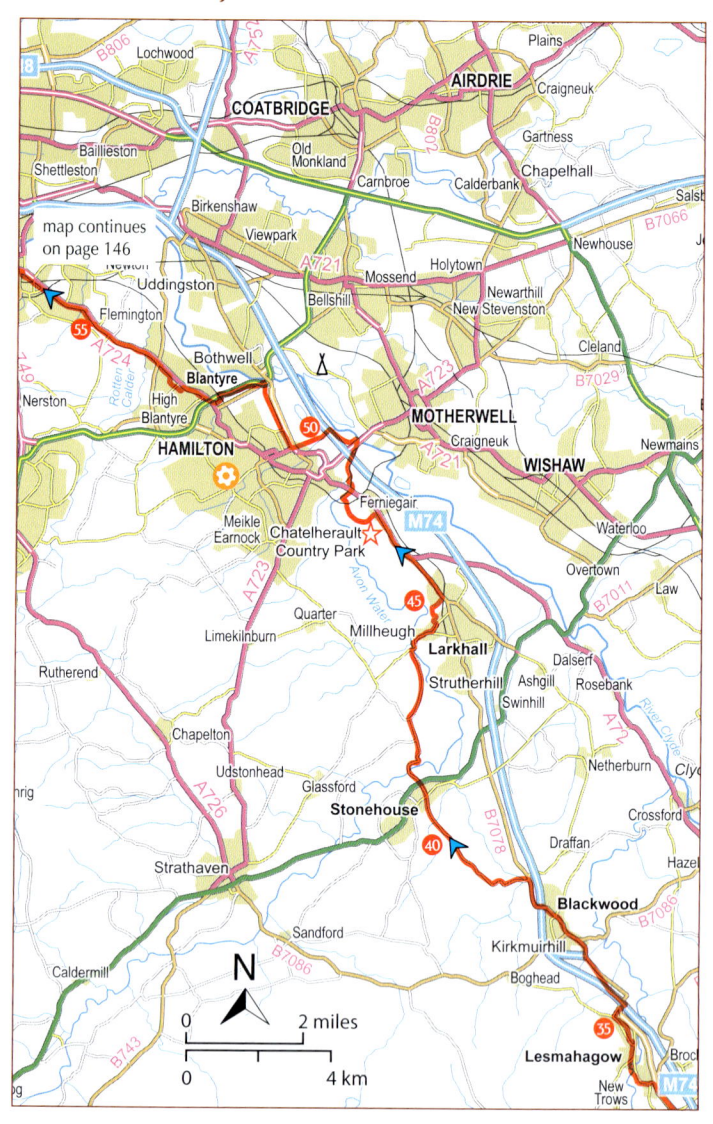

centred on the Palladian Hamilton Palace which was started by the 3rd Duke of Hamilton in 1695 and was still being enhanced by the family nearly two centuries later.

At its height, Hamilton Palace was packed with exquisite furniture, famous paintings and coveted objets d'art on a scale that rivalled the Royal Collection. But what created their huge fortune also nearly destroyed them. Excessive coalmining during the Victorian era caused subsidence and the cost of repairs far outstripped the family's wealth, much of which had already been squandered. Two enormous house sales in 1882 and 1919 saved the Hamilton fortune and saw most of their treasures passed into private and public collections across the globe. But nothing could save Hamilton Palace and it was demolished.

All that remains is the Hamilton Mausoleum which was built by the 10th Duke between 1842 and 1858. It is guarded by two fierce sandstone lions, one awake and the other sleeping representing life and death. To enter the Mausoleum, you

The Hamilton Mausoleum showing the three archways crowned with statues of Life, Death and Immortality

CYCLING LAND'S END TO JOHN O' GROATS

must choose one of three archways crowned with statues of Life, Death and Immortality with only Death giving entry into the tomb. Once complete the remains of 16 members of the Hamilton family were moved into the Mausoleum from the nearby collegiate church. However, they didn't stay for long. Just like Hamilton Palace, the mausoleum suffered from subsidence and its inmates were transferred to a nearby cemetery.

Follow NCN 75 past the Mausoleum and out of the park. Join a shared-use path along The Furlongs then turn right at the roundabout and ride along Bothwell Road.

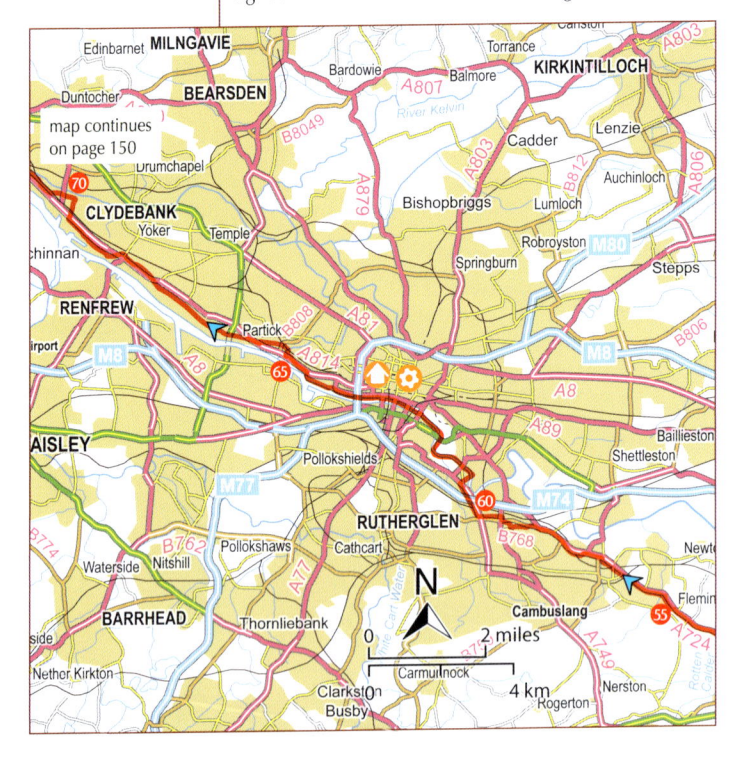

STAGE 9A – MOFFAT TO BALLOCH

After 1 mile, turn left along a shared-use path just before the River Clyde and follow it alongside and then beneath the East Kilbride Expressway to meet the A724. Turn right towards Glasgow and right again at the roundabout and follow NCN 74 through **Blantyre** (53/30 miles) occasionally crossing to the other carriageway or making a detour along a backstreet.

Continue following NCN 74 alongside the A724 which after crossing Rotten Calder (54/29 miles) becomes Hamilton Road. Ride through Halfway (56/27 miles), **Cambuslang** (57/28 miles), where there is another detour along a quieter back street, using shared-use paths whenever they are provided. ▶

At the roundabout after Cambuslang, follow NCN 74 left alongside the B768 through **Rutherglen** (59/24 miles) again making detours along quieter backstreets either side of the main road. After following NCN 74 for almost 60 miles, it peters out ignominiously at the end of King Street in Rutherglen where our route turns right briefly following NCN 756 alongside the busy Glasgow Road under the M74 to Magenta Office Park. Follow NCN 756 right in front of the large office block, cross the Dalmarnock Smart Bridge over the River Clyde. ▶

Turn immediately left along the Clyde Walkway along the north bank of the river joining NCN75. Follow it around the sports fields on Flesher's Haugh, across Glasgow Green and through the centre of **Glasgow** (62/19 miles) along miles of well provisioned shared-use path.

> Having been gifted to the people of Glasgow by King James II in 1450, **Glasgow Green** holds a special place in the hearts of the city's residents. Down the centuries they used the park for grazing cattle, washing and bleaching linen and drying fishing nets. It was substantially remodelled in the early 19th century when the city fathers employed 324 jobless workers to drain and level the ground and divert burns through underground culverts. Since then, besides using it for recreation, the park has

By population Cambuslang is the 27th largest town in Scotland, although never having had a town hall, it also has a claim to being the largest village in Scotland.

Dalmarnock Smart Bridge got its name because it carries telecommunications and IT connections over the river to nearby business parks.

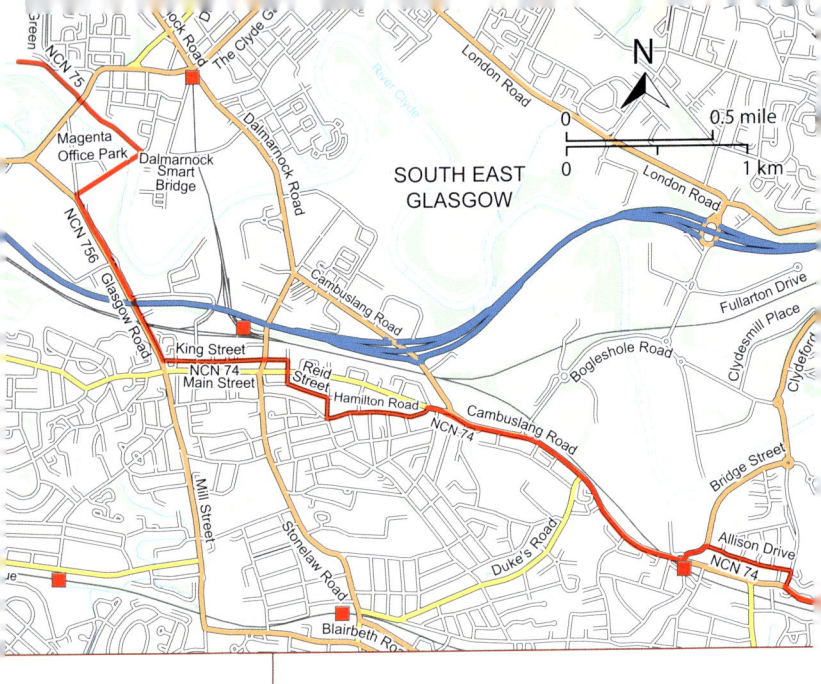

been the place where the populace traditionally congregate to demonstrate against all manner of perceived injustices.

Continue past SSE Hydro, a multi-purpose indoor arena, and the Clyde Auditorium that was soon rebranded as the SEC Armadillo on account of its roof which represent an interlocking series of ship's hulls, in reference to the Clyde's shipbuilding heritage. Here NCN 75 turns south across the Clyde and our route picks up NCN 7 which it follows to the end of this stage and beyond to its end in Inverness.

GLASGOW

From a small rural settlement Glasgow slowly grew to become a medieval bishopric and a royal burgh, with the first bridge over the Clyde being recorded in 1285 and the University of Glasgow being founded in 1451.

STAGE 9A – MOFFAT TO BALLOCH

When the author Daniel Defoe (1660–1731) visited the city in the early 18th century when its population was about 12,000 he recorded that it was 'the cleanest and beautifullest, and best built city in Britain, London excepted'. Little did he know that the city was soon to experience massive growth that would last for two centuries.

Its position on the western seaboard helped the city become the UK's main hub for transatlantic trade with the Americas and by 1821 Glasgow's population had surpassed that of Edinburgh. By the end of the 19th century it was known as the 'Second City of the Empire', producing a fifth of the world's shipping tonnage and a quarter of world's locomotives. Many of the city's architectural masterpieces, such as the City Chambers and Kelvingrove Art Gallery and Museum, were built during this golden era. During the 1920s Glasgow became one of the first cities in Europe to reach a population of one million but today the city's population is about half that at its peak.

The decline set in with the manufacturing recession after World War I and the Great Depression during the 1930s with only a brief respite during and immediately after World War II. By the 1960s industrial growth in countries such as Japan and West Germany weakened the city's pre-eminent position of many of the core industries, such as shipbuilding and Glasgow went into an extended period of economic decline which led to high unemployment, urban decay and population decline, which was exacerbated by the Scottish Office focusing inward investment on new towns such as Livingston and East Kilbride.

Throughout these difficult years Glasgow Corporation set out on an ambitious programme of rebuilding and regeneration By the late 1980s, these initiatives started to pay off with a significant resurgence in Glasgow's economic fortunes as a major centre for business services and finance resulting in a virtuous cycle of increased tourism and inward investment. This economic revival persists with ongoing regeneration of inner-city areas such as the Clyde waterfront leading to more affluent people moving back to live in the centre of Glasgow. Despite its economic renaissance, some parts of the city still endure high levels of unemployment and social deprivation. However, Glasgow is now recognized as an attractive tourist centre and was recently described by the travel guide publisher Lonely Planet as 'disarmingly blending sophistication and earthiness'.

Follow NCN 7 westwards along the north bank of the Clyde towards Clydebank, Dumbarton and Loch Lomond looping around under the Clydeside Expressway and

CYCLING LAND'S END TO JOHN O' GROATS

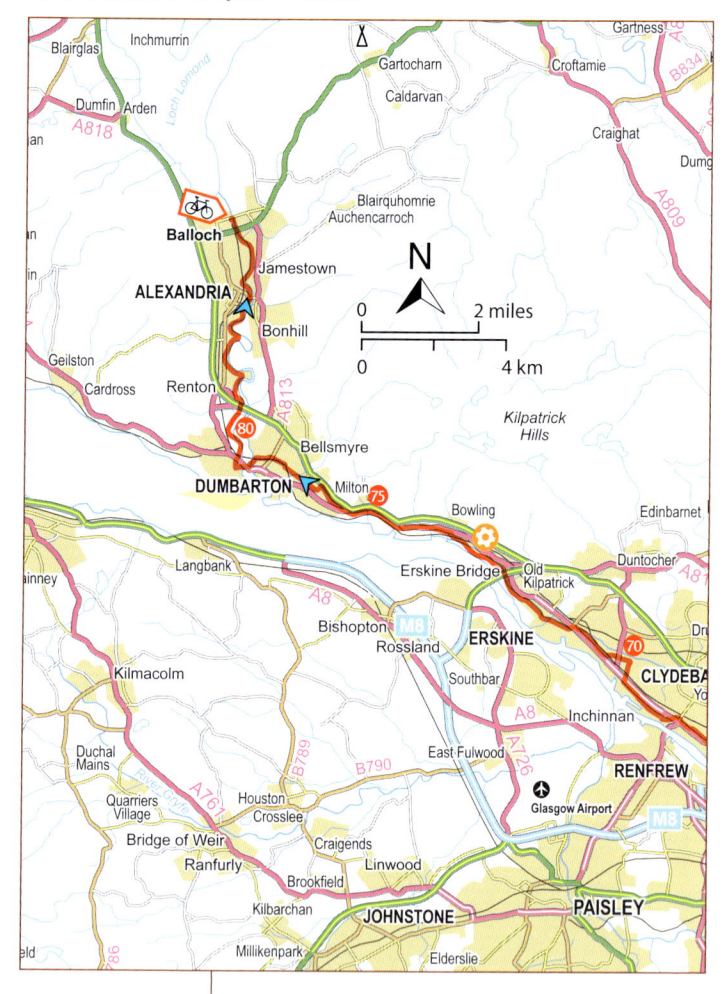

then crossing the footbridge over the River Kelvin only to loop bank under the expressway ½ mile further on. This is urban cycling at its best following a wide shared-use path along long stretches of repurposed railway track.

STAGE 9A – MOFFAT TO BALLOCH

Bankies Bike stands alongside the Forth and Clyde Canal in Clydebank

The local council commissioned the artist John Crosby to produce the larger-than-life Bankies Bike that stands alongside the Forth and Clyde Canal in **Clydebank** (69/14 miles) to celebrate the rejuvenation of the area and promote cycling. However, it has achieved limited success and you will encounter relatively few cyclists.

Follow NCN 7 along the canal towpath for 4 miles passing under the Erskine Bridge to arrive at Bowling Harbour (74/9 miles) where you will find Magic Cycles which has a cycle workshop and café. ▶

Continue following NCN 7 westwards along another stretch of disused railway track bed and through the centre of **Dumbarton** (77/6 miles) and along Bridge Street over the River Leven, a short but remarkably fast-flowing river that is very popular with anglers trying to catch migratory salmon and sea trout going up to Loch Lomond. ▶

Turn right at the end of the bridge and follow NCN 7 along the bank of the River Leven, past Renton (80/3 miles) and around **Alexandria** (81/2 miles) to **Balloch** where the stage ends on the bridge over the outflow of Loch Lomond.

Its easily accessible location at the southern end of Loch Lomond and just off the main road from Glasgow to the West Highlands (A82) meant

Bowling Harbour, which opened in 1790, is the birthplace of Clyde puffers – small coal-fired, single-masted, cargo ships that transported essential supplies around the west coast of Scotland.

David Byrne, the founding member of the new wave band Talking Heads and pro-cycling activist, was born in Dumbarton in 1952. But you're not on the road to nowhere; you're heading for John o' Groats.

CYCLING LAND'S END TO JOHN O' GROATS

Balloch was destined to become a tourist hotspot for day-trippers from Glasgow and Dumbarton particularly after the railway arrived in 1850. Despite its relatively small size, the village has a number of hotels, inns, pubs and B&Bs. There are also cruises along Loch Lomond, which is both the largest expanse of fresh water in the British Isles and contains Inchmurrin, the largest freshwater island in the British Isles, which is 2½ miles to the north of Balloch.

Set above the eastern shore of the loch is Balloch Castle, which was built as a residence on the site of an earlier castle in 1808–1809 by John Buchanan of Ardoch (1761–1839), who was a partner in the Ship Bank, Glasgow's oldest banking house. In 1915 the Corporation of the City of Glasgow purchased the estate as a civic amenity.

RIDING NORTH TO SOUTH – JOGLE

With most of the first 25 miles through Greater Glasgow being along shared-use paths, you may wish to start out early to avoid local commuters cycling and walking into work.

Built for distributing coal, Bowling Harbour is now used by leisure craft sailing and cruising on the Clyde

STAGE 10A
Balloch to Pitlochry

Start	Bridge over the River Leven in Balloch (NS 391 819)
Finish	Junction of Atholl Road and West Moulin Road, Pitlochry (NN 939 582)
Distance	92 miles (147 km)
Ascent	2000m
Time	11–12hrs
OS Maps	OS Landranger 56, 57, 51 and 52
Refreshments	Drymen, Aberfoyle, Callander, Kingshouse, Killin, Kenmore and just off route in Aberfeldy
Accommodation	Lots of accommodation of all types in and around Pitlochry

When it comes to navigation this stage is remarkably easy as it follows NCN 7 throughout. However, it is probably the most arduous as it is both the longest and has the most climbing. With nearly 21 miles of unpaved path this stage has the most off-road cycling too. But don't let that deter you from riding it as it is certainly more scenic, and I would argue more satisfying, than the standard route.

First you will probably ride and climb faster than the 12mph horizontal and 500 vertical metres per hour used to estimate riding times. Second, although Sustrans have erected a sign at the start of the longest off-road stretch in the Queen Elizabeth Forest Park warning cyclists on road bikes that the next 9 miles may not be suitable for them, most of the path is firetrack made from well-compacted fine shale. I rode it in the wet on a laden lightweight audax/touring bike fitted with 25c tyres without any problems. So sensible folk riding on wider tyres should just ignore the Sustrans sign and press on. But if you really don't fancy 9 miles of off-road, there is an alternative detailed in the route description.

Cross the River Leven and then turn left following signs for NCN 7 and ride through Balloch Park into the ornamental woodland of **Balloch Country Park**. Turn right at

Cycling Land's End to John o' Groats

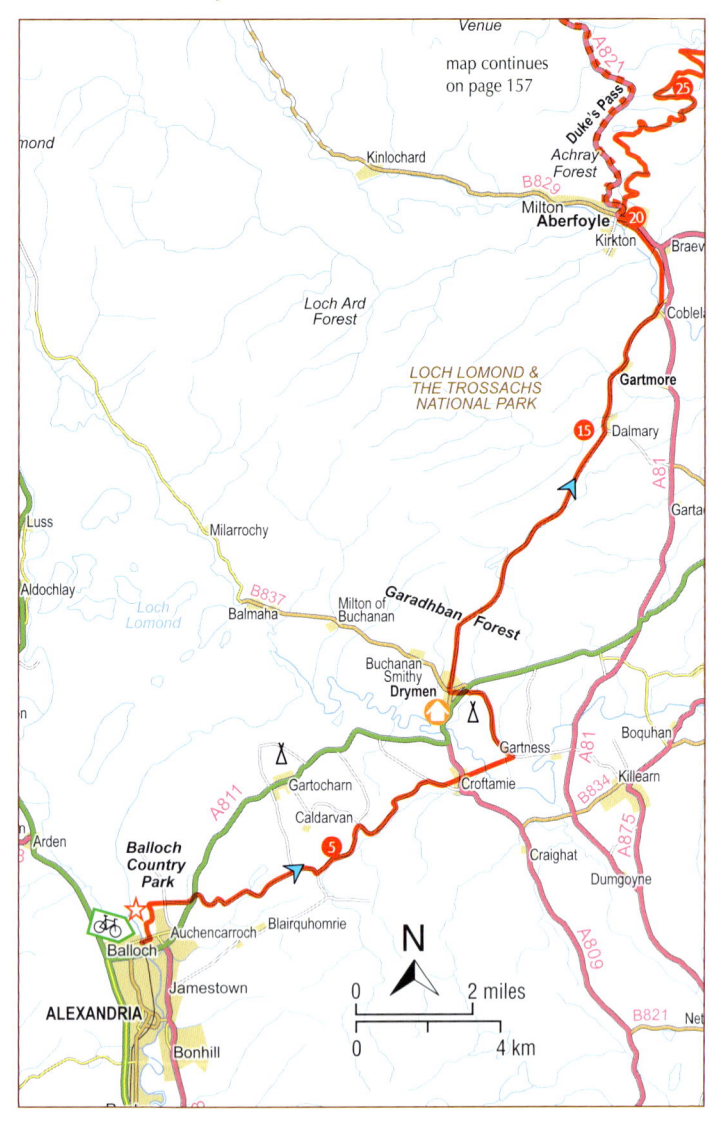

STAGE 10A – BALLOCH TO PITLOCHRY

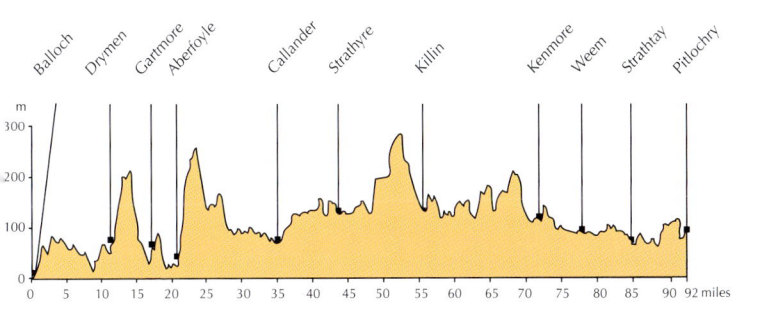

the crossroads before Balloch Castle and follow the drive past the old lodge and out onto the road. After ½ mile turn left along the A811 and after just 200 metres, turn right and climb up around the bend into the open countryside enjoying pleasant cycling on quiet roads. After 5 miles follow signs for NCN 7 left along a 2-mile stretch of railway track that was formerly the Forth and Clyde Junction Railway. ▶

Turn left at its end, briefly joining the West Highland Way, and ride up through **Drymen** (10/84 miles) and a section of the **Garadhban Forest** and then the Loch Ard Forest, following waymarkers for NCN 7. Once across the open moor, enjoy the long descent then climb up through the pleasant village of **Gartmore** (17/76 miles) and join a 2-mile stretch of the former Strathendrick and Aberfoyle Railway to **Aberfoyle** (20/74 miles). With an abundance of cafés it is a good place for a break, especially as there is nothing for the next 14 miles until Callander.

Aberfoyle describes itself as 'The Gateway to the Trossachs', an area of wooded glens, braes, and lochs which is a microcosm of a typical highland landscape. The area first be came popular in the 1820s after Sir Walter Scott published a poem called '*The Lady of the Lake*' that lists many local places and it has remained popular ever since,

The Forth and Clyde Junction Railway was built in the 1850's to carry coal from the Fife coalfields to Bowling on the Clyde; however that never happened leaving the line a commercial failure.

much of its attraction being due to its proximity to both Edinburgh and Glasgow.

The outlaw and folk-hero Robert Roy MacGregor (1671–1734), who is more often remembered as Rob Roy, was born at Glengyle at the head of Loch Katrine and died in Balquhidder on Loch Voil. He is said to have once escaped from the law by climbing and hiding in a tree that still stands in the Aberfoyle.

Ride through Aberfoyle and follow the A821 uphill for 500 metres through the more attractive part of the village and then turn right at a bike-shaped barrier for the 9-mile off-road section through Queen Elizabeth Forest Park.

Alternative to Queen Elizabeth Forest Park

If you want to follow the on-road alternative rather than the off-road section through the Queen Elizabeth Forest Park, continue along the A821 heading north through the **Duke's Pass**. After 5 miles follow the sharp bend right towards Callander now heading east past Loch Achray and **Loch Venachar**. After another 6½ miles, turn right towards Invertrossachs and re-join the route after crossing **Gartchonzie Bridge** by turning left towards Callander. It is the same distance and has the same amount of ascent, but you will encounter a fair amount of traffic touring through The Trossachs.

If you stick to NCN7 through Queen Elizabeth Forest Park follow the twisting trail uphill for 2½ miles and then enjoy a long descent around the western shore of Loch Drunkie and down the Achray Forest Drive to join a trail through the woods along the southern shore of **Loch Venachar**. Continue through Invertrossachs (29/64 miles), where the route follows a single-track road through Gartchonzie (32/62 miles) to the eastern end of the loch and then turn left along the A81 at the mini-roundabout and ride into **Callander** (34/60 miles).

Stage 10a – Ballach to Pitlochry

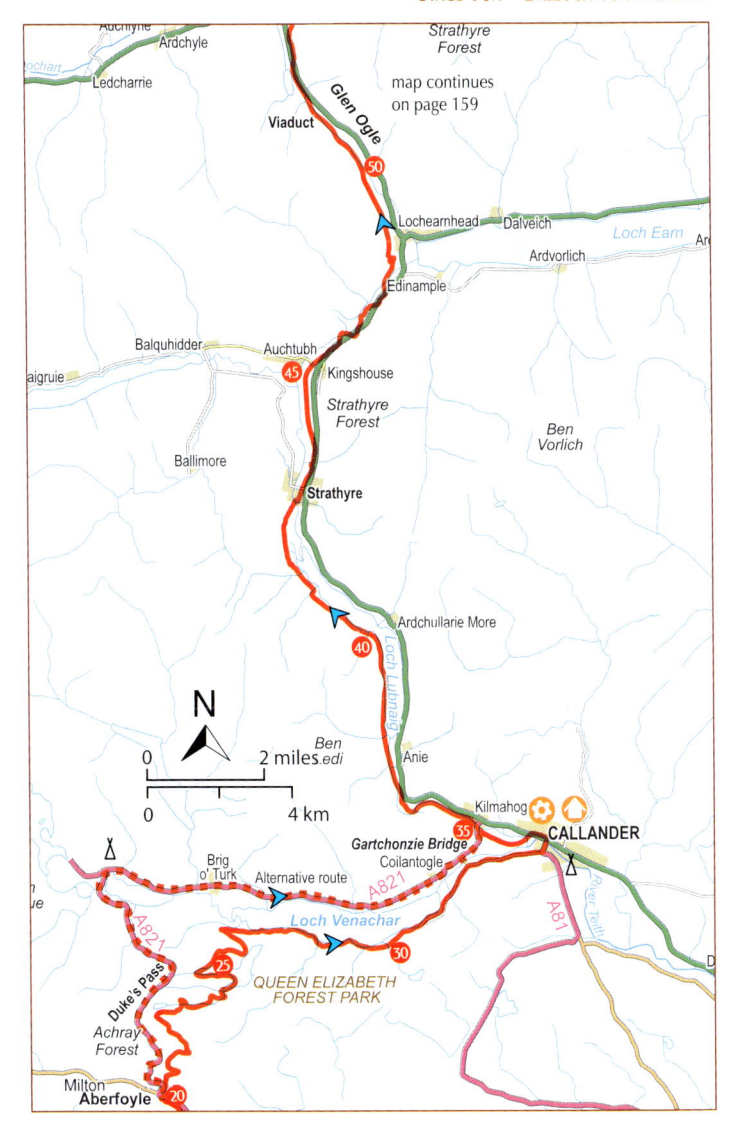

The octagonal watch house in Bridgend Graveyard in Callander was built as a lookout to guard against 'body snatchers' who until the early 19th century made money by illegally supplying anatomists with fresh corpses

Situated immediately south of the Highland Boundary Fault that is traditionally seen as the boundary between the highlands and the lowlands, **Callander** is a bustling little town that is a popular base for tourists exploring the Loch Lomond & The Trossachs National Park or stopping off on their way up into the Highlands.

Follow NCN 7 alongside L on the north bank of the River Teith, cross an open area called The Meadows and along the repurposed track bed of the former Callander and Oban Railway, stretches of which the route follows for the next 20 miles until just before Killin. Cross the A821 and continue following NCN 7 along the track bed of the old railway through the woodland along the western shore of Loch Lubnaig, through the quiet village of **Strathyre** (43/51 miles) and parallel to the A84 to Kingshouse, where you can take a break in the popular café at Mhor 84 (see www.mhor84.net).

Follow NCN 7 along a tarmac track through cool woodlands crossing an arched bridge (47/47 miles) that replaced part of the old viaduct which once carried the old railway line from Balquhidder to Crieff over Kendrum Burn. The bridge was built to commemorate Nigel Hester,

STAGE 10A – BALLOCH TO PITLOCHRY

a young organist, music teacher and cyclist who was killed while riding along the A9 in 1997. Then climb the short zigzags that give good views eastwards down Loch Earn that were once said to be the very finest in the UK that could be seen from a railway carriage, re-join the track bed of the Callander and Oban Railway and continue up Glen Ogle. ▶

Cross the **Glen Ogle viaduct** and then at the top of what has been a long, slow climb, cross the A84 opposite Lochan Lairig Cheile and descend through the conifer woods following an excellent path to **Killin** (55/39

> After visiting Glen Ogle in September 1842, Queen Victoria (1819–1901) wrote in her diary that it reminded her of prints she had seen of the Khyber Pass.

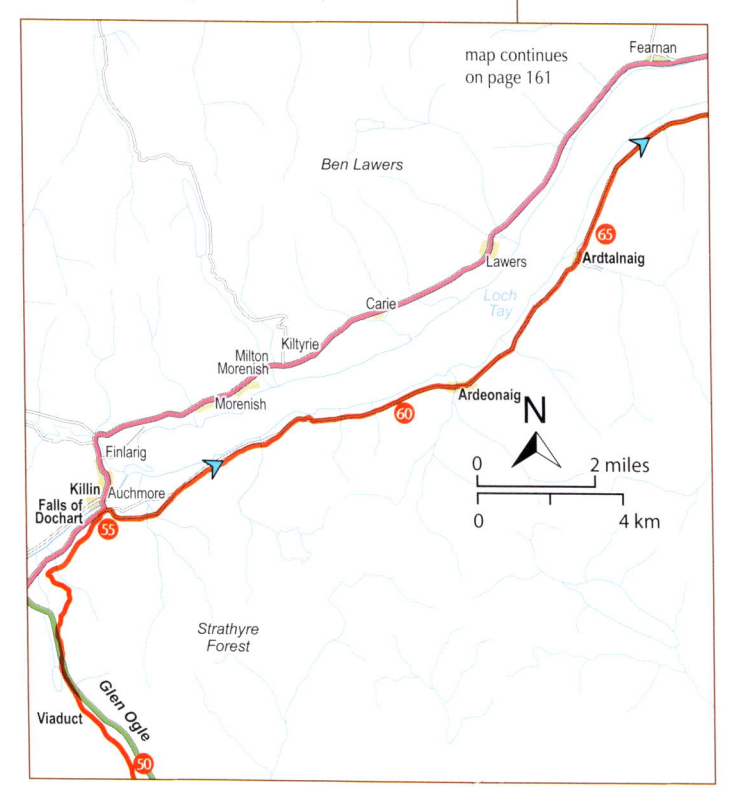

CYCLING LAND'S END TO JOHN O' GROATS

The Category B listed 150-yard (140 m) long Glen Ogle viaduct, which runs parallel to the valley across an area of low ground, was completed in 1880 and used until the line closed in 1965.

miles) including another stretch of track bed of the Killin Railway which was built with funds raised by local trades people to connect the tourist village to the Callander and Oban Railway at Glenoglehead. ◄

The **Falls of Dochart** in Killin are really cascades where the River Dochart drops over serried tiers of flat rocks, but I guess 'falls' does more to attract tourists than 'cascades' ever would. This straggling village, which is overshadowed by the mighty mass of Ben Lawers, (1214m/ 3984 ft), sprung up at the junction of routes from all points of the compass. Such easy access makes it a popular destination for tourists today, stopping off to quickly photograph the Falls from the five-arched Bridge of Dochart before continuing to the next stop on their itinerary. As our route does not cross the bridge it would be easy to do the same, but if you do make a short

The Falls of Dochart where the River Dochart drops over serried tiers of flat rocks

Stage 10a – Balloch to Pitlochry

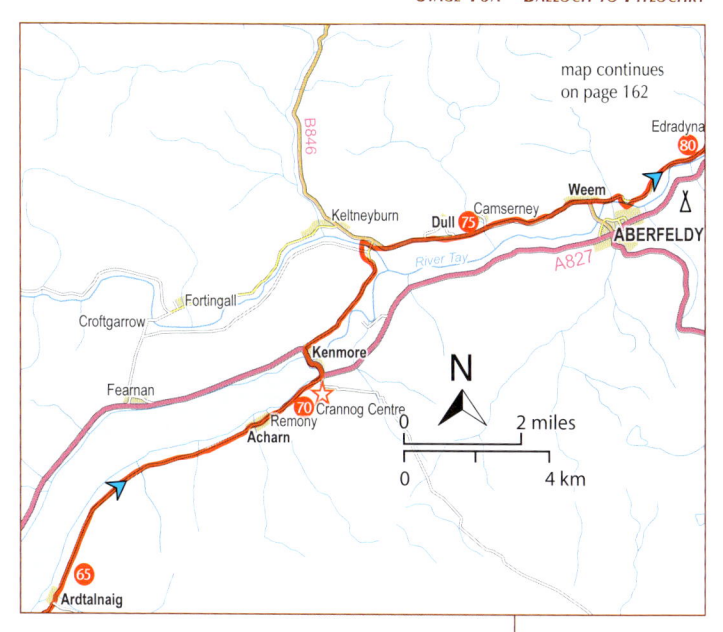

detour across into the more-populated eastern end of the village, you will find many well-provisioned shops, several hotels and a number of cafés.

Take the minor road towards Ardeonaig alongside The Fall of Dochart Inn and follow NCN 7 through woodland and then along the southern shore of the 14½ mile (23.42 km) long Loch Tay. It is pleasant riding on a single track road passing through **Ardeonaig** (61/33 miles), where there is a hotel, and **Ardtalnaig** (65/29 miles) and **Archarn** (70/24 miles), which are quiet hamlets, with good views of Ben Lawers and its neighbouring summits above the opposite shore. ▶

Turn left towards Killin at end of the loch, follow the A827 through the centre of **Kenmore** (71/23 miles) and over the bridge across the River Tay and then turn right towards Tummel Bridge all the time following

The reconstructed loch dwelling at The Scottish Crannog Centre at the eastern end of Loch Tay is based on findings from underwater excavation of a 2,500 year-old crannog near Fearnan on the opposite shore.

161

CYCLING LAND'S END TO JOHN O' GROATS

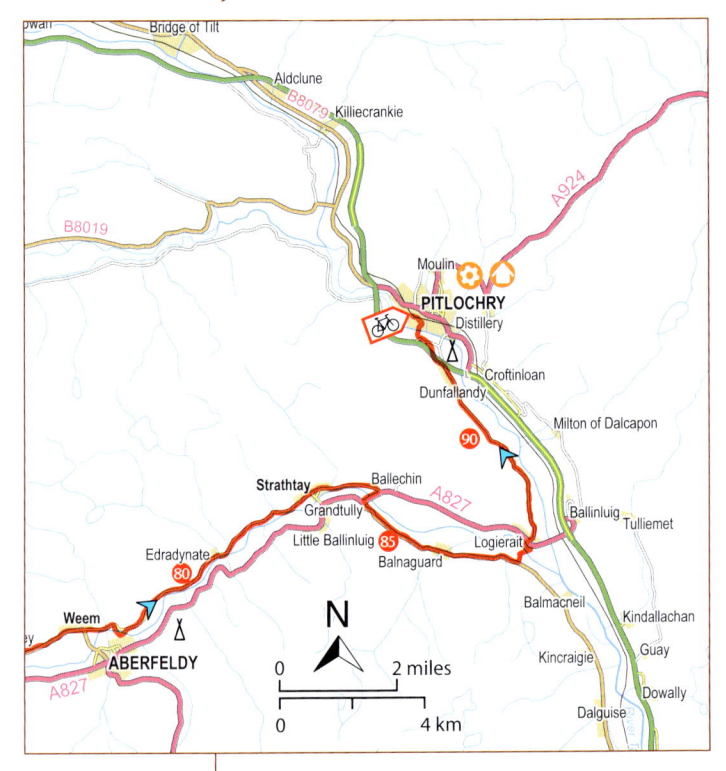

General George Wade (1673–1748), who after the Jacobite uprising of 1715, built barracks, roads and bridges to secure order in Scotland, considered 'Wade's Bridge' in Aberfeldy his finest achievement.

waymarkers for NCN 7. Immediately after crossing the iron bridge across the River Lyon, turn right along the B846 in the direction of Aberfeldy and ride through **Dull** (75/19 miles), a non-descript place that is appropriately twinned with both the American town of Boring and Australia's Bland Shire. Continue past the 16th century Castle Menzies, where Bonnie Prince Charlie, (1720–1788), the Stuart pretender to the throne stayed for two nights while on his way to a devastating defeat at the battle of Culloden in April 1746. Continue following the B846 if you wish to visit Aberfeldy which is on the opposite bank of the River Tay and return the same way. ◄

Otherwise turn left owards Strathtay by a toll house on a sharp bend in **Weem** and follow a quiet road along the north bank of the River Tay. After passing through **Strathtay** (83/11 miles), which has an abundance of Victorian villas with fine mature gardens that were once the retreats of wealthy Dundee merchants, follow signs for NCN 7 along a section of shared-use path besides the A827 and cross the River Tay to follow a quieter road along the opposite bank.

After 3 miles, follow signs for NCN left back across the River Tay to Logierait (88/6 miles) and then northwards along the west bank of the River Tummel to **Pitlochry** where this stage ends at the junction of Atholl Road and West Moulin Road.

16th century Castle Menzies, near Aberfeldy, where Bonnie Prince Charlie stayed for two nights before his devastating defeat at Culloden in 1746

RIDING NORTH TO SOUTH – JOGLE

Enjoy the final 3 miles of fire-tracks down through the Queen Elizabeth Forest to Aberfolyle which drop at a steady gradient of just less than 5 per cent but take care as the surface can be loose on the corners.

CYCLING LAND'S END TO JOHN O' GROATS

STAGE 11
Pitlochry to Aviemore

Start	Junction of Atholl Road and West Moulin Road, Pitlochry (NN 939 582)
Finish	Where NCN 7 crosses Dalfaber Drive in Aviemore (NH 902 136)
Distance	60 miles (96 km)
Ascent	900m
Time	6–7hrs
OS Maps	OS Landranger 52, 43, 42 and 35
Refreshments	Blair Atholl, House of Bruar, Dalwhinnie, Ralia Café, Newtonmore and Kingussie
Accommodation	Lots of accommodation of all types in and around Aviemore

At the Pass of Drumochter, 25 miles into this stage, the route enters the area covered by The Highland Council and stays within its boundaries all the way to John o' Groats. It was created in 1984 by amalgamating all the previous mainland county councils to the north and west, and covers nearly a third of Scotland's land area but has less than 5 per cent of its population. Cycle shops are few and far between and the next café may be two hours up the road, so plan accordingly. Check you have sufficient emergency spares and energy-giving snacks to get you between the main centres of population. You are into the last quarter of your End-to-End and it would be a disaster to fail due to a simple mechanical or 'bonking' (what cyclists and other endurance sportspeople call hypoglycaemia) in the middle of nowhere.

This far into your LEJOG you are probably very tired and the final four stages have been kept deliberately short so you can take them at a more relaxed pace. However if you are still feeling good you could save a day and the expense of a night's accommodation by riding Pitlochry to Inverness (100 miles) and Inverness to Tongue (91 miles), effectively switching to the final 3 days of the 12 day schedule set out on the Main Route Schedule, found at the front of this guide.

STAGE 11 – PITLOCHRY TO AVIEMORE

Head northwards along Atholl Road following the A924 and pass under the A9. After passing the turning for the trunk road, the road first becomes the B8019 and then after 1½ miles the B8079. It is one of General Wade's Military Roads and jostles for space through the Pass of Killiecrankie together with the River Garry, the A9 and the Highland Main Line railway. ▶

Continue through **Killiecrankie** (4/56 miles) and **Blair Atholl** (7/53 miles) to the **House of Bruar** (10/50 miles) and then turn right along the B847 following NCN 7 towards Calvine. Ensure you have enough energy-giving snacks to get you through the next section which consists of 20 miles of steady climbing up through the Pass of Drumochter, which is the highest point on the whole route at an altitude of 456m (1495ft), followed by 6 miles of descending into Dalwhinnie before you encounter another shop or café.

General Wade's Military Roads were mostly built by his successor William Caulfield (1698 - 1767) who famously said, 'Had you seen these roads before they were made, you would lift up your hands and bless General Wade'.

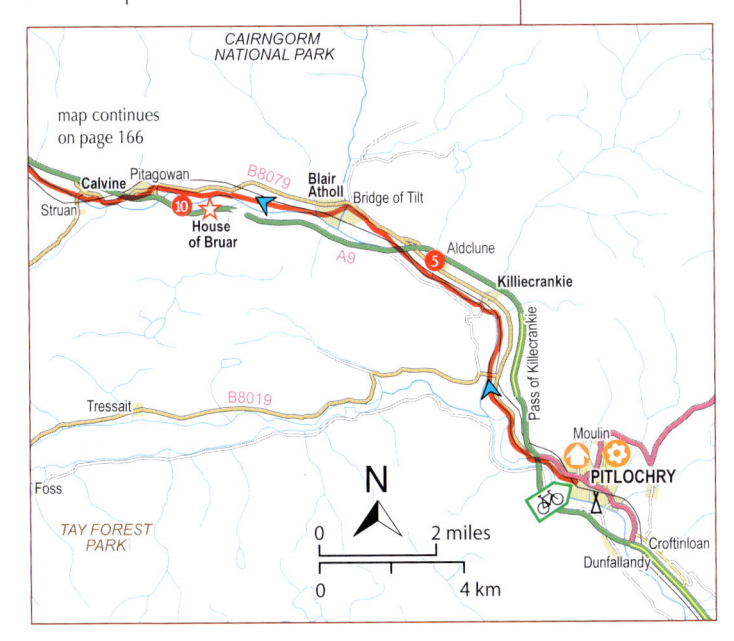

Cycling Land's End to John o' Groats

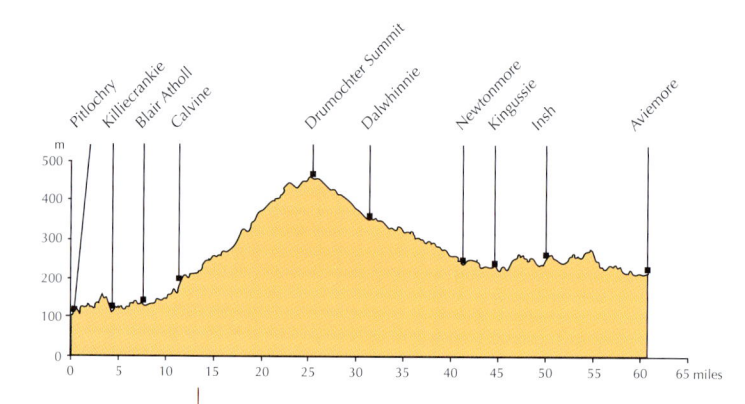

After passing through **Calvine** (11/49 miles) follow signs for NCN 7, bear left onto a traffic-free path and knuckle down for a long haul. Although it is never steep, it is relentless and unless you have nice light the landscape is not exactly memorable. There is nothing else to

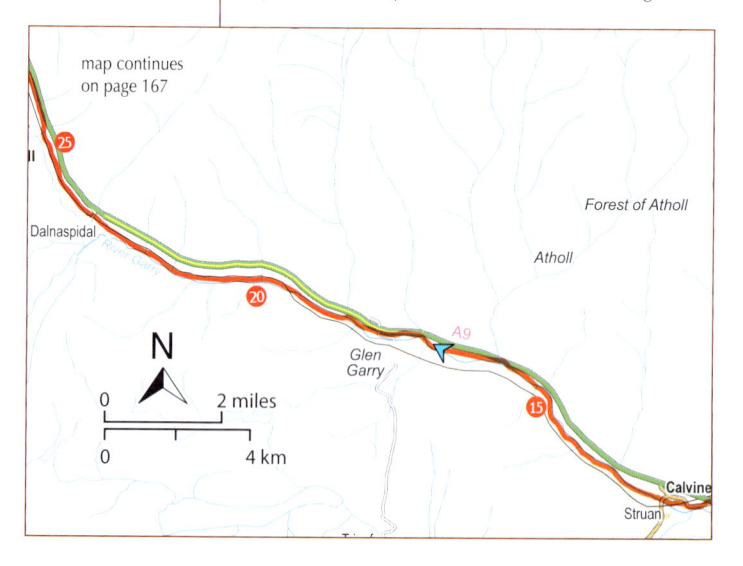

Stage 11 – Pitlochry to Aviemore

do, but pedal. If you're thinking that it's a pig of a climb then you're in good company. The conical hill just to the west of the route after Dalnaspisdal (23/37 miles) is known as **The Sow of Atholl**, which does not relate to its Gaelic name - Meall an Dobharchain – which translates as Watercress Hill and is thought to refer to the marshy ground on the lower SE flanks of the hill where watercress would have grown in the past. Rather, it is thought to be a more recent renaming to give a partner to the neighbouring summit of The Boar of Badenoch (An Torc) which lies 2.5 km to the north.

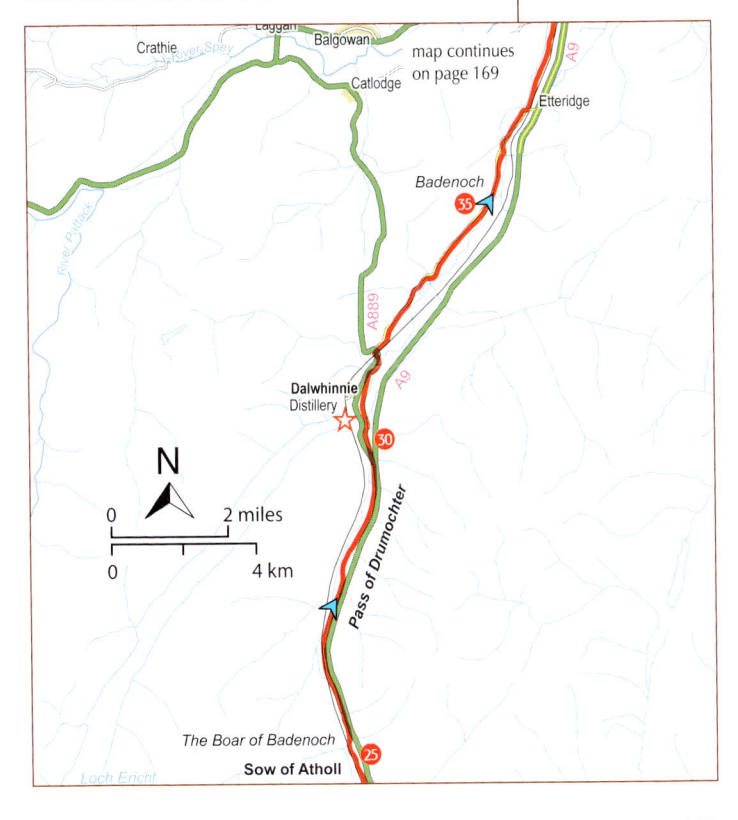

Following the old road near the summit of the Pass of Drumochter at the highest point on the route

Sitting at an altitude of 351m (1,152 ft) and with little shelter, Dalwhinnie has what is classified as a subpolar oceanic climate and is frequently the coldest place in the UK with winter temperatures below -20°C.

Continue following the free-rolling, traffic-fee path through the **Pass of Drumochter**, enjoy a long downhill stretch sometimes alongside the busy A9 and sometimes a few hundred yards to its west, and then swing left and follow the A889 into **Dalwhinnie** (30/30 miles). ◀

Follow NCN 7 through the village and then turn right towards Crubenmore first following a single-track road and then after Crubenmore Lodge a shared-use path alongside the A9. Pass the **Ralia Café** (39/21 miles) – or not depending on how hungry you are – and then turn left and follow NCN 7 along the B9150 over the River Spey into **Newtonmore** (40/20 miles).

Newtownmore Camanachd Club are stars of the sport of shinty, a testosterone-loaded version of hockey that derives from the Irish game of hurling. Since the club was formerly founded in 1890 it has won the Camanachd Cup by topping the national league no fewer than 34 times. This record has yet to be bettered. Neither is their record of winning the sport's knock-out competition to claim the MacTavish Cup a record 43 times. By comparison

STAGE 11 – PITLOCHRY TO AVIEMORE

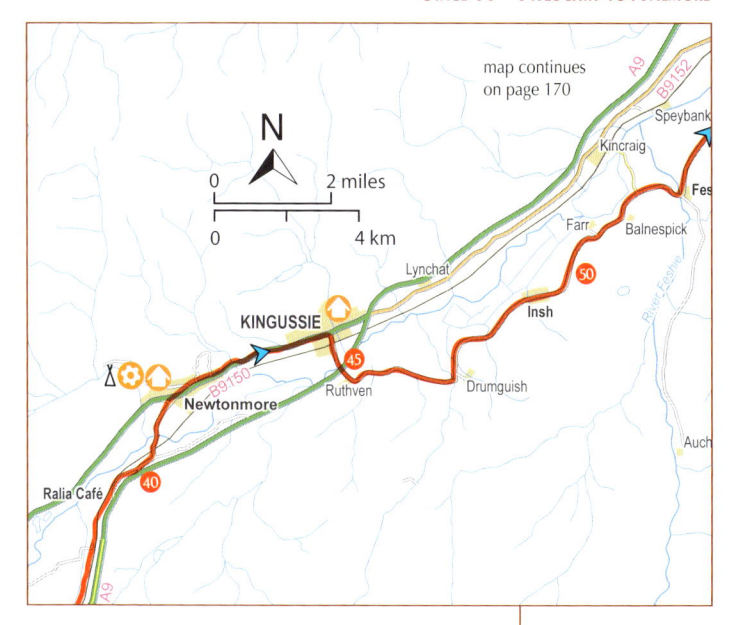

Manchester United's 20 wins of the Football League Cup and Arsenal's 14 Football Association Cup wins seem modest achievements.

Ride through the village and then once past the Highland Folk Museum join a shared-use path alongside the opposite carriageway and follow NCN 7 into

Ruthven Barracks near Kingussie were occupied for less than 30 years and have stood empty since 1746

Cycling Land's End to John o' Groats

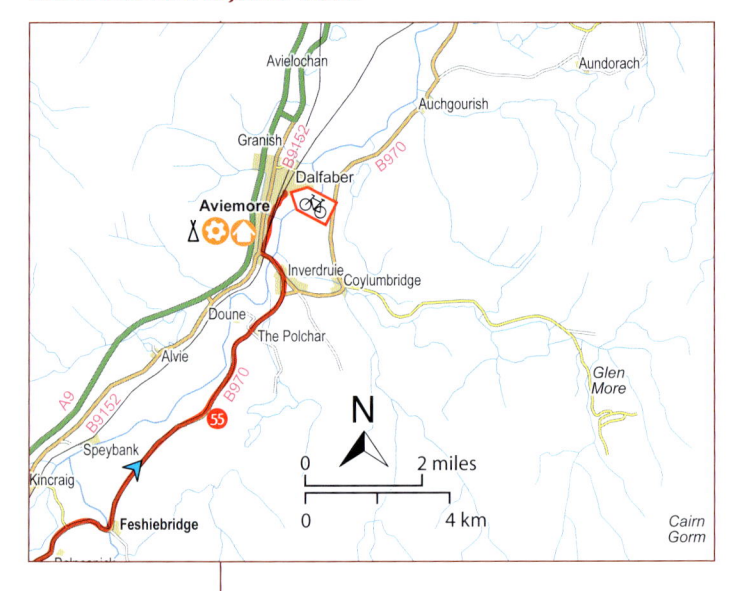

Built by General Wade in 1720 to suppress any Jacobite rising, Ruthven Barracks was captured and torched by Bonnie Prince Charlie's forces in 1746 and has never been reoccupied.

Kingussie (44/16 miles). Just before the town centre, turn right along Ruthven Road. Follow NCN 7 along the B970 first over the railway and River Spey, then under the A9 and past Ruthven Barracks (45/15 miles), which stand atop a small hill to the north of the road. Continue through **Insh** (49/11 miles) and **Feshiebridge** (53/7 miles) to Inverdruie (58/2 miles). ◄

If you are continuing past Aviemore today you could turn right and follow a loop of NCN 7 through Coylumbridge and join Stage 12 at Boat of Garten. Otherwise turn left, follow NCN 7 alongside B970 and then, immediately after crossing the River Spey, turn right along Dalfaber Road where this stage ends at the junction with Dalfaber Drive which leads straight into the centre of **Aviemore**.

> The arrival of the railway in 1898 saw **Aviemore** grow from a sleepy village into a fledging tourist destination. But after the chairlift into the northern

corries of Cairn Gorm was opened in 1961 its popularity grew and it rapidly became Britain's most visited ski resort. Today the town is a popular resort all year round providing both outdoor enthusiasts and tourists with a base for exploring the Cairngorms National Park.

RIDING NORTH TO SOUTH – JOGLE

After the Pass of Drumochter, the final 25 miles is predominantly downhill all the way to Pitlochry, making for an easy afternoon.

Pleasant early morning riding through the forest between Aviemore and Boat of Garten

CYCLING LAND'S END TO JOHN O' GROATS

STAGE 12
Aviemore to Alness

Start	Where the NCN 7 crosses Dalfaber Drive in Aviemore (NH 902 136)
Finish	Junction of High Street and Ardross Street in Alness (NH 656 696)
Distance	64 miles (102 km)
Ascent	700m
Time	6–7hrs
OS Maps	OS Landranger 36, 27, 26 and 21
Refreshments	Boat of Garten, Carrbridge, Tomatin, Inverness, Dingwall and Evanton
Accommodation	Only one hostel just before the end of this stage but plenty of choices of other types of accommodation

Another day with modest mileage to give you time to restock on essential supplies and perhaps even indulge in a leisurely lunch in Inverness before the final couple of days, which statistics suggest could well be the wettest and windiest of the journey. I hope they're not and that you are blessed with cloudless skies and the merest hint of a breeze that is wafting in from the south. But let's be realistic, six of the 10 wettest years in the UK since records began in 1862 have occurred since 1998, so it's probably going to rain sometime before your journey's end. But with only short days remaining you may find you can sit out the showers by retreating into a café or sheltering under a tree – if only they weren't quite so scarce this far north.

Re-join NCN 7 on Dalfaber Drive, turn left along Spey Avenue and ride away from Aviemore along a gravel track alongside the railway before joining a single track road through ancient pine forest that leads to **Boat of Garten** (5/59 miles). ◄

Turn left, follow NCN 7 for 1 mile along Deshar Road and then turn left along a shared-use path alongside the westbound carriageway of the A95 and then northwards along the B9153 towards Carrbridge. It is pleasant cycling

Boat of Garten gets its name from an old ferry that crossed the River Spey here, but today it is also known as 'Osprey village' due to the growing population of osprey that breed locally.

Stage 12 – Aviemore to Alness

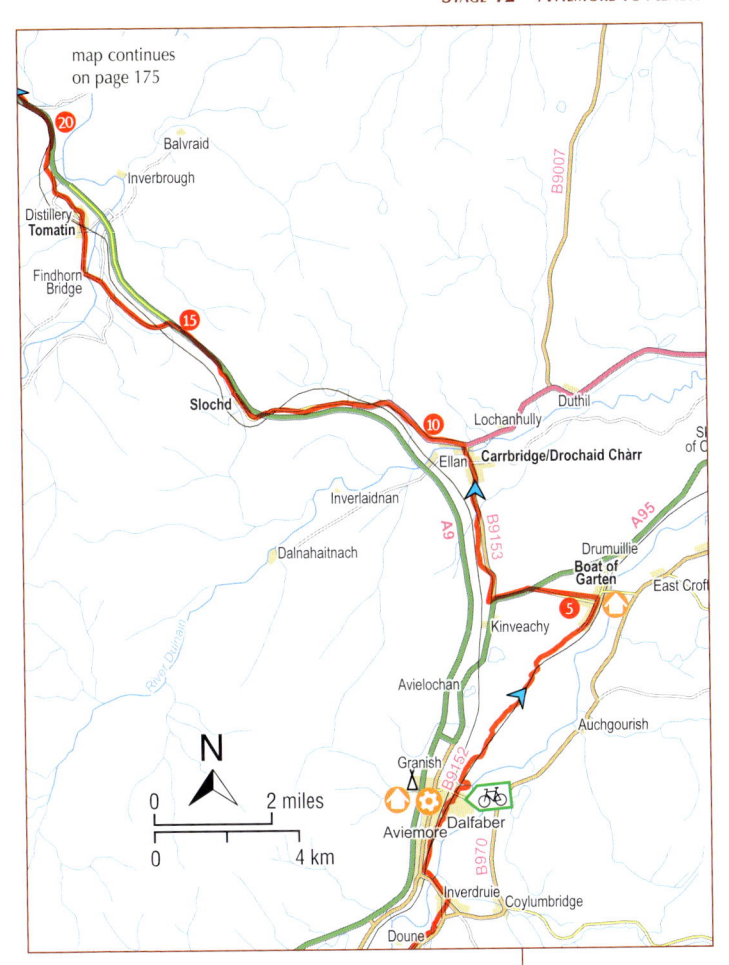

through the western section of the Abernethy Forest most of which is now managed by the Royal Society for the Protection of Birds who work to maintain the local populations of birds which include buzzards, tawny owls, great spotted woodpeckers and sparrowhawks. Ride into

Cycling Land's End to John o' Groats

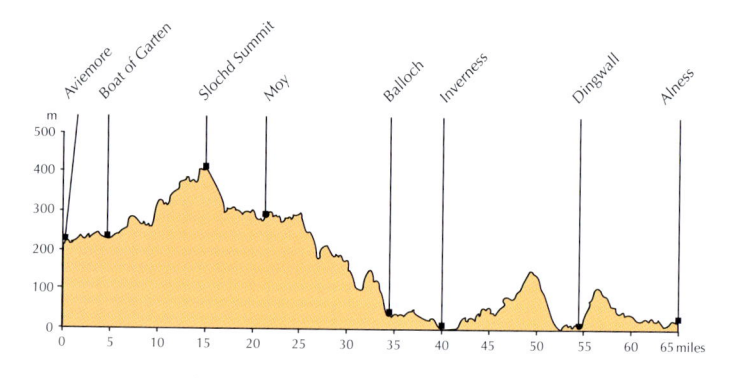

> The Old Bridge of Carr was built by local mason John Nicolson in 1717 at a cost of £100 and was used until the great 'Muckle Spate' of August 1829 left it and others across the region in ruins.

Carrbridge (9/55 miles). Ignore the first turning where NCN 7 goes out on a loop past the station and out along a gravel track through Sluggan adding and extra 1.6 miles to the stage. Stop at the bridge across the River Dulnan to view the Old Bridge of Carr which is just upstream. Then continue to the junction and turn left along the A938 towards Inverness. ◄

Continue over **The Slochd** (15/49 miles), where the road reaches 405m (1,328 ft) above sea level and get ready for 18 miles of net descent right down to the Moray Firth. Follow the road down through Findorn Bridge and **Tomatin** (18/46 miles) where there is a distillery and then briefly follow a stretch of shared-use path alongside the A9 before joining the B9154. Ride past **Loch Moy** (22/42 miles) and then 4½ further on turn right following a waymarker sign for NCN 7 towards Culloden.

Continue along this pleasant road that gives occasional glimpse out towards the Moray Firth for 3 miles and then turn left following NCN 7 towards Culloden first through a farmyard and then under the railway to merge with NCN 1, which the route follows for the final 164 miles to John o' Groats albeit with a shortcut to bypass Tain that saves nearly 10 miles. A mile further on you can detour to visit Culloden Battlefield which is just 600 metres off-route.

Stage 12 – Aviemore to Alness

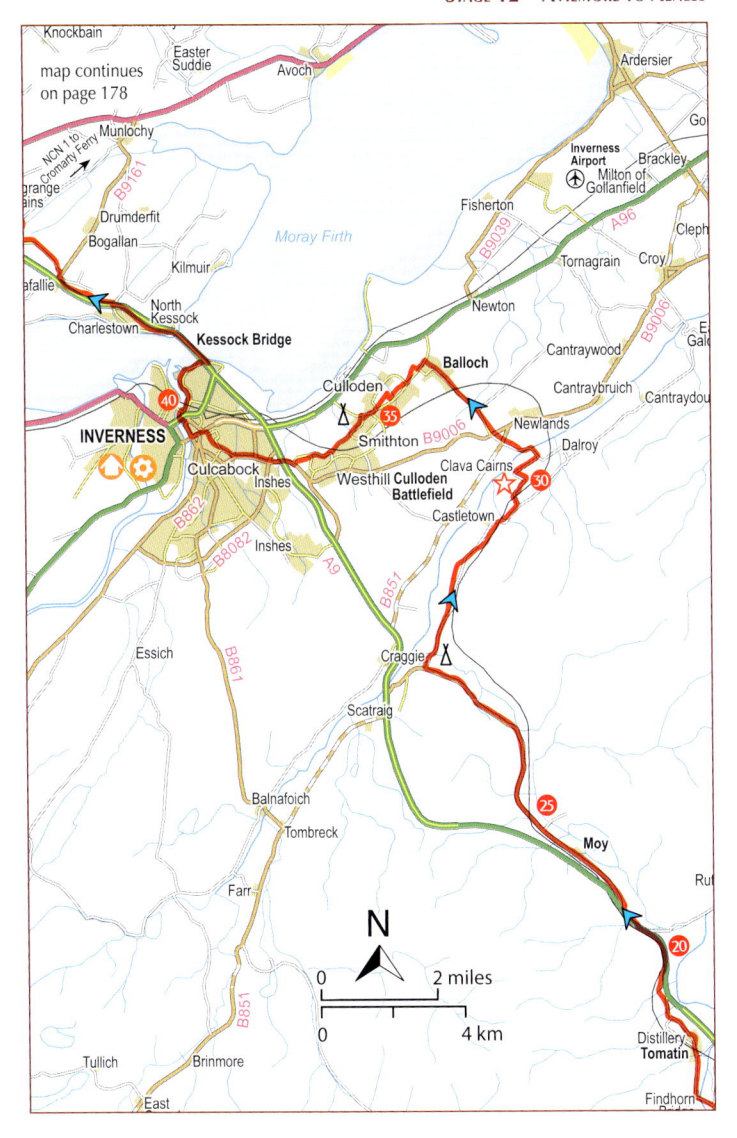

Clava Cairns, adjacent to the route between Loch Moy and Culloden, are a well-preserved Bronze Age cemetery in a beautiful wooded glade

Alternatively if you don't fancy the full multi-media re-enactment at the Culloden Battlefield Visitor Centre you could ride 100 metres along the B9006 towards Cawdor Castle and visit **Cumberland's Stone**, a flat glacial erratic where the victorious Duke of Cumberland (1721–1765) is said to have had his breakfast, or was it his lunch, before decisively defeating Bonnie Prince Charlie and his Jacobite army on the nearby battlefield on 16 April 1746. It may not provide the same immersive experience, but what do you expect for free?

On **Culloden Battlefield** the Jacobite forces of Charles Edward Stuart, (1720–1788) aka Bonnie Prince Charlie, were decisively defeated by Hanoverian forces commanded by the Duke of Cumberland. Between 1,500 and 2,000 Jacobites, but only about 300 government soldiers, were killed or wounded in a battle that lasted barely an hour, effectively putting an end to plots and uprisings to restore descendants of the Stuart dynasty to the British throne. However, should an independent Scotland ever want its own sovereign, there are direct descendants of James II's sister, Henrietta Anne Stuart (1644–1670) through her marriage to Philippe, Duke of Orléans (1640–1701), still alive today. And if they were to decline, there are also

STAGE 12 – AVIEMORE TO ALNESS

living descendants of Bonnie Prince Charlie's illegitimate daughter, Charlotte Stuart (1753–1789).

When you're done, return to the route and continue into **Balloch** (33/31 miles) and then turn left along Cherry Park and follow NCN 1 through the eastern suburbs of Inverness It is well waymarked throughout. Continue over the A9, past the Inshes Retail Park and onward into the centre of **Inverness** (39/25 miles).

Long regarded as the capital of the Highlands, **Inverness** is the most northerly city in the United Kingdom. Despite its location, during the first two decades of the 21st century, the city's population grew by nearly 80 per cent making it one of Europe's fastest growing cities. Much of this growth came from a concerted programme of attracting inward investment which helped replace traditional industries such as distilling and fishing with high-tech, medical and biotechnology businesses. Good communication links by rail and air, excellent schools and easy access to all parts of the Highlands make it an attractive place to live and in a 2019 survey it ranked fifth out of 189 British cities for its quality of life, the highest of any Scottish city.

Turn right along the eastern bank of the River Ness, first past an eclectic mix of old sandstone houses and then past industrial units along Shore Road. After 2 miles, cross the **Kessock Bridge** that spans the narrows between Beauly Forth to the west and Moray Forth to the east, where bottlenose dolphins and harbour porpoises are frequently spotted. ▶

Continue along the rather narrow segregated path alongside the northbound carriageway of the A9 then after 1½ miles follow signs for NCN 1 through the subway and follow the path and then a minor road alongside the southbound carriageway. A mile further on turn right and then left across the B9161 following the NCN 1 towards Tore. Ignore the junction where a branch of NCN

Prior to the Kessock Bridge opening in 1982, travellers had the choice of heading inland to Beauly or taking the Kessock Ferry which had crossed the narrows since the 15th century.

177

Cycling Land's End to John o' Groats

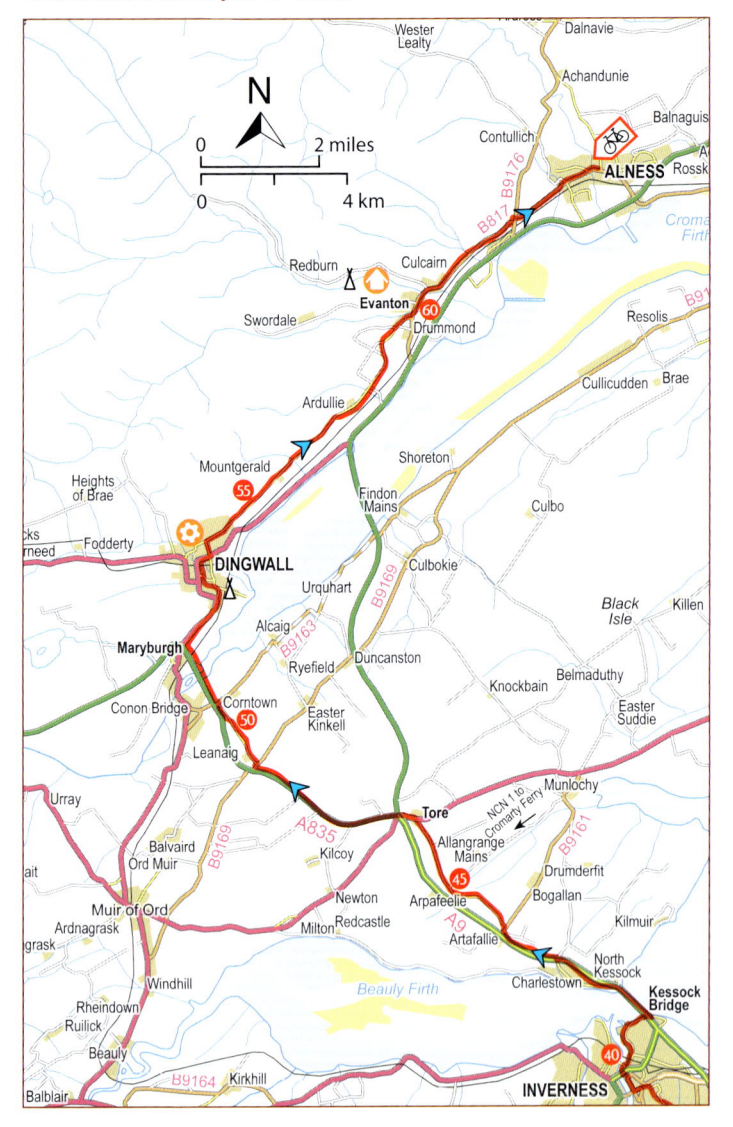

178

STAGE 12 – AVIEMORE TO ALNESS

1 turns right for a loop along the Black Isle that involves taking the Cromarty Ferry and continue towards **Tore**. ▶

At the end of this road, turn left towards Conon Bridge, join a shared-use path around Tore Roundabout (47/17 miles) and follow it alongside the A835 for the next 2½ miles.

Turn right along the B9169 and then quickly left along a minor road and follow NCN 1 downhill towards Conon Bridge where the route once again joins a shared-use path alongside the A835. Cross the bridge over the River Conan, follow the path around the roundabout to the north of **Maryburgh** (52/12 miles) and continue first riding alongside the A862 and then along Greenhill Street into the centre of **Dingwall** (53/11 miles). If you are heading northwards the NCN 1 sticks to the Greenhill Road and Newton Road that together form the ring road which passes a superstore with a café. However you can easily make a detour into the town centre which has plenty of other eateries by turning right along High Street. ▶

Continue along Newton Road and then turn left along Tulloch Road following waymarker signs for NCN 1 towards The Tulloch Castle Hotel. After ¼ mile turn right towards Evanton and continue climbing along the hillside with good views south of Cromarty Bridge which carries the A9 across the Cromarty Firth. Turn left along the B817 on the outskirts of **Evanton** (60/4 miles) and ride through

The Cromarty Ferry only runs from the 1st June until 15th September leaving Cromarty every 30 minutes from 8am till 6.00pm and leaving Nigg every 30 minutes from 8.15am till 6.15 pm.

Dingwall is the home of Ross County, (The Staggies), the most northerly full-time professional football team in the British Isles.

Heading down the NCN 1 towards Conon Bridge

Cycling Land's End to John o' Groats

> To by-pass Alness and save a mile, stay on the B9176 heading towards Ardross and join Stage 13 two miles north of the town.

the village which was established in the early 19th century by local landowner Alexander Fraser who named it after his son Evan.

At the edge of Evanton, join a shared-use path and follow it alongside the B817, across the B9176 and into **Alness** where this stage ends at the junction of High Street and Ardross Street. ◀

Initially a small port and important crossing point over the River Averon **Alness** grew into a town once the main road was constructed in 1715. Thomas Telford dramatically improved the quality of the original road and oversaw the building of the first bridge over the River Averon in the first decades of the 19th century. Around the same time, two distilleries were established in the town, Teaninich Distillery in 1817 and Dalmore Distillery in 1839. Both remain in production although the Diageo-owned Teaninich Distillery is less well known as it only produces malts for blending.

Far better-known is the Dalmore Distillery which sits on the banks of the Cromarty Firth to the south east of the town. During World War I, the distillery was commandeered by the military so that the US Navy could use it as a base for the assembly of mines that were shipped across the Atlantic to Kyle of Lochalsh, transported to Alness by rail and then shipped out along a newly-built pier that is still known locally as Yankee Pier. You can visit the distillery although it is essential to book in advance. See www.thedalmore.com for details.

RIDING NORTH TO SOUTH – JOGLE

Keep your windproof jacket, neck-ware and full-fingered gloves handy for the second half of this stage up into the Cairngorms which may be chilly as it includes stretches with altitudes above 400m/1300ft.

STAGE 13
Alness to Tongue

Start	Junction of High Street and Ardross Street in Alness (NH 656 696)
Finish	Junction of Main Street and A838 in the centre of Tongue (NC 591 677)
Distance	66 miles (106 km)
Ascent	1100m
Time	7–8hrs
OS Maps	OS Landranger 21, 16 and 10
Refreshments	Falls of Shin, Lairg, Crask Inn, Altnaharra Hotel
Accommodation	Although there is accommodation of all types along this stage, there is not much of it so book early to avoid disappointment

From Alness, NCN 1 continues northeast alongside the Cromarty Firth and Nigg Bay to Tain before swinging back northwest along the Dornoch Firth to Ardgay. Our route takes a shortcut to Ardgay by following B9176 inland saving roughly 9 miles and something like 45 minutes in the saddle without any additional climbing. Going over 'The Struie', as the B9176 is known locally, is just steady pedalling at barely noticeable gradients of just a couple of percent through wonderful scenery that gives magnificent views out across the Cromarty Firth to the south and eventually the Kyle of Sutherland to the north.

Head north up Ardross Street towards Ardross and then after 2 miles, turn right along the B9176. ▶ Climb steadily through Dalnavie (3/64 miles), **Stittenham** (4/63 miles) and Aultnamain (7/60 miles). Enjoy the open views across a mixed terrain of rugged moorland and pastures peppered with patches of Scots Pine and mixed conifers. Then stop at the viewpoint on **Cadha Mor** (12/55 miles) for what many consider to be one of the finest vistas in the Highlands. On a clear day you can see Carbisdale

Drovers once used this road to drive cattle to markets in the more populous south.

Cycling Land's End to John o' Groats

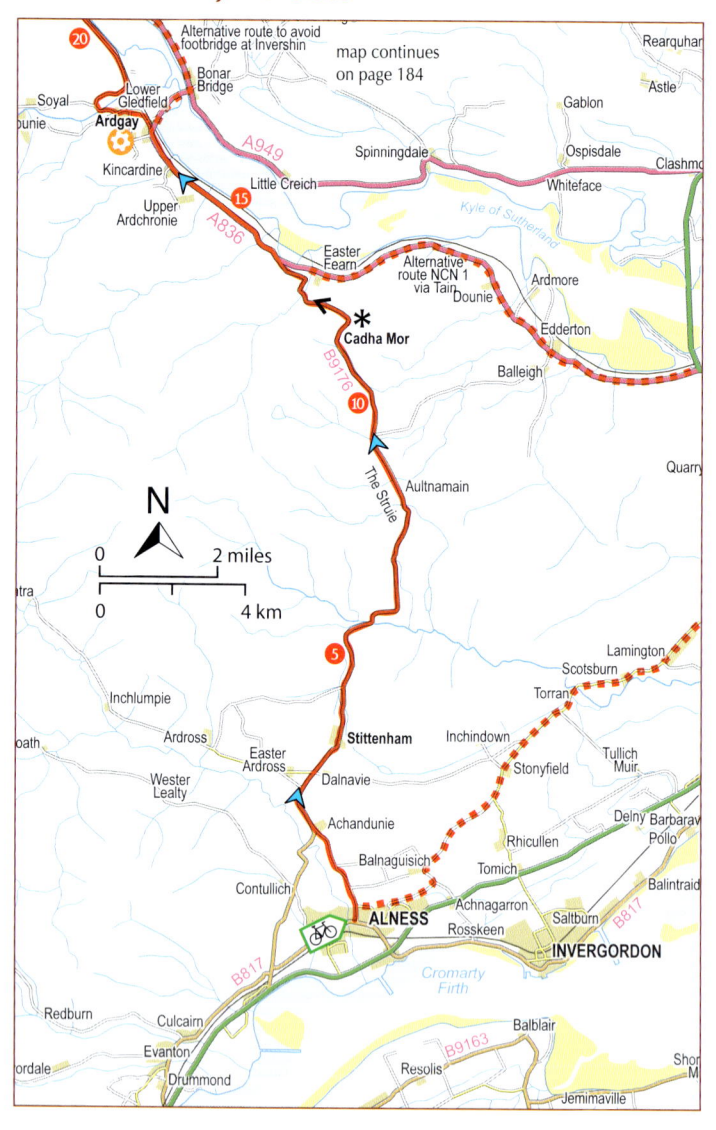

STAGE 13 – ALNESS TO TONGUE

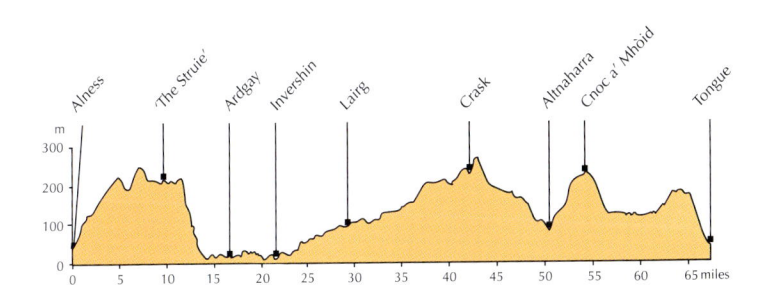

Castle on the Kyles of Sutherland at the head of the estuary, Ben More Assynt (998m/3,274 ft) which is the highest point in the former county of Sutherland and Ben Klibreck (962m /3,165ft), which the route passes 30 miles further along.

Enjoy the 2 miles descent to the Dornoch Firth where gradients briefly reach 20% and then turn left along the A836 towards Lairg re-joining NCN 1. Continue through the hamlets alongside Dornoch Firth to **Ardgay** (17/50 miles) and then turn left towards Culrain. Just after crossing the River Carron, turn right still following NCN 1 towards Culrain. ▶

Ardgay owes its existence to the 3rd Duke of Sutherland (1828–1892) who insisted the railway went along the southern shore of the Kyle of Sutherland so he could commercially develop that part of his estate.

Southbound riders passing the Cadha Mòr viewpoint at the top of The Struie

Cycling Land's End to John o' Groats

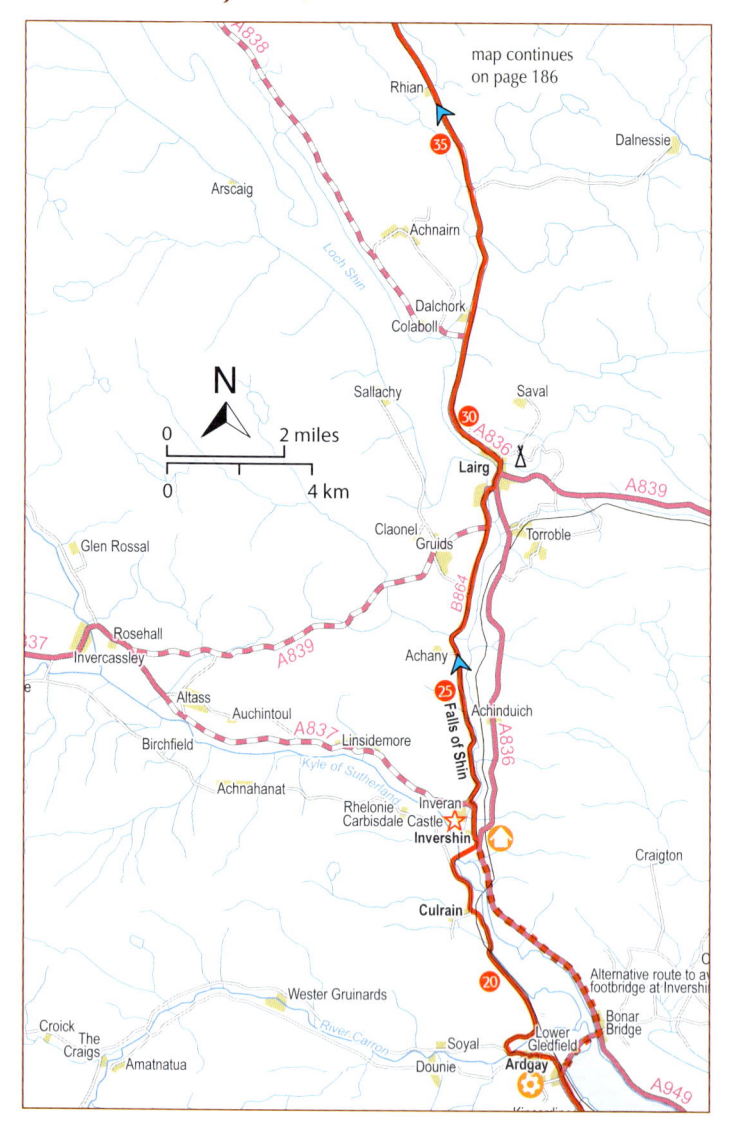

Stage 13 – Alness to Tongue

Pass the station in **Culrain** (21/46 miles) and then turn right and follow NCN 1 alongside the railway and across the Kyles of Sutherland by a footbridge where you may need to carry your bike as it has 50 steps down for those heading north and 50 steps up for those heading south.

CARBISDALE CASTLE

Set high in the woods above the Kyles of Sutherland, Carbisdale Castle was built for the widowed Duchess of Sutherland between 1905 and 1917. As plain Mary Blair, she was the wife of the 3rd Duke of Sutherland's land agent who died in a shooting accident in 1883 that many suspected may have been suicide or perhaps even murder. Widow Blair married the 3rd Duke in 1889 just three months after his estranged first wife had died but was only married to him for four years before he died at the age of 63.

Shortly before his death the Duke had disinherited his children and tried to leave his wealth to his second wife, who was later found guilty of destroying documents and imprisoned for six weeks in Holloway Prison. The family eventually made a substantial settlement in her favour that enabled her to build Carbisdale Castle which soon became known as the 'Castle of Spite' as it was widely considered that the Duchess located the castle in a prominent position just outside the Sutherland estates to spite her late husband's family.

Turn left along the A836 and ride through **Invershin** (22/45 miles). After a mile, turn left along the A837 towards Lochinver. Continue for 1 mile and then, immediately after crossing the River Shin, turn right following NCN1 along the B864 toward Lairg. Stop and visit the **Falls of Shin** (24/43 miles) where salmon can be seen leaping up the falls from the viewing platform between May and October. Then 4 miles further along this pleasant road, turn right and follow the A839 across the River Shin and left into the centre of **Lairg** (29/38 miles), which is the last place on this stage to top up on snacks and supplies.

Turn left and follow NCN 1 along what is now the A836 towards Tongue first beside Loch Shin and then through mixed pasture and moorland with frequent plantations of conifer and birch. Despite being designated

Cycling Land's End to John o' Groats

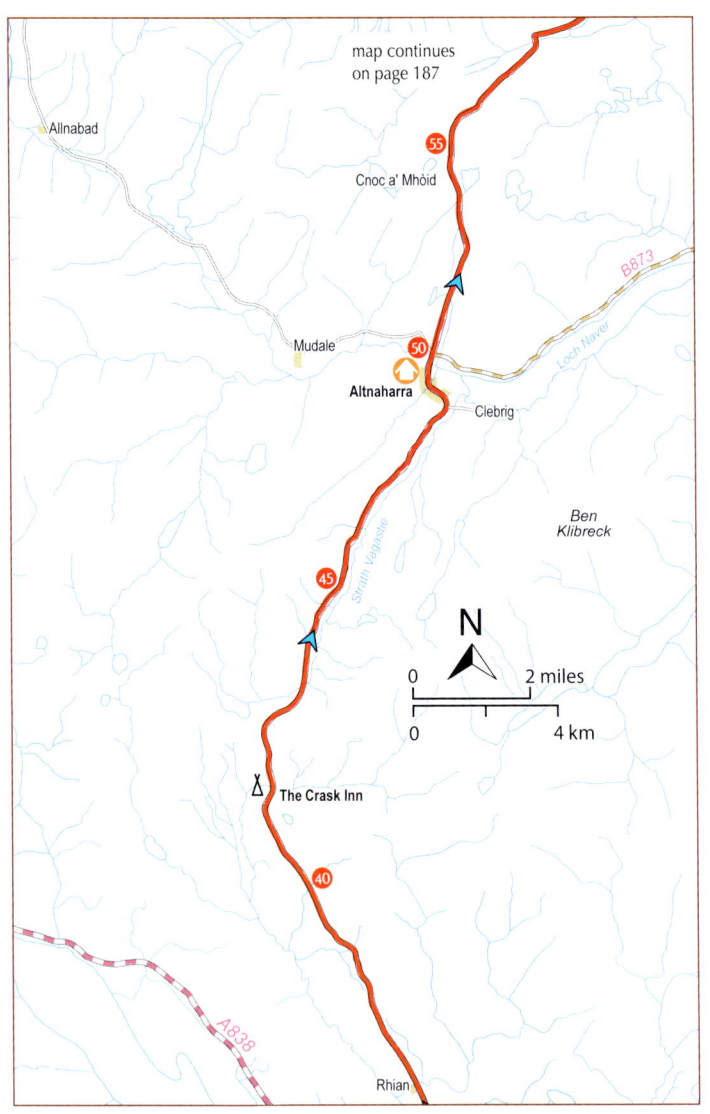

Stage 13 – Alness to Tongue

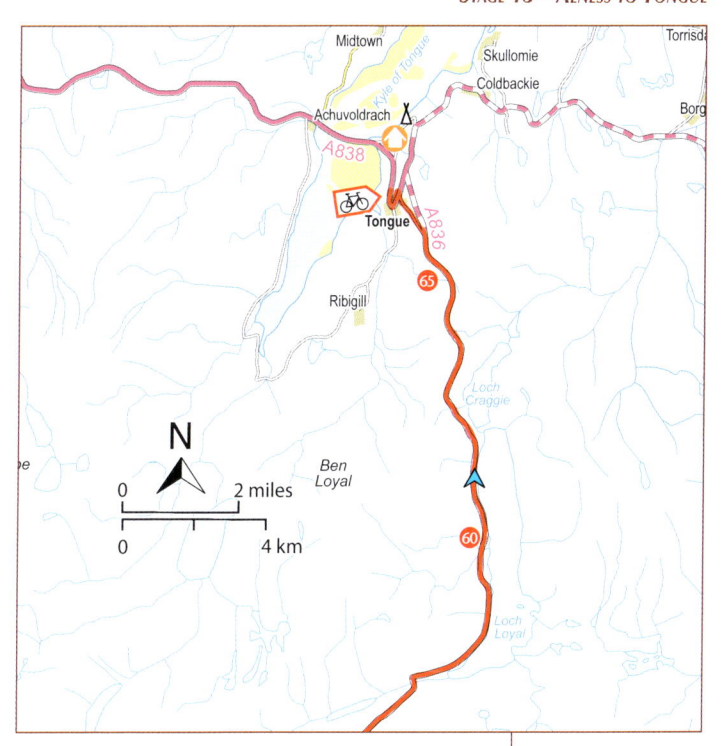

The National Cycle Network waymarker post outside The Crask Inn

Cycling Land's End to John o' Groats

Heading north on NCN1 along the A836 towards The Crask Inn

Now owned and used as a place of worship by the Scottish Episcopalian Church, the Crask Inn, which was built by the Sutherland Estate around 1815, still provides food, drink, camping and B&B accommodation.

Tongue gets its name from the Old Norse word for a spit of land – this one being the terminal moraine that projects into the eastern shore of the Kyle of Tongue by the causeway.

as an A road, it soon becomes single track with passing places so keep an eye out for vehicles coming from behind and allow them to pass as soon as possible.

Take a break at the remote **Crask Inn** (42/25 miles) that has been a traditional stop-off for generations of End-to-Enders and then enjoy a long downhill stretch along Strath Vagastie towards Loch Naver with Ben Klibreck high above you to the right. ◄

Continue through **Alltnarra** (50/17 miles), climb steadily for 4 miles up the southern slopes of Cnoc a' Mhòid which gives good views of Ben Hope and Ben Loyal and then descend to Loch Loyal. Continue past Loch Loyal and then Loch Craggie before one final gentle climb over to **Tongue**. Turn left just before the sign for Braetongue and ride down into the centre of the village where the stage ends. ◄

RIDING NORTH TO SOUTH – JOGLE

You may wish to avoid the steep gradients of 'The Struie' by following NCN 1 south through Tain adding an extra 9 miles and just under 1 hour of riding time.

STAGE 14
Tongue to John o' Groats

Start	Junction of Main Street and A838 in the centre of Tongue (NC 591 677)
Finish	By the pier in John o' Groats (ND 380 734)
Distance	64 miles (102 km)
Ascent	1300m
Time	7–8hrs
OS Maps	OS Landranger 10, 11 and 12
Refreshments	Bettyhill, Melvich, Thurso, Thurso and Castletown
Accommodation	The limited supply of accommodation particularly in John o' Groats makes it essential to book early to avoid disappointment

In Scotland, north-facing coasts are typically riven by valleys formed by retreating glaciers. This makes such roads a bit like a roller-coaster in that you are repeatedly losing height to cross north-flowing streams. Although the gradients are rarely severe, it may be a tiring day so beware of setting yourself unrealistic goals, such as arriving at John o' Groats by lunchtime so you can catch an afternoon train from Thurso or Wick. Better to take your time and enjoy the final day of a journey you may never repeat again but will remember for the rest of your life. It may involve the expense of another night's accommodation, but it'll be worth it. Needless to say the scenery is magnificent.

Head out of Tongue along the A838 towards Thurso, passing the war memorial by where the road becomes the A836 and our route re-joins NCN 1, which it stays with all the way to John o' Groats. There are wonderful views north along the Kyle of Tongue to the eponymously named Rabbit Islands and the larger Eilean Nan Ron. ▶

Views of the sea disappear once the road swings eastwards through typical Flow Country landscape of expanses of blanket bog and are not regained until the

Eilean Nan Ron (The Island of Seals) which had a population of 73 in 1881 and was only evacuated in 1938, now has a colony of grey seals that produces about 350 calves each year.

CYCLING LAND'S END TO JOHN O' GROATS

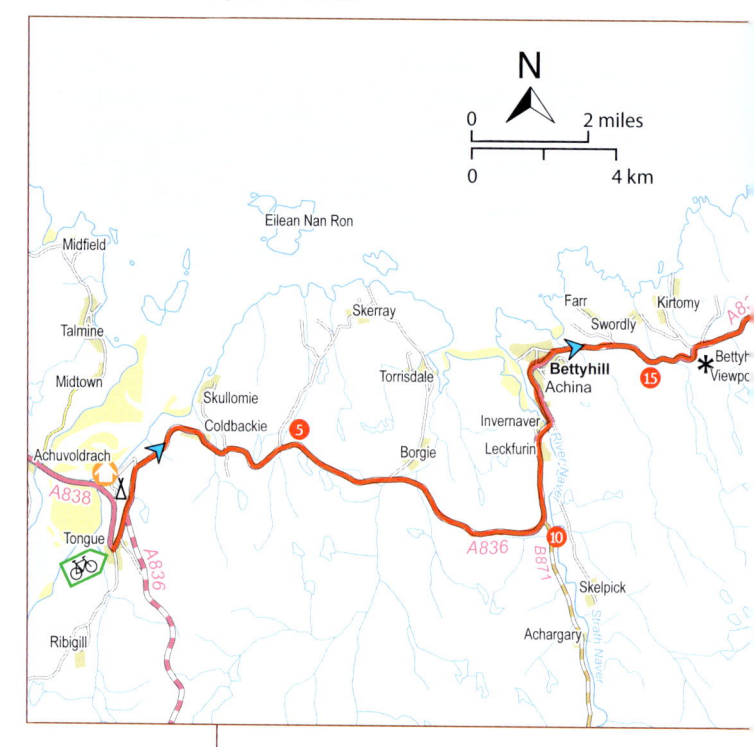

road swings northwards along Strath Naver towards **Bettyhill** (13/51 miles) where you get a magnificent view out across the white sands of Torrisdale Bay.

After 3 miles, the Bettyhill viewpoint gives excellent views across to Ben Loyal, Ben Hope, which is the most northern Munro, and neighbouring summits to the west. Further along the route there are views to the sea near **Armadale** (19/45 miles), Strathay (23/41 miles), **Melvich** (26/38 miles) and **Reay** (32/32 miles), which are all small communities of crofts and farmsteads scattered above sheltered sandy bays. After passing through Reay, turn right and follow NCN 1 inland through Achvarasdal (33/31 miles), Shebster (35/29 miles) and Westfield

Stage 14 – Tongue to John o' Groats

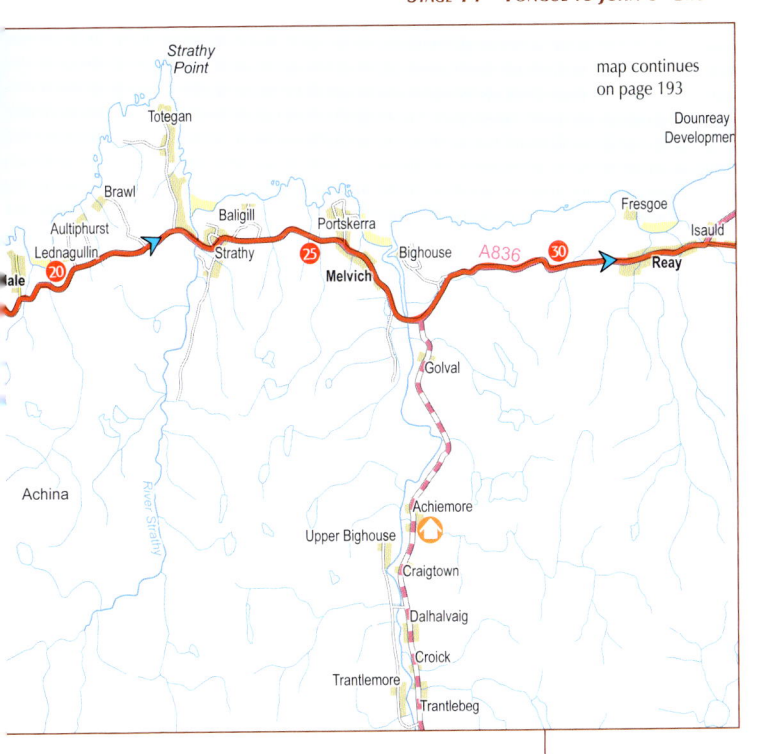

(38/26 miles). Taking this backroad temporarily avoids some of the traffic following the North Coast 500 touring

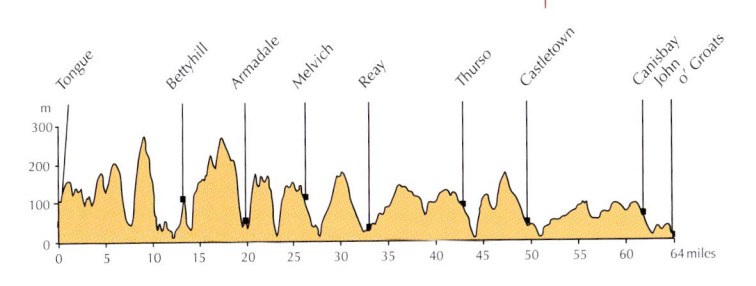

Cycling Land's End to John o' Groats

> Launched in 2015, the North Coast 500 has bought considerable economic benefits to the north of Scotland albeit with considerably more traffic during the peak summer months.

route along the A836 and sight of Dounreay Nuclear Power Development Establishment which ceased production in 1994 when the reactors were shut down but still employs a substantial workforce involved in decommissioning the site. ◄

Follow NCN 1 along this quiet road through **Thurso** (43/21 miles) and across the River Thurso to Thurso East. Bear left following NCN 1 along the A836 towards Castletown and then turn right along Mount Pleasant Road and ride out into the countryside.

COLONISATION AND DISPLACEMENT IN THE EXTREME NORTH

Between the 8th and 15th centuries, Viking and Norse settlers invaded and colonised the remote north and west parts of modern Scotland, establishing settlements such as Thurso, which is just 320 miles to the west of the Norwegian city of Stavanger. In favourable conditions historians suggest it would have taken them just 1 to 2 days to make the crossing to lands they called *Suðrland* ('southern land') and *Katanes* ('headland of the Catt people') which over time became Sutherland and Caithness. Norse and Viking rule was probably at its height in the mid-11th century when it covered between a fifth and a quarter of the land area of modern Scotland. By the middle of the 15th century the Scandinavians finally relinquished any remaining control they had to the Scottish crown. However, their presence persists in place names, such as Thurso which translates as Thor's River. Evidence collected in recent times suggests that the Vikings and Norse were not so much warriors as homemakers in that they both settled their families in their new colonised lands and married local Gaels so that the Viking genetic marker M17 is still prevalent in the local population.

500 years later the reverse of colonisation was happening in the extreme north of Scotland. Between 1750 and 1860 a significant proportion of the population of the Scottish Highlands and Islands were either assisted to emigrate or forcibly evicted during what are now known as the Highland Clearances. Despite the clearances, the populations of both Sutherland and Caithness peaked in 1851 at over 25,000 and 40,000 respectively. Today the populations of these two former counties are already half that at their peak making the region the least densely populated in the whole of the UK. And with young people continuing the long tradition of heading south in search of employment, the population of the extreme north continues to decline compromising the viability of many local communities.

STAGE 14 – TONGUE TO JOHN O' GROATS

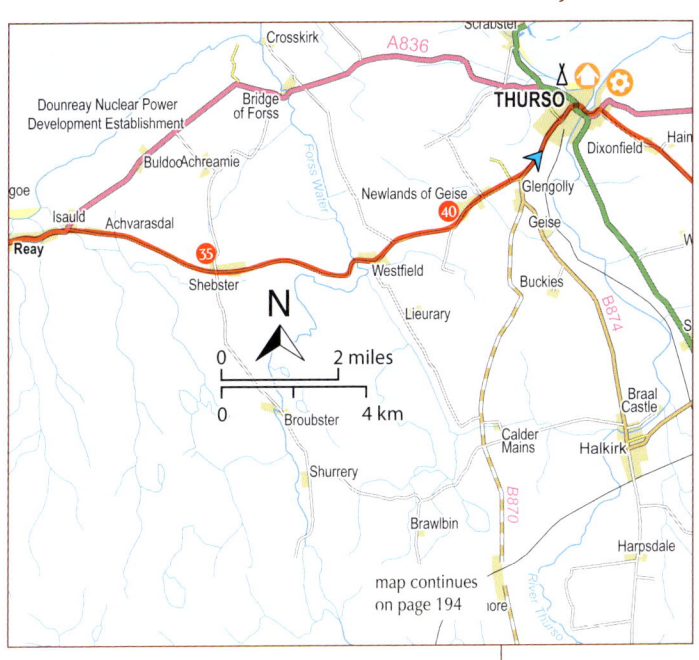

Remains of flagstone quarrying near the harbour at Castletown with the cliffs of Dunnet Head in the distance

CYCLING LAND'S END TO JOHN O' GROATS

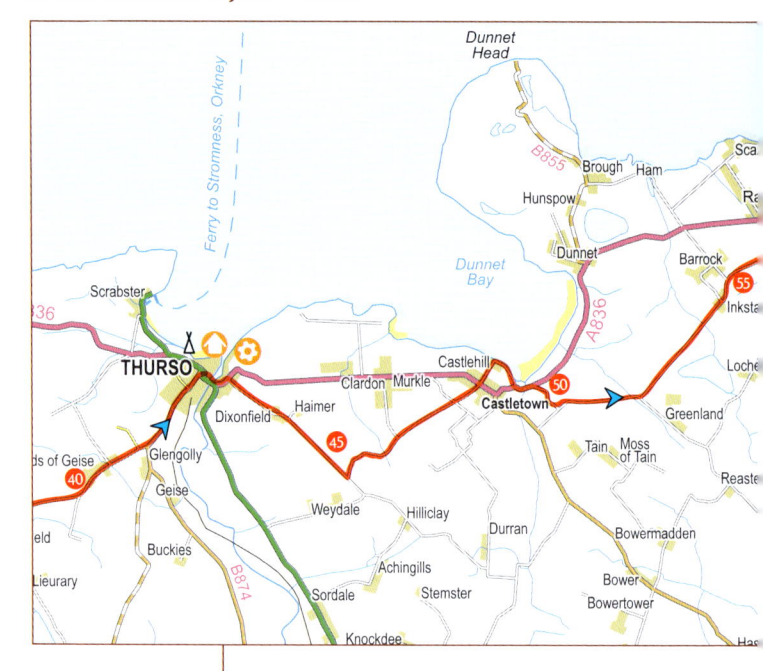

Turn left after 2½ miles and follow NCN 1 to **Castletown** (49/15 miles). Either turn right along Main

The John o' Groats Hotel from the harbour

STAGE 14 – TONGUE TO JOHN O' GROATS

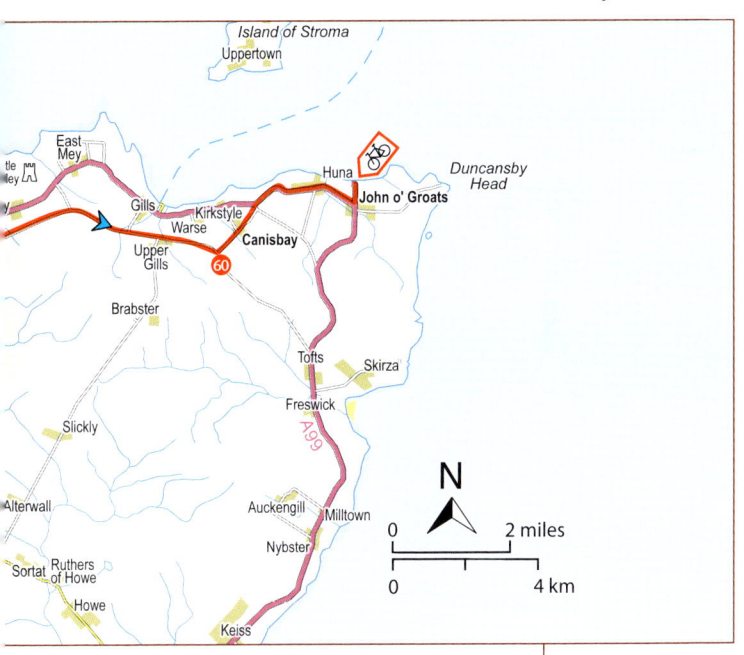

Street or cross the junction and cycle around by the harbour – both will bring you out on the A836 on the east side of the village – and then turn right and follow NCN 1 back inland. After ¾ mile, turn left and then a mile further on turn left towards Barrock opposite Lower Greenland Farm (52/12 miles).

Continue along this quiet and often dead straight road for 8 miles and then turn left through **Canisbay** (61/3 miles) and follow NCN 1 back to the A836. ▶

Turn left and then immediately right and follow NCN 1 through Huna (62/2 miles) to meet the A99. Turn left towards **John o' Groats**, where this stage; this route, and your journey end at the road end by the pier. After months of planning and training, a thousand miles of cycling and probably a few moments of self-doubt, you have done it. All that remains is to grab a selfie beneath the iconic

The headstone of the Dutch ferryman Jan De Groot man, who founded John o' Groats in the late 15th century, is in the porch of the Grade A-listed Canisbay Kirk, the most northerly church on mainland Britain.

195

Cycling Land's End to John o' Groats

fingerpost by the harbour wall, post it to social media and savour the moment.

RIDING NORTH TO SOUTH – JOGLE

If start your JOGLE by reversing this stage you will be just 10 miles further south at the end of your first day. To get more miles under your belt, head south after Bettyhill following the B871 and B873 through Strath Naver ending the day at Altnaharra (75 miles) or Crask (83 miles).

The author digs in for the last few miles (Photo by Mari Harrod)

APPENDIX A
Accommodation

The following is a list of selected accommodation on or near the route.

Stage 1
Hostels
Land's End
Land's End Hostel and B&B: tel 07585 625 774, www.landsendholidays.co.uk
YHA Land's End: tel 0345 371 9643, www.yha.org.uk

Penzance
YHA Penzance: tel 0345 371 9653, www.yha.org.uk

St Austell
Edens Yard Backpackers: tel 01726 814 907, www.edensyard.uk
YHA Eden Project: (Bodelva PL24 2SG), tel 0345 3719573, www.yha.org.uk

Hotels
Land's End
Land's End Hotel: tel 01736 871 844, www.landsendhotel.co.uk
Whitesands Hotel: tel 07375 514 597, www.whitesandshotel.co.uk

Penzance
Hotel Penzance: tel 01736 363 117, www.hotelpenzance.com
Queen's Hotel: tel 01736 362 371, www.queens-hotel.com

Fowey
Fowey Harbour Hotel: tel 01726 832551, www.harbourhotels.co.uk
The Old Quay House Hotel: tel 01726 833302, www.theoldquayhouse.com

Bed and Breakfast
Land's End
Treeve Moor House: tel 01736 871 284, www.treevemoorhouse.co.uk
Sea View House: tel 07581 417 595, www.seaviewhousebandbsennencornwall.com

Penzance
Bay Lodge Guest House: tel 01736 351 090, www.baylodgepenzance.com
Torwood House: tel 01736 360 063, www.torwoodhousehotel.co.uk

Fowey
Trethewey House: tel 07368 557 665, www.tretheweyguesthouse.co.uk
The Well House: tel 01726 833 832, www.wellhousefowey.co.uk

Cycling Land's End to John o' Groats

Camping

Land's End
Sea View Holiday Park: tel 01736 871 266, www.seaview.org.uk
Trevedra Farm Caravan and Camping: tel 01736 871818, www.trevedrafarm.co.uk

Penzance
Bone Valley Holiday Park: tel 01736 360 313
Vellanhoggan Summer Campsite/Vellanhoggan Cottage: tel 01736 351 777, www.ponsandane.co.uk

St Austell
Carlyon Bay Camping Park: tel 01726 812 735, www.carlyonbay.net
Doubletrees Farm: tel 01726 812 266, www.doubletreesfarm.co.uk

Fowey
Penhale Caravan and Camping Park: tel 01726 833 425
www.penhale-fowey.co.uk

Stage 2

Hostels

Okehampton
YHA Okehampton: tel 03452 602 791, www.yha.org.uk
YHA Okehampton Bracken Tor: tel 03452 602 863, www.yha.org.uk

Hotels

Crediton
The Ship Hotel: tel 01363 894 020, www.theshiphotelcrediton.co.uk

Bed and Breakfast

Crediton
Hillside B&B (Sandford): tel 01363 772 050, www.creditonbandb.co.uk
The Lamb Inn (Sandford): tel 01363 773 676, www.lambinnsandford.co.uk

Campsites

Liskeard
Fursdon Farm Caravan and Campsite: tel 01579 342 403, fursdonfarmcornwall.co.uk
Penbugle Farm Glamping and Camping (St Keyne PL14 4RS): tel 01579 326 709
www.penbuglefarm.co.uk

Callington
Compton Park: tel 01579 383 069, www.comptonpark.co.uk
Keadeen B&B and Camping (Golberdon): tel 01579 384 197, www.keadeen.co.uk

Okehampton
Bundu Camping and Caravan Park (Sourton Down): tel 01837 861 747, www.bundu.co.uk
Lydford Caravan and Camping Park: tel 01822 820 497, www.lydfordsite.co.uk

Crediton
Langford Bridge Camping & Caravan Park (EX5 5AQ): tel 01392 851 459, www.langfordbridge.co.uk

Stage 3
Hostels
Street
YHA Street: tel 0345 371 9143, www.yha.org.uk (10 miles off route)

Cheddar
YHA Cheddar Hillfield: tel 0345 371 9730, www.yha.org.uk (5 miles off route)

Hotels
Clevedon
Walton Park Hotel: tel 01275 874253, www.waltonparkhotel.co.uk

Bed and Breakfast
Clevedon
Cavell House: tel 01275 874 477, www.cavellhouse.com

Warren's Village Self-Catering Motel, Kenn tel 01275 871 666 www.warrensholidayvillage.com

Camping
Wellington
Minnows Touring Park Sampford Peverell Tiverton EX16 7EN tel 01884 821 770 www.minnowstouringpark.co.uk (3 miles off route)

Nunnington Park Farm Wiveliscombe Taunton TA4 2AD tel 01984 629 073 www.nunningtonparkfarm.co.uk (3 miles off route)

Taunton
Cornish Farm Touring Park Shoreditch tel 01823 327 746, www.cornishfarm.com

Tanpits Farm Campsite Dyers Lane Bathpool tel 01823 974 845, www.tanpitsfarmcampsite.co.uk

Bridgwater
Withy Water Caravan and Camping Park Withy Grove East Huntspill Highbridge TA9 3NP tel 01278 783 700 www.withywater.co.uk

Newton Brook Caravan and Camping Holmwood Farm North Newton tel 01278 664 422 www.newtonbrookcaravanandcamping.com

Cycling Land's End to John o' Groats

Congresbury
Oak Farm Touring Park tel 01934 833 246,
www.campingandcaravanningclub.co.uk

Clevedon
Bullock Farm Fishery and Campsite Kingston Seymour tel 01934 835 020,
www.bullockfarm.co.uk

Cranmoor Campsite Kingston Seymour tel 01934 838 397,
www.cranmoorcampsite.co.uk

Stage 4

Hostels

Slimbridge
Wild Goose Lodge Shepherds Patch tel 01453 890 275,
www.wild-goose-lodge.igloucestershire.com

Stourport on Severn
Haye Farm Sleeping Barn Ribbesford Bewdley DY12 2TP tel 01299 403371
www.haye-farm.co.uk (4 miles off-route)

Hotels

Worcester
Premier Inn Worcestershire County Cricket Club: tel 08715 279 456,
www.premierinn.com
Severn View Hotel: tel 0190 527 600, www.severnview-hotel.co.uk

Bed and Breakfast

Worcester
Walter de Cantelupe Inn (Kempsey): tel 01905 820 572, www.walterdecantelupe.co.uk
Ye Olde Talbot: tel 01905 235 730, www.greeneking-pubs.co.uk

Camping

Slimbridge
Tudor Caravan Park (Shepherds Patch): tel 01453 890 483, www.tudorcaravanpark.com

Tirley
The Haw Bridge Inn: tel 01452 780 272, www.hawbridgeinntirley.co.uk

Tewkesbury
Croft Farm Water Park (Bredons Hardwick): tel 01684 772 321,
www.croftfarmwaterpark.com

Worcester
Mill House Caravan & Camping Hawford: tel 01905 451 283,
www.millhousecaravanandcamping.co.uk
(1.7 miles off Stage 5 along the Droitwich Canal)

Stage 5
Hostels
None on this stage

Hotels

Nantwich
The Cheshire Cat: tel 01270 623 020, www.thecatat.com
The Crown Hotel: tel 01270 625 283, www.crownhotelnantwich.com

Bed and Breakfast

Nantwich
Moss Cottage B&B (Edleston): tel 07801 125 007
Mile House Barn (Worleston): tel 07946 165 520, www.milehousebarn.co.uk

Camping

Kidderminster
Wolverley Camping & Caravanning Club Site (Brown Westhead Park DY10 3PX):
tel 01562 850909, www.campingandcaravanningclub.co.uk

Newport
Ted's Caravan and Campsite Hungerhill Farm (Sheriffhales, Shifnal TF11 8SA):
tel 07923 132 219, www.hungerhillfarm.co.uk

Nantwich
The Cotton Arms (Wrenbury): tel 01270 780 377, www.cottonarmswrenbury.co.uk

The Willows Touring Park: tel 01270 812 754, www.willowstouringpark.co.uk

Stage 6
Hostels
None on this stage

Hotels

Garstang
Crofter Hotel: tel 01995 604 128, www.croftershotel.co.uk

Bed and Breakfast

Garstang
Kenlis Arms Hotel (Barnacre): tel 01995 603 307, www.kenlisarms.co.uk

Camping

Northwich
Belmont Hall (Great Budworth): tel 07530 450 019 or 07871 160 647,
www.belmontcamping.co.uk

Comberbach
Shrubbery Cottage: tel 01606 892 299 or 07710 066 496,
www.shrubberycottage.co.uk

Garstang
Wyreside Farm Park (St Michaels On Wyre): tel 01995 679 797,
www.wyresidefarmpark.co.uk

Stage 7

Hostels

Penrith
Wayfarers Independent Hostel: tel 01768 866 011, www.wayfarershostel.com

Hotels

Penrith
Foundary-34 Hotel: tel 01768 210 099, www.foundry-34.co.uk
Premier Inn: tel 08715 279 642, www.premierinn.com

Bed and Breakfast

Penrith
Acorn Guest House: tel 01768 868 696, www.acorn-guesthouse.co.uk
Ashberry Guest House: tel 01768 868 601, www.ashberry-guesthouse.co.uk

Camping

Bay Horse, Lancaster
Wyreside Lakes Sunnyside Farmhouse: tel 01524 792093, www.wyresidelakes.co.uk

Kirkby Lonsdale
Kirkby Lonsdale RUFC Campsite (Underley Park): tel 01524 259 162,
www.klrufc.co.uk

Sedbergh
Holme Open Farm: tel 01539 620 654, www.holmefarmcamping.co.uk

Shap
Crown Inn: tel 01931 716 562

Stage 8
Hostels

Carlisle
Carlisle City Hostel: tel 07914 720 821, www.carlislecityhostel.com

Carlisle West
Hillside Farm B&B and Bunkbarn (Boustead Hill, Burgh by Sands):
tel 01228 576 398, www.hadrianswalkbnb.co.uk (7 miles off route)

Moffat
Rivox Bunkhouse (Evan Water): www.rivox.net (Basic bunkhouse 1½ miles off route)

Hotels

Moffat
Black Bull Hotel: tel 01683 221 150, www.theblackbullmoffat.co.uk

Bed and Breakfast

Moffat
Dell Mar Guesthouse: tel 01683 220 260, www.dell-marmoffat.com
29 Well Street B&B: tel 01683 221 905, www.29wellstreet.co.uk

Camping

Annan
Broom Farm Estate (Newbie): tel 01461 700 386, www.broomfisheries.co.uk

Hoddom Mains
Hoddom Castle Caravan Park: tel 01576 300 251, www.hoddomcastle.co.uk

Lochmaben
Kirk Loch Caravan and Camping Site: tel 07824 528 467,
www.dumgal.gov.uk/kirklochcs

Moffat
Moffat Camping and Caravanning Club Site: tel 01683 220 436
www.campingandcaravanningclub.co.uk

Stage 9
Hostels

Edinburgh
Cowgate Tourist Hostel: tel 0131 226 5716, www.cowgate-hostel.edinburgh-hotel.org
(10 miles off-route along NCN 754)

Edinburgh Central Youth Hostel: tel 0131 524 2090, www.hostellingscotland.org.uk
(10 miles off-route along NCN 754)

Cycling Land's End to John o' Groats

Edinburgh Metro Cowgate: tel 0131 556 8718,
www.edinburgh-metro-youth-hostel.bedspro.com (10 miles off-route along NCN 754)

Euro Hostel Edinburgh: tel 0845 490 0461, www.eurohostels.co.uk
(10 miles off-route along NCN 754)

Hotels

South Queensferry
Premier Inn South Queensferry: www.premierinn.com

Bed and Breakfast

South Queensferry
Ravenous Beastie: tel 0131 319 1447
The Queens B&B: tel 0131 331 4345, www.thequeensbandb.co.uk

Camping

Livingston (East Calder)
Linwater Caravan Park (West Clifton): tel 0131 333 3326, www.linwater.co.uk
(2 miles off route)

Stage 10

Hostels

Perth
Perth Youth Hostel SYHA: tel 01738 877 800, www.hostellingscotland.org.uk

Pitlochry
Pitlochry Backpackers: tel 01796 470 044, www.pitlochrybackpackershotel.com
Pitlochry Youth Hostel SYHA: tel 01796 472 308, www.hostellingscotland.org.uk

Hotels

Pitlochry
Acarsaid Hotel: tel 01796 472 389, www.acarsaidhotel.com
Rosemount Hotel: tel 01796 472 302, www.scottishhotels.co.uk

Bed and Breakfast

Pitlochry
Atholl Villa Guest House: tel 01796 473 820, www.athollvilla.co.uk
Woodburn House B&B: tel 01796 473 818, www.woodburnhouse.co.uk

Camping

Kinross
Gallowhill Caravan and Camping Park: tel 01577 862364

Perth
Noahs Ark Caravan Park: tel 01738 580 661, www.noahsarkcaravanpark.co.uk

Dunkeld
Invermill Farm Caravan Park (Inver): tel 01350 727 477, www.invermillfarm.com

Pitlochry
Faskally Caravan Park: tel 01796 472 007, www.faskally.co.uk
(2 miles outside town along Stage 11)
Milton of Fonab Caravan Park: tel 01796 472 882, www.fonab.co.uk

Stage 9a
Hostels

Glasgow
Clyde Hostel: tel 0141 248 5207, www.clydehostel.co.uk
Euro Hostel Glasgow: tel 0845 539 9956, www.eurohostels.co.uk
Glasgow Youth Hostel SYHA: tel 0141 332 3004, www.hostellingscotland.org.uk

Campsites

Abington
Mount View Caravan Park: tel 01864 502 808, www.mountviewcaravanpark.co.uk

Bothwell (Hamilton)
Strathclyde Country Park: tel 01342 327 490, www.caravanclub.co.uk

Balloch (Gartocharn)
Lagganbeg Caravan and Camping Park (Mill Loan): tel 01389 830 281,
www.lagganbegcaravanandcampingpark.com

Stage 10a
Hostels

Drymen
Kip in the Kirk The Old Church Hall: tel 07734 394 315, www.kipinthekirk.co.uk
Rowardennan Lodge Youth Hostel SYHA (Rowardennan by Drymen):
tel 01360 870 259, www.hostellingscotland.org.uk (11 miles off-route)

Callander
Callander Hostel: tel 01877 331 465, www.callanderhostel.co.uk

Pitlochry
Pitlochry Backpackers: tel 01796 470 044, www.pitlochrybackpackershotel.com
Pitlochry Youth Hostel SYHA: tel 01796 472 308, www.hostellingscotland.org.uk

Campsites

Drymen
Drymen Camping: tel 07494 144 064, www.drymencamping.co.uk

Trossachs
Loch Achray Campsite (A821, Callander FK17 8HX): tel 01389 722600
www.lochlomond-trossachs.org
(On A821 alternative route around Queen Elizabeth Forest Park)

Callendar
Callendar Woods Holiday Park: tel 01250 878 123, www.woodleisure.co.uk

Aberfeldy
Aberfeldy Caravan Park: tel 01887 822 108, www.aberfeldycaravanpark.co.uk

Pitlochry
Faskally Caravan Park Faskally: tel 01796 472 007, www.faskally.co.uk
Milton of Fonab Caravan Park: tel 01796 472 882, www.fonab.co.uk

Stage 11

Hostels

Newtonmore
Newtonmore Hostel Craigellachie House: tel 01540 673 360,
www.newtonmorehostel.co.uk
Strathspey Mountain Hostel: tel 01540 673 694, www.strathspeymountainhostel.com

Aviemore
Aviemore Bunkhouse: tel 01479 811 181, www.aviemore-bunkhouse.com
Aviemore Youth Hostel SYHA: tel 1479 810 345, www.hostellingscotland.org.uk
Cairngorm Lodge SYHA (Glenmore): tel 01479 861 238, www.hostellingscotland.org.uk

Hotels

Aviemore
Cairngorm Hotel: tel 01479 810 233, www.cairngorm.com
Macdonald Aviemore Hotel: tel 0344 879 9152, www.macdonaldHotels.co.uk

Bed and Breakfast

Aviemore
Carn Mhor (The Shieling): tel 01479 812 464, www.carnmhor.co.uk
The Park Guesthouse: tel 01479 810 941, www.theparkguesthouseaviemore.co.uk

Campsites

Newtonmore
Invernahavon Caravan Site (Glentruim): tel 01540 673 534, www.invernahavon.com

Aviemore
Dalraddy Holiday Park (Kincraig): tel 01479 810 330, www.dalraddy.co.uk

Rothiemurchus Camp & Caravan Park (Coylumbridge): tel 01479 812 800, www.rothiemurchus.net

Stage 12
Hostels
Boat of Garten
Fraoch Lodge: tel 01479 831 331, www.scotmountainholidays.com

Nethy Bridge
Lazy Duck Hostel: tel 07846 291 154, www.lazyduck.co.uk (5 miles off-route)

Inverness
Bazpackers: tel 01463 717 663, www.bazpackershostel.co.uk
Black Isle Hostel: tel 01463 233 933, www.blackislehostel.com
Inverness Hostel: tel 07581 111 200, www.invernesshostel.co.uk
Inverness Youth Hostel SYHA: tel 01463 231 771, www.hostellingscotland.org.uk

Alness
The Bunkhouse Black Rock Caravan Park (Evanton): tel 01349 830 917, www.blackrockscotland.com (4 miles before end of stage)

Hotels
Alness
The Commercial Hotel: tel 01349 882 202, www.commercialhotelalness.co.uk
The Station Hotel: tel 01349 882 230, www.stationhotelalness.com

Bed and Breakfast
Alness
Beechwood Lodge, Ardross: tel 07876 683 999, www.beechwoodlodge.co.uk
(5 miles off route)
Westmore: tel 01349 884 647, www.westmorebandb.co.uk

Campsites
Inverness
Ardtower Caravan Park: tel 01463 790 555/07773 359 032, www.ardtower-caravanpark.com
Auchnahillin Holiday Park (Daviot East): tel 01463 772 286, www.auchnahillin.co.uk

Dingwall
Dingwall Camping and Caravanning Club: tel 01349 862 236, www.campingandcaravanningclub.co.uk

Cycling Land's End to John o' Groats

Alness
Black Rock Caravan Park (Evanton): tel 01349 830 917, www.blackrockscotland.com
(4 miles before end of stage)

Stage 13
Hostels

Ardgay
Invershin Hotel and Bunkhouse (Lairg): tel 01549 421 202, www.invershin.com
(4 miles beyond village)

Altnaharra
LeJog Cabin Altnaharra Hotel: tel 01549 411222, www.altnaharra.com

Tongue
Kyle of Tongue Hostel: tel 01847 611 789, www.tonguehostelandholidaypark.co.uk

Hotels

Tongue
Ben Loyal Hotel: tel 01847 611 216, www.benloyal.co.uk
Tongue Hotel: tel 01847 611 206, www.tonguehotel.co.uk

Bed and Breakfast

Tongue
The Bothy B&B: tel 01847 611 293, www.thebothytongue.co.uk
Tigh Nan Ubhal Guesthouse: tel 01847 611 281, www.tigh-nan-ubhal.co.uk

Camping

Lairg
Pondside Camping & Accommodation: tel 01549 402 109/07902 947 331
www.pondside.co.uk
Woodend Caravan & Camping Site (Achnairn): tel 01549 402 248 (No website)

Crask
The Crask Inn By Lairg (Sutherland): tel 01549 411 241, www.thecraskinn.com

Tongue
Kyle of Tongue Hostel: tel 01847 611 789, www.tonguehostelandholidaypark.co.uk

Stage 14
Hostels

Strath Halladale
Corn Mill Bunkhouse (Achumore): tel 01641 571 219, www.independenthostels.co.uk
(7 miles off-route)

Appendix A – Accommodation

Thurso
Sandra's Backpacker's Hostel: tel 01847 894 575, www.sandras-backpackers.co.uk

Hotels

John o' Groats
Castle Arms Hotel (Mey): tel 01847 851 244, www.castlearmshotel.co.uk
(Just off route, 6 miles west of John o' Groats)
Seaview Hotel: tel 01955 611 220, www.seaviewjohnogroats.co.uk

Bed and Breakfast

John o' Groats
Hamnavoe B&B: tel 01955 611 776, www.johnogroatsbnb.com
The Anchorage East End: tel 01955 611384, www.theanchoragejohnogroats.co.uk

Camping

Bettyhill
Craigdhu Caravan Camping Site: tel 01641 521 273

Melvich
North Coast Touring Park: tel 01641 531 282, www.northcoasttouringpark.co.uk

Thurso
Thurso Bay Caravan & Camping Park (Scrabster): tel 01847 892 244, www.thursobaycamping.co.uk

John o' Groats
John o' Groats Caravan and Camping Site: tel 01955 611 329, www.johnogroatscampsite.co.uk
Stroma View (Huna): tel 01955 611 313, www.stromaview.co.uk

APPENDIX B
Cycle shops

The following is a list of cycle shops on or near the route.

Stage 1
Penzance
Halfords: tel 01736 335 910, www.halfords.com
The Cycle Centre: tel 01736 351 671, www.cyclecentre.net
Bike Tech Cornwall: tel 01736 806135, www.biketechcornwall.com

St Austell
Halfords: tel 01726 68981, www.halfords.com

Stage 2
Liskeard
Liskeard Cycles: tel 01579 347 696, www.liskeardcycles.co.uk

Callington
Callington Cycles: tel 01579 386 824, www.callingtoncycles.co.uk

Okehampton
Okehampton Cycles The Pump and Pedal: tel 01837 861 488, www.okecycles.co.uk

Crediton
The Bike Shed: tel 01363 774 773, www.bikesheduk.com

Stage 3
Wellington
Kings Cycles: tel 01823 662 260, www.kingscycles.co.uk

Taunton
Bicycle Chain: tel 01823 252 499, www.bicyclechain.co.uk
Halfords: tel 01527 914 298, www.halfords.com
On Your Bike: tel 01823 259 035, www.on-your-bike.org

Bridgwater
Bicycle Chain: tel 01278 423 640, www.bicyclechain.co.uk
Halfords: tel 01278 411 590, www.halfords.com
St John Street Cycles: tel 01278 441 500, www.sjscycles.co.uk

Axbridge
Strawberry Line Cycles: tel 07795 547 446, www.strawberrylinecycles.co.uk

Appendix B – Cycle shops

Clevedon
Bike Style: tel 01275 876 572, www.bike-style.co.uk
Halfords: tel 01275 345 880, www.halfords.com

Stage 4
Henbury
AD Cycle Repairs: tel 07831 328 063, www.adcyclerepairs.co.uk

Thornbury
Pete's Cycles: tel 01454 281 548

Gloucester
Eastgate Cycles: tel 01452 300 366, www.eastgatecycles.co.uk
Mitchell's Cycles: tel 01452 411 888, www.mitchellscyclesgloucester.co.uk
Striking Bikes: tel 01452 522 100, www.striking-bikes.co.uk

Tewkesbury
Halfords: tel 01684 854 990, www.halfords.com

Worcester
Barbourne Bicycles: tel 01905 729535, www.barbournebicycles.co.uk
Halfords: tel 01905 754 044, www.halfords.com
Worcester Cycle Centre: tel 01905 611 123, www.worcestercyclecentre.com

Stage 5
Droitwich Spa
Bicycles4u: tel 01905 778751

Stourport-on-Severn
Stourport Specialist Cycles: tel 01299 826 470, www.stourportspecialistcycles.co.uk

Kidderminster
Halfords: tel 01562 861 993, www.halfords.com

Wombourne
Fishface Cycles: tel 01902 892 014, www.fishfacecycles.com

Audlem
Audlem Cyclesport: tel 01270 811 333, www.audlemcyclesport.co.uk

Nantwich
Rock Garden Cycles: tel 01270 361 908, www.rockgardencycles.co.uk

Cycling Land's End to John o' Groats

Stage 6
Northwich
Dave Hinde: tel 01606 41333, www.hinderacingltd.com
G & B Cycles: tel 01606 783 484, www.northwichcycles.co.uk
Halfords: tel 01606 42532, www.halfords.com
Jack Gee Cycles: tel 01606 43029, www.cyclescheme.co.uk/retailer/jack-gee-cycles-northwich

Warrington
Cyclehouse Warrington: tel 01925 575 999, www.cyclehouse.co.uk
Halfords: tel 01925 411 595, www.halfords.com
Ron Spencer Cycles: tel 01925 632 668, www.ronspencercycles.com

Golborne
Golborne Cycle Centre: tel 01942 677 989

Wigan
Halfords: tel 01942 825 060, www.halfords.com
Leon Cycle: tel 01942 932 115, www.leoncycle.co.uk

Chorley
Halfords: tel 01257 260408, www.halfords.com
The Bike Cabin: tel 07479 188 030, www.thebikecabin.com

Buckshaw Village
Merlin Cycles: tel 01772 432431, www.merlincycles.com

Preston
Broadgate Cycles: tel 01772 746 448, www.broadgatecycles.co.uk
Evans Cycles: tel 01772 542 300, www.evanscycles.com
Halfords: tel 01772 769 160, www.halfords.com
Leisure Lakes Bikes: tel 01772 200 944, www.leisurelakesbikes.com

Garstang
Bowland Cycles: tel 01995 600 194, www.bowlandcycles.co.uk

Stage 7
Lancaster
Halfords: tel 01524 846 889, www.halfords.com
Leisure Lakes Bikes: tel 01524 844 389, www.leisurelakesbikes.com
On Yer Bike: tel 01524 60554, www.onyerbike.com

Appendix B – Cycle shops

Penrith
Arragons Cycle Centre: tel 01768 890 344, www.arragons.com
Halfords: tel 01768 892 960, www.halfords.com

Stage 8
Carlisle
Bikeseven: tel 01228 739 926, www.bikeseven.co.uk
Halfords: tel 01228 514 041, www.halfords.com
Palace Cycles: tel 01228 523 142, www.palacecycles.co.uk
Scotby Cycles: tel 01228 546 931, www.scotbycycles.co.uk
Whiteheads: tel 01228 511 303, www.whiteheads.biz

Moffat
Annandale Cycles: tel 01683 220 033, www.annandalecycles.com

Stage 9
Livingston
Scot Cycles: tel 01506 674 379, www.scotcycles.com

Alternative Stage 9
Hamilton
Halfords: tel 01698 283 323, www.halfords.com

Glasgow East
Halfords: tel 0141 647 4911, www.halfords.com

Glasgow Central
Billy Bilsland Cycles: tel 0141 552 0841, www.billybilslandcycles.co.uk
Cycle Republic: tel 0141 847 0531, www.cyclerepublic.com
Evans Cycles: tel 0141 233 0200, www.evanscycles.com
Gear Bikes: tel 0141 339 1179, www.gearbikes.com
Philip Lang Cycles: tel 0141 552 5103, www.philiplangcycles.co.uk

Glasgow West
Halfords: tel 0141 951 1165, www.halfords.com
West End Cycles: tel 0141 357 1344

Glasgow (Bowling)
Magic Cycles: tel 01389 298 100, www.magiccycles.co.uk

Dumbarton
Halfords: tel 01389 734 372, www.halfords.com

Cycling Land's End to John o' Groats

Stage 10

Inverkeithing
Ryans Bike Surgery: tel 01383 420 777, www.ryansbikesurgery.com

Dunfermline
The Bike Shop Scotland: tel 01383 621 999

Halfords: tel 01383 620 853, www.halfords.com

Singletrack Bikes: tel 01383 733 219, www.singletrackbikes.co.uk

Kinross
Loch Leven Cycles: tel 01577 862 839, www.lochlevencycles.co.uk

Perth
Halfords: tel 01738 622 181, www.halfords.com

J. M. Richards Cycles: tel 01738 626 860, www.jmrichardscycles.com

Dunkeld
Progression Bikes: tel 01350 727 629, www.progressionbikesscotland.com

Pitlochry
Escape Route: tel 01796 473 859, www.escape-route.co.uk

Alternative Stage 10

Callender
Wheels Cycling Centre: tel 01877 331 100, www.wheelscyclingcentre.com

Stage 11

Newtonmore
Bike Worx: tel 01540 673 791

Aviemore
Bothy Bikes: tel 01479 810 111, www.bothybikes.co.uk

Mikes Bikes: tel 01479 810 478, www.aviemorebikes.co.uk

Stage 12

Inverness
Alpine Bikes: tel 01463 729 171, www.alpinebikes.com

Bikes of Inverness: tel 01463 225 965, www.bikesofinverness.co.uk

Halfords: tel 01527 914 294, www.halfords.com

Highland Bikes: tel 01463 234 789, www.highlandbikes.com

Velocity Café and Bicycle Workshop: tel 01463 419 956, www.velocitylove.co.uk

Dingwall
Dryburgh Cycles: tel 01349 862 163, www.dryburghcycles.com

Appendix B – Cycle shops

Stage 13

Ardgay
Heaven Bikes: tel 07543 466 699, www.heavenbikes.co.uk/

Stage 14

Thurso
The Bike Shop: tel 01847 895 385

Wick
(17 miles from John o' Groats down the A92)
The Spot Cycle Shop: tel 01955 602 698

APPENDIX C
Facilities summary

Main route

Stage		Miles from Land's End	Miles from John o' Groats	Hostel	Campsite	B&B	Hotel	Bike shop	Rail station near route	Notes
1	**Land's End**	0	1000	x	x	x	x			
	Penzance	11	989	x	x	x	x	x	x	
	St Austell	57	943	x	x	x	x	x	x	
	Fowey	65	935		x*	x	x			*Campsite at Bodinnick
2	Liskeard	79	921		x	x	x	x	x	
	Callington*	87	913		x	x		x		*2 miles off route
	Okehampton	111	889	x	x	x	x	x	x	
	Crediton	130	870		x	x	x	x	x	
3	Wellington	157	843		x	x	x	x	x	
	Taunton	165	835		x	x	x	x	x	
	Bridgewater	177	823		x	x	x	x	x	
	Axbridge*	202	798	x		x	x	x		*4 miles off route

Appendix C – Facilities summary

Stage		Miles from Land's End	Miles from John o' Groats	Hostel	Campsite	B&B	Hotel	Bike shop	Rail station near route	Notes
	Clevedon	216	784		x	x	x	x		
4	Portishead*	224	776			x	x	x		*2 miles off route
	Henbury*	229	771			x	x	x		*1 mile off route
	Thornbury*	243	757			x	x	x		*2 miles off route
	Slimbridge	258	742	x	x	x				
	Gloucester	271	729		x	x	x	x	x	
	Tewkesbury*	288	712		x	x	x	x	x	*1 mile off route
	Worcester	307	693		x	x	x	x	x	
5	Ribbesford*	324	676	x						*4 miles off route
	Kidderminster	327	673		x	x	x	x	x	
	Wombourne*	340	660					x		*3 miles off route
	Albrighton	350	650			x			x	
	Newport	362	638		x	x	x			
	Audlem	383	617					x		

CYCLING LAND'S END TO JOHN O' GROATS

Stage		Miles from Land's End	Miles from John o' Groats	Hostel	Campsite	B&B	Hotel	Bike shop	Rail station near route	Notes
	Nantwich	391	609		x	x	x	x	x	
6	Northwich	408	592		x	x	x	x	x	
	Warrington*	422	578			x	x	x	x	*1 mile off route
	Golbourne	430	570					x		
	Wigan	436	564				x	x	x	
	Chorley*	445	555				x	x	x	*1 mile off route
	Preston*	456	544			x	x	x	x	*1 mile off route
	Garstang	476	524		x	x	x	x	x	
7	Lancaster*	487	513		x	x	x	x	x	*2 miles off route
	Kirkby Lonsdale	504	496		x	x	x			
	Sedbergh	516	484		x	x	x			
	Shap	534	466	x	x	x	x			
	Penrith	546	454	x		x	x	x	x	
8	Carlisle	566	434	x		x	x	x	x	
	Annan	586	414		x	x	x			

APPENDIX C – FACILITIES SUMMARY

Stage		Miles from Land's End	Miles from John o' Groats	Hostel	Campsite	B&B	Hotel	Bike shop	Rail station near route	Notes
	Lochmaben	601	399		x	x	x			
	Moffat	616	384	x*		x	x	x		*Hostel 1½ miles off route
9	Livingston*	669	331		x*	x	x	x	x	*2 miles off route
	South Queensferry	680	320	x*	x**	x	x	x	x	*10 miles off route in Edinburgh **7 miles off route
10	Inverkeithing	684	316			x	x	x	x	
	Dumfermline	688	312			x	x	x	x	
	Kinross	700	300		x	x	x	x	x	
	Perth	716	284	x	x	x	x	x	x	
	Dunkeld	733	267	x	x	x	x	x	x	
	Pitlochry	746	254	x	x	x	x	x	x	
11	Newtonmore	787	213	x	x	x	x	x	x	
	Kingussie	790	210	x		x	x		x	
	Aviemore	806	194	x	x	x	x	x	x	

CYCLING LAND'S END TO JOHN O' GROATS

Stage		Miles from Land's End	Miles from John o' Groats	Hostel	Campsite	B&B	Hotel	Bike shop	Rail station near route	Notes
12	Boat of Garten	811	189	x*	x	x	x		x	*Also hostel at Nethy Bridge – 5 miles off route
	Inverness	845	155	x	x	x	x	x	x	
	Dingwall	860	140		x	x	x	x	x	
	Alness	870	130	x*	x*	x	x		x	*Both at Evanton – 4 miles before end of stage
13	Ardgay	887	113	x		x	x	x	x	
	Lairg	899	101		x	x	x		x	
	Crask	912	88		x	x				
	Altnaharra	920	80	x			x			
	Tongue	937	63	x	x	x	x			
14	Bettyhill	950	50		x	x	x			
	Melvich	963	37	x*	x					*7 miles off route in Strath Hallade
	Thurso	980	20	x	x	x	x	x	x	
	John o' Groats	1000	0		x	x	x			

Appendix C – Facilities summary

Stage		Miles from Land's End	Miles from John o' Groats	Hostel	Campsite	B&B	Hotel	Bike shop	Rail station near route	Notes
Alternative route										
9a	Abington	636	410		x		x			
	Larkhall	661	385			x	x			
	Hamilton	666	380		x	x	x		x	
	Glasgow	678	368	x		x	x	x	x	
	Dumbarton	693	353			x	x	x	x	
	Balloch	699	347		x	x	x		x	
10a	Drymen	709	337	x	x	x	x			
	Callender	733	313	x	x	x	x			
	Aberfeldy*	777	269		x	x	x			*1 mile off route
	Pitlochry	792	254	x	x	x	x	x	x	

APPENDIX D
Useful resources and contacts

Land's End to John o' Groats Association
The Land's End to John o' Groats Association (www.lejog.org) is an organization for anyone who has completed the trip as a continuous journey in either direction. Applicants are asked to provide evidence of their trip by collecting dated signatures, stamps and till receipts from hostels, B&Bs, garages and post offices along their route.

Cycle Route Planning Apps

You can use the basic mapping functionality, save and download files on most apps for free, although you may have to register first. The more popular ones that are generally more compatible with GPX devices are listed below but there are plenty of others.
www.connect.garmin.com www.cycletravel.org
www.komoot.com www.mapmyride.com
www.ridewithgps.com www.strava.com

Alternative accommodation
Airbnb (www.airbnb.co.uk) is an online marketplace for accommodation brokerage.

Warm Showers (www.warmshowers.org) is a free worldwide hospitality exchange for touring cyclists.

Hostels
Independent Hostel Guide (www.independenthostels.co.uk) is the UK's network of independently owned bunkhouses and hostels.

Scottish Youth Hostel Association (www.hostellingscotland.org.uk) is Scotland's largest provider of hostel accommodation for people of all ages.

Youth Hostel Association (www.yha.org) is England's largest provider of hostel accommodation for people of all ages.

Camp sites

The following organisations have websites that list campsites along the route:
The Camping and Caravanning Club www.campingandcaravanningclub.co.uk
Cool Camping www.coolcamping.co.uk
UK Campsite www.ukcampsite.co.uk

Selected companies offering supported End-to-End Holidays
Bike Adventures www.bikeadventures.co.uk
Contours Cycling Holidays www.contourscycle.co.uk

APPENDIX D – USEFUL RESOURCES AND CONTACTS

CTC Cycling Holidays www.cyclingholidays.org
More Adventure www.moreadventure.co.uk
Peak Tours www.peak-tours.com
Pedal Britain www.pedlabritain.com
Pedal Nation www.pedalnation.co.uk
Skedaddle www.skedaddle.com
Trailbrakes www.trailbrakes.co.uk
Yellow Jersey Cycling Holidays www.yellowjerseycyclingholidays.co.uk

Selected companies offering self-guided End-to-End Holidays
Drover Holidays www.droverholidays.co.uk
Green Traveller www.greentraveller.co.uk
Wheely Wonderful Cycling www.wheelywonderfulcycling.co.uk

APPENDIX E
Official tourist information contacts

Stages	Area	Website
1–14	Britain	www.visitbritain.com – Covers all of Great Britain
1–8	England	www.visitengland.com – Covers all of England
1,2	Cornwall	www.visitcornwall.com
2,3	Devon	www.visitdevon.co.uk
3,4	Somerset	www.visitsomerset.co.uk
4	Bristol	www.visitbristol.co.uk
4	Gloucestershire	www.visitgloucester.co.uk
4,5	Worcestershire	www.visitworcestershire.org
5	Staffordshire	www.enjoystaffordshire.com
5	Shropshire	www.shropshiretourism.co.uk
5,6	Cheshire	www.visitcheshire.com
6,7	Lancashire	www.visitlancashire.com
7,8	Cumbria	www.visitcumbria.com
8–14	Scotland	www.visitscotland.com – Covers all of Scotland
8,9	South West Scotland	www.visitsouthwestscotland.com
8,9	Moffat	www.visitmoffat.co.uk
9	West Lothian	www.visitwestlothian.co.uk
9, 9a	Lanarkshire	www.visitlanarkshire.com
10	Fife	www.welcometofife.com
10a	Loch Lomond and the Trossachs	www.lochlomond-trossachs.org
11,12	Cairngorms	www.visitcairngorms.com
11,12	Aviemore	www.visitaviemore.com
12	Inverness	www.visitinvernesslochness.com
12,13	Dornoch and Alness	www.exploreeasterross.co.uk
13	Lairg	www.lairgandrogart.co.uk
13	Sutherland	www.heartofsutherland.co.uk
13,14	Sutherland and Caithness	www.venture-north.co.uk

APPENDIX F
Additional contacts for rail travel

Trainline
Trainline (www.trainline.com), the online booking system for rail travel, can make bike reservations for every leg of your journey where one is required but advise that you contact them first before purchasing your ticket by calling 0871 244 1545 (Calls cost 13p a minute plus your phone company's access charge).

London North East Railway
Regardless of where you are coming from or going to, London North East Railway (www.lner.co.uk) has a bike-friendly booking system where you can buy tickets and make bike reservations for all train operating companies. All they ask is that before you book your train tickets, phone their Web Support Team on 03457 225 333 to check bike space availability and to reserve your space. If there are no bike spaces available on the train you had in mind, they will help you choose an alternative train that does.

Great Western Railway
Regardless of your origin station, you can also book your journey and make a bike reservation with Great Western Railway (www.gwr.com) – the train operator that provides intercity services into Penzance – either online or by calling 0345 7000 125.

CrossCountry Trains
Although some of their trains have a separate goods compartment with numerous bike spaces, CrossCountry Trains (www.crosscountrytrains.co.uk), the operator that provides regional services into Penzance advises that you always reserve a space for your bike. You can do this on their website, although you may have to wait up to 24 hours for a confirmation. Alternatively, if you require a reservation at short notice, you can contact them through their Twitter handle (@CrossCountryUK) or through Facebook and a member of staff will reply within 30 mins, 24 hours a day, 7 days a week.

Scotrail
Scotrail (www.scotrail.co.uk), which provides services to and from destinations nearest to John o' Groats, recommends that you reserve a space for your bike, which you can do on their website when purchasing your ticket.

APPENDIX G
What to take

Below is a check list of things to take together the typical weights of items that are carried.

Riding gear
Helmet
Balaclava or Buff®
Cycling glasses
S/S base layer
S/S cycling jersey
Arm warmers
Cycling gloves (full-fingered and fingerless)
Cycling shorts
Leg warmers
Socks Waterproof Jacket (350gm)
W/P over-trousers (300gm)
Overshoes (150gm)

Leisurewear
Long sleeved T shirt x2 (150gm x2)
Underwear x2 (100gm x2)
Micro-fleece top (420gm)
Travel trousers (450gm)
Socks x2 (60gm x2)
Trainers/Crocs/espadrilles (600gm)
Couple stuff bags (40gm x2)

Additional leisurewear for cooler months
Fleece jacket (550gm)
Heavier travel trousers (550gm)

Tools and accessories
Rear light (55gm)
Front light (100gm)
Pump (110gm)
Multi-tool (120gm)
Spoke key (17gm)
Spare inner tube (120gm)
Spare folding tyre or a 'boot' – section of old tyre for reinforcing splits and holes (350gm/50gm)
Self-adhesive patches (20gm) or traditional puncture repair kit (40gm)
Tyre levers (26gm)
Powerlink (5gm)
Set of cables (50gm)
Latex gloves (3gm)
Spare bolts x2 (4gm)
Cable ties x2 (3gm)
Mini-bottle of chain oil (30gm)

Extras
Toiletries/Shaving kit (300gm)
Travel towel (135gm)
Sun cream (45gm)
Lip salve (15gm)
Wet wipes (50gm)
Small amount of liquid, non-biological, laundry detergent (50gm)
Compact first aid kit (200gm)
Map or GPS and charger (150gm)
Guidebook (235gm)
Itinerary (10gm)
Pen (10gm)
Compact camera and charger (265gm)
Phone and charger (270gm)
Wallet/cards (100gm)

APPENDIX H
Further reading

Elgar the Cyclist, Kevin Allen (Print Matters, 1997). Only for those with an interest in early cycling, classical music – or both.

How to Ride a Bike: From Starting Out to Peak Performance, Sir Chris Hoy (Hamlyn, 2018). Full of practical advice about everything a cyclist needs to know about training, maintenance and riding safely.

Land's End to John o' Groats - End to End Cycle Route - A Safer Way, Royston G Wood, (CreateSpace Independent Publishing Platform, 2014). Not a traditional guidebook but a list of links to a series of online Google maps and gpx files.

Land's End to John o' Groats: On the National Cycle Network: Official Sustrans Guide, (Sustrans, 2017). This book details a slightly wandering 1,173-mile LEJOG that takes in many of the National Cycle Network's flagship routes.

The End to End Cycle Route: Land's End to John o' Groats, Nick Mitchell (Cicerone, 2012). This now out of print Cicerone guide is superseded by this guidebook.

Ultra-Distance Cycling: An Expert Guide to Endurance Cycling Paperback, Simon Jobson and Dominic Irvine (Bloomsbury Sport, 2017). The definitive manual for those wanting to ride long distances.

Selected LEJOG Travelogues

End to End: John o' Groats, Broken Spokes and a Dog called Gretna, Alistair McGuinness, (Half a World Away Publication, 2016). An amusing solo travelogue of riding LEJOG for a very worthy cause.

Free Country: A Penniless Adventure the Length of Britain Paperback, George Mahood, (CreateSpace Independent Publishing Platform, 2014). A laugh-out-loud account of how with no bikes, no food and no money, George and his pal strip off to their boxer shorts and rely on other people's generosity for everything they need to ride to John o' Groats.

Land's End to John o' Groats: On a beer mat, Dave Lewis, (Lulu, 2017). Another travelogue of riding LEJOG, albeit quite a funny one as Dave and his mate do it on a wing and a prayer.

Mud, Sweat and Gears: Cycling From Land's End to John o' Groats (Via the Pub), Ellie Bennett (Summersdale Publishers, 2012). Entertaining travelogue of a couple with a keen interested in sampling the different beers available along the route.

DOWNLOAD THE ROUTES IN GPX FORMAT

All the routes in this guide are available for download from:

www.cicerone.co.uk/1025/GPX

as standard format GPX files. You should be able to load them into most online GPX systems and mobile devices, whether GPS or smartphone. You may need to convert the file into your preferred format using a conversion programme such as gpsvisualizer.com or one of the many other such websites and programmes.

When you follow this link, you will be asked for your email address and where you purchased the guidebook, and have the option to subscribe to the Cicerone e-newsletter.

CICERONE
www.cicerone.co.uk

LISTING OF CICERONE GUIDES

BRITISH ISLES CHALLENGES, COLLECTIONS AND ACTIVITIES
Cycling Land's End to John o' Groats
Great Walks on the England Coast Path
The Big Rounds
The Book of the Bivvy
The Book of the Bothy
The Mountains of England & Wales:
 Vol 1 Wales
 Vol 2 England
The National Trails
Walking The End to End Trail

SCOTLAND
Ben Nevis and Glen Coe
Cycle Touring in Northern Scotland
Cycling in the Hebrides
Great Mountain Days in Scotland
Mountain Biking in Southern and Central Scotland
Mountain Biking in West and North West Scotland
Not the West Highland Way
Scotland
Scotland's Mountain Ridges
Scottish Wild Country Backpacking
Skye's Cuillin Ridge Traverse
The Borders Abbeys Way
The Great Glen Way
The Great Glen Way Map Booklet
The Hebridean Way
The Hebrides
The Isle of Mull
The Isle of Skye
The Skye Trail
The Southern Upland Way
The Speyside Way
The Speyside Way Map Booklet
The West Highland Way
The West Highland Way Map Booklet
Walking Ben Lawers, Rannoch and Atholl
Walking in the Cairngorms
Walking in the Pentland Hills
Walking in the Scottish Borders
Walking in the Southern Uplands
Walking in Torridon, Fisherfield, Fannichs and An Teallach
Walking Loch Lomond and the Trossachs
Walking on Arran
Walking on Harris and Lewis
Walking on Jura, Islay and Colonsay
Walking on Rum and the Small Isles
Walking on the Orkney and Shetland Isles
Walking on Uist and Barra
Walking the Cape Wrath Trail

Walking the Corbetts
 Vol 1 South of the Great Glen
 Vol 2 North of the Great Glen
Walking the Galloway Hills
Walking the Munros
 Vol 1 – Southern, Central and Western Highlands
 Vol 2 – Northern Highlands and the Cairngorms
Winter Climbs Ben Nevis and Glen Coe

NORTHERN ENGLAND ROUTES
Cycling the Reivers Route
Cycling the Way of the Roses
Hadrian's Cycleway
Hadrian's Wall Path
Hadrian's Wall Path Map Booklet
The C2C Cycle Route
The Coast to Coast Map Booklet
The Coast to Coast Walk
The Pennine Way
The Pennine Way Map Booklet
Walking the Dales Way
Walking the Dales Way Map Booklet

NORTH-EAST ENGLAND, YORKSHIRE DALES AND PENNINES
Cycling in the Yorkshire Dales
Great Mountain Days in the Pennines
Mountain Biking in the Yorkshire Dales
St Oswald's Way and St Cuthbert's Way
The Cleveland Way and the Yorkshire Wolds Way
The Cleveland Way Map Booklet
The North York Moors
The Reivers Way
Trail and Fell Running in the Yorkshire Dales
Walking in County Durham
Walking in Northumberland
Walking in the North Pennines
Walking in the Yorkshire Dales: North and East
Walking in the Yorkshire Dales: South and West

NORTH-WEST ENGLAND AND THE ISLE OF MAN
Cycling the Pennine Bridleway
Isle of Man Coastal Path
The Lancashire Cycleway
The Lune Valley and Howgills
Walking in Cumbria's Eden Valley
Walking in Lancashire
Walking in the Forest of Bowland and Pendle

Walking on the Isle of Man
Walking on the West Pennine Moors
Walks in Silverdale and Arnside

LAKE DISTRICT
Cycling in the Lake District
Great Mountain Days in the Lake District
Joss Naylor's Lakes, Meres and Waters of the Lake District
Lake District Winter Climbs
Lake District: High Level and Fell Walks
Lake District: Low Level and Lake Walks
Mountain Biking in the Lake District
Outdoor Adventures with Children – Lake District
Scrambles in the Lake District – North
Scrambles in the Lake District – South
Trail and Fell Running in the Lake District
Walking The Cumbria Way
Walking the Lake District Fells –
 Borrowdale
 Buttermere
 Coniston
 Keswick
 Langdale
 Mardale and the Far East
 Patterdale
 Wasdale
Walking the Tour of the Lake District

DERBYSHIRE, PEAK DISTRICT AND MIDLANDS
Cycling in the Peak District
Dark Peak Walks
Scrambles in the Dark Peak
Walking in Derbyshire
Walking in the Peak District – White Peak East
Walking in the Peak District – White Peak West

SOUTHERN ENGLAND
20 Classic Sportive Rides in South East England
20 Classic Sportive Rides in South West England
Cycling in the Cotswolds
Mountain Biking on the North Downs
Mountain Biking on the South Downs
Suffolk Coast and Heath Walks
The Cotswold Way
The Cotswold Way Map Booklet
The Kennet and Avon Canal

The Lea Valley Walk
The North Downs Way
The North Downs Way
  Map Booklet
The Peddars Way and Norfolk
  Coast Path
The Pilgrims' Way
The Ridgeway National Trail
The Ridgeway Map Booklet
The South Downs Way
The South Downs Way Map Booklet
The Thames Path
The Thames Path Map Booklet
The Two Moors Way
The Two Moors Way Map Booklet
Walking Hampshire's Test Way
Walking in Cornwall
Walking in Essex
Walking in Kent
Walking in London
Walking in Norfolk
Walking in the Chilterns
Walking in the Cotswolds
Walking in the Isles of Scilly
Walking in the New Forest
Walking in the North
  Wessex Downs
Walking on Dartmoor
Walking on Guernsey
Walking on Jersey
Walking on the Isle of Wight
Walking the Jurassic Coast
Walking the South West Coast Path
Walking the South West Coast Path
  Map Booklets
  Vol 1: Minehead to St Ives
  Vol 2: St Ives to Plymouth
  Vol 3: Plymouth to Poole
Walks in the South Downs
  National Park

WALES AND WELSH BORDERS
Cycle Touring in Wales
Cycling Lon Las Cymru
Glyndwr's Way
Great Mountain Days in Snowdonia
Hillwalking in Shropshire
Hillwalking in Wales – Vols 1&2
Mountain Walking in Snowdonia
Offa's Dyke Path
Offa's Dyke Path Map Booklet
Ridges of Snowdonia
Scrambles in Snowdonia
Snowdonia: 30 Low-level and Easy
  Walks – North
Snowdonia: 30 Low-level and Easy
  Walks – South
The Cambrian Way
The Ceredigion and Snowdonia
  Coast Paths
The Pembrokeshire Coast Path
The Pembrokeshire Coast Path
  Map Booklet

The Severn Way
The Snowdonia Way
The Wye Valley Walk
Walking in Carmarthenshire
Walking in Pembrokeshire
Walking in the Brecon Beacons
Walking in the Forest of Dean
Walking in the Wye Valley
Walking on Gower
Walking the Shropshire Way
Walking the Wales Coast Path

INTERNATIONAL CHALLENGES, COLLECTIONS AND ACTIVITIES
Europe's High Points

AFRICA
Kilimanjaro
Walks and Scrambles in the
  Moroccan Anti-Atlas
Walking in the Drakensberg

ALPS CROSS-BORDER ROUTES
100 Hut Walks in the Alps
Alpine Ski Mountaineering
  Vol 1 – Western Alps
  Vol 2 – Central and Eastern Alps
The Karnischer Hohenweg
The Tour of the Bernina
Trail Running – Chamonix and the
  Mont Blanc region
Trekking Chamonix to Zermatt
Trekking in the Alps
Trekking in the Silvretta and
  Ratikon Alps
Trekking Munich to Venice
Trekking the Tour of Mont Blanc
Walking in the Alps

PYRENEES AND FRANCE/SPAIN CROSS-BORDER ROUTES
Shorter Treks in the Pyrenees
The GR10 Trail
The GR11 Trail
The Pyrenean Haute Route
The Pyrenees
Walks and Climbs in the Pyrenees

AUSTRIA
Innsbruck Mountain Adventures
Trekking in Austria's Hohe Tauern
Trekking in the Stubai Alps
Trekking in the Zillertal Alps
Walking in Austria
Walking in the Salzkammergut:
  the Austrian Lake District

EASTERN EUROPE
The Danube Cycleway Vol 2
The Elbe Cycle Route
The High Tatras
The Mountains of Romania
Walking in Bulgaria's National Parks
Walking in Hungary

FRANCE, BELGIUM AND LUXEMBOURG
Camino de Santiago – Via Podiensis
Chamonix Mountain Adventures
Cycle Touring in France
Cycling London to Paris
Cycling the Canal de la Garonne
Cycling the Canal du Midi
Cycling the Route des
  Grandes Alpes
Mont Blanc Walks
Mountain Adventures in
  the Maurienne
Short Treks on Corsica
The GR5 Trail
The GR5 Trail – Benelux
  and Lorraine
The GR5 Trail – Vosges and Jura
The Grand Traverse of the
  Massif Central
The Moselle Cycle Route
The River Loire Cycle Route
Trekking in the Vanoise
Trekking the Cathar Way
Trekking the GR20 Corsica
Trekking the Robert Louis
  Stevenson Trail
Via Ferratas of the French Alps
Walking in Provence – East
Walking in Provence – West
Walking in the Ardennes
Walking in the Auvergne
Walking in the Briançonnais
Walking in the Dordogne
Walking in the Haute Savoie: North
Walking in the Haute Savoie: South
Walking on Corsica
Walking the Brittany Coast Path

GERMANY
Hiking and Cycling in the
  Black Forest
The Danube Cycleway Vol 1
The Rhine Cycle Route
The Westweg
Walking in the Bavarian Alps

IRELAND
The Wild Atlantic Way and
  Western Ireland
Walking the Wicklow Way

ITALY
Alta Via 1 – Trekking in
  the Dolomites
Alta Via 2 – Trekking in
  the Dolomites
Italy's Sibillini National Park
Shorter Walks in the Dolomites
Ski Touring and Snowshoeing in
  the Dolomites
The Way of St Francis
Trekking in the Apennines

Trekking the Giants' Trail: Alta Via 1 through the Italian Pennine Alps
Via Ferratas of the Italian Dolomites Vols 1 & 2
Walking and Trekking in the Gran Paradiso
Walking in Abruzzo
Walking in Italy's Cinque Terre
Walking in Italy's Stelvio National Park
Walking in Sicily
Walking in the Aosta Valley
Walking in the Dolomites
Walking in Tuscany
Walking in Umbria
Walking Lake Como and Maggiore
Walking Lake Garda and Iseo
Walking on the Amalfi Coast
Walking the Via Francigena Pilgrim Route – Parts 2 & 3
Walks and Treks in the Maritime Alps

MEDITERRANEAN
The High Mountains of Crete
Trekking in Greece
Walking and Trekking in Zagori
Walking and Trekking on Corfu
Walking in Cyprus
Walking on Malta
Walking on the Greek Islands – the Cyclades

NEW ZEALAND & AUSTRALIA
Hiking the Overland Track

NORTH AMERICA
Hiking and Cycling the California Missions Trail
The John Muir Trail
The Pacific Crest Trail

SOUTH AMERICA
Aconcagua and the Southern Andes
Hiking and Biking Peru's Inca Trails
Torres del Paine

SCANDINAVIA, ICELAND AND GREENLAND
Hiking in Norway – South
Trekking in Greenland – The Arctic Circle Trail
Trekking the Kungsleden
Walking and Trekking in Iceland

SLOVENIA, CROATIA, SERBIA, MONTENEGRO AND ALBANIA
Mountain Biking in Slovenia
The Islands of Croatia
The Julian Alps of Slovenia
The Mountains of Montenegro
The Peaks of the Balkans Trail
The Slovene Mountain Trail
Walking in Slovenia: The Karavanke
Walks and Treks in Croatia

SPAIN AND PORTUGAL
Camino de Santiago: Camino Frances
Coastal Walks in Andalucia
Costa Blanca Mountain Adventures
Cycling the Camino de Santiago
Cycling the Ruta Via de la Plata
Mountain Walking in Mallorca
Mountain Walking in Southern Catalunya
Portugal's Rota Vicentina
Spain's Sendero Historico: The GR1
The Andalucian Coast to Coast Walk
The Camino del Norte and Camino Primitivo
The Camino Ingles and Ruta do Mar
The Camino Portugues
The Mountains of Nerja
The Mountains of Ronda and Grazalema
The Sierras of Extremadura
Trekking in Mallorca
Trekking in the Canary Islands
Trekking the GR7 in Andalucia
Walking and Trekking in the Sierra Nevada
Walking in Andalucia
Walking in Catalunya – Barcelona
Walking in Portugal
Walking in the Algarve
Walking on Gran Canaria
Walking on La Gomera and El Hierro
Walking on La Palma
Walking on Lanzarote and Fuerteventura
Walking on Madeira
Walking on the Azores
Walking on the Costa Blanca
Walking the Camino dos Faros

SWITZERLAND
Switzerland's Jura Crest Trail
The Swiss Alpine Pass Route – Via Alpina Route 1
The Swiss Alps
Tour of the Jungfrau Region
Walking in the Bernese Oberland
Walking in the Engadine – Switzerland
Walking in the Valais
Walking in Zermatt and Saas-Fee

CHINA, JAPAN AND ASIA
Hiking and Trekking in the Japan Alps and Mount Fuji
Hiking in Hong Kong
Japan's Kumano Kodo Pilgrimage
Trekking in Tajikistan

HIMALAYA
Annapurna
Everest: A Trekker's Guide
Trekking in Bhutan
Trekking in Ladakh
Trekking in the Himalaya

MOUNTAIN LITERATURE
8000 metres
A Walk in the Clouds
Abode of the Gods
Fifty Years of Adventure
The Pennine Way – the Path, the People, the Journey
Unjustifiable Risk?

TECHNIQUES
Fastpacking
Geocaching in the UK
Map and Compass
Outdoor Photography
Polar Exploration
The Mountain Hut Book

MINI GUIDES
Alpine Flowers
Navigation
Pocket First Aid and Wilderness Medicine
Snow

For full information on all our guides, books and eBooks, visit our website:
www.cicerone.co.uk

CICERONE

Trust Cicerone to guide your next adventure, wherever it may be around the world...

Discover guides for hiking, mountain walking, backpacking, trekking, trail running, cycling and mountain biking, ski touring, climbing and scrambling in Britain, Europe and worldwide.

Connect with Cicerone online and find inspiration.

- buy books and ebooks
- articles, advice and trip reports
- podcasts and live events
- GPX files and updates
- regular newsletter

cicerone.co.uk